GUIDANCE IN ELEMENTARY SCHOOLS

GUIDANCE IN ELEMENTARY SCHOOLS

Ruth Martinson

Associate Professor of Education
Long Beach State College

Harry Smallenburg

Director, Division of Research
and Guidance, Office of the Los Angeles
County Superintendent of Schools

PRENTICE-HALL, INC.

Englewood Cliffs, N. J. ⊂⊃ 1958

Library of Congress Catalog Card No.: 58-8709

Printed in the United States of America
36634

DEDICATION

The authors dedicate this book to Miss Alma Jaekel, Head Clerk, Division of Research and Guidance, Office of the Los Angeles County Superintendent of Schools, who for more than twenty years has provided generous, efficient, and helpful service to the staff of the Division of Research and Guidance, and through them to the many counselors, psychologists, and other pupil personnel workers in Los Angeles County.

PREFACE

Guidance in the elementary school is not a phenomenon of the present day, despite the recency of attention to this field. Good teachers throughout the history of education have served as guides and counselors to their pupils. The guidance provided by these master teachers, however, was based upon personal concern and interest rather than upon study and knowledge gained through modern guidance techniques.

The development of psychological tools for the study of individuals has led inevitably to classroom application. Planning for individual children has become an organized and integral part of the total educational program. Realization of the uniqueness of the individual has increased the need for trained personnel to serve teachers and children at all school levels.

The present book presents guidance at the elementary school level as an organized program of activities that will benefit every school child. The program and the relationships of personnel within the program are discussed with the hope that the reader may visualize and appreciate the proper contributions of all.

Many persons have contributed to the writing of this volume. Appreciation is due to the many school personnel, students, and publishers who have permitted so willingly the use of guidance materials. Special thanks are due to the staff of the Division of Research and Guidance, Office of the Los Angeles County Superintendent of Schools, for intellectual stimulation and moral support.

Ruth Martinson
Harry Smallenburg

TABLE
OF CONTENTS

PREFACE   vii

ELEMENTARY GUIDANCE—AN OVERVIEW   xiii

1. DEFINITION OF ELEMENTARY GUIDANCE   1

   Guidance involves special materials and may involve special
   personnel. Guidance requires a planned program. Values
   of a planned guidance program.

2. THE DEVELOPMENT OF ELEMENTARY GUIDANCE   7

   Educators who influenced the guidance movement. The
   contributions of measurement to guidance. Child study de-
   velopments. Vocational guidance. Growth of elementary
   guidance programs.

3. GUIDANCE MATERIALS AND COST IN MODERN EDUCA-
   TION   17

   Physical facilities. Basic materials. Cost.

4. MATERIALS, METHODS, AND ROLES OF PERSONNEL IN
   INDIVIDUAL CHILD STUDY   28

   Problems involved in individual study. Outcomes of indi-
   vidual study. An approach to the study of individual chil-
   dren. Teachers begin to study the individual. Anecdotal
   records. Time sample and running account. Children's
   work. Informal interviews. Teacher's description. Roles of
   personnel. Case conference. Individual therapy. Follow-up.

                                                                 ix

5. INFORMAL METHODS OF GROUP STUDY   66

Values in group study. Materials for group study. Criteria for use of group study materials. Questionnaires and interest surveys. Questionnaires for children. Questionnaires for parents. Panels and discussions by pupils. Measures of social relations. Biographical data. Rating scales and check lists. Reaction forms and dramatizations. Roles of personnel in group study.

6. TESTING PROGRAM   126

Values. Criteria for use. A planned program. Preparation for the use of tests. Use of test results. Roles of personnel in effective use of tests.

7. SCHOOL RECORDS   141

Importance of records. Content of records. Planning of records. Effective use of records. Roles of personnel in effective development and use of records.

8. THE NEED FOR GUIDANCE PERSONNEL   166

From the standpoint of parents. From the standpoint of the administrator. From the standpoint of the teacher. Personnel arrangements.

9. QUALIFICATIONS AND DUTIES OF PERSONNEL   173

Personal qualifications. Educational qualifications. Duties of guidance personnel. The study of children. Group work in school. Work with parents and community. Research. The importance of teamwork.

10. RELATIONSHIPS OF SCHOOL PERSONNEL IN GUIDANCE   190

The school administrator. The physician and/or nurse. The curriculum consultant. The teacher. The total staff.

11. GUIDANCE OF EXCEPTIONAL CHILDREN   194

Needs of exceptional children. Problems in identification of needs. Helping the exceptional child in the classroom. Contributions of the guidance worker.

12. IN-SERVICE STUDY OF GUIDANCE TECHNIQUE   214

Roles of personnel. Types of programs. Desired outcomes. Guidance professional groups. Out-of-district resources.

13. WORKING WITH PARENTS 222

*Importance of home-school contacts. Kinds of contacts.
Preparation for two-way group communication. Panels.
Group participation. Trends in home reporting. Bases for
changes. Developments in reporting. Planning for changes
in reporting practices. Individual conferences. Advantages.
Criteria for planning. Training procedures. Conference
schedules. Conference guides.*

14. CHARACTERISTICS OF AN EFFECTIVE GUIDANCE PRO-
GRAM 271

15. EVALUATION OF GUIDANCE SERVICES IN ELEMENTARY
SCHOOLS 275

*Purposes of evaluation. Procedures. General evaluative
forms. Benefits of evaluation.*

16. ORIENTATION TO THE SECONDARY SCHOOL 289

*Orientation of school personnel. Orientation of parents.
Orientation of students.*

APPENDIX *A* FILMS FOR GUIDANCE 297

APPENDIX *B* PAMPHLET MATERIALS 304

APPENDIX *C* BIBLIOGRAPHY 306

INDEX 309

ELEMENTARY GUIDANCE—
AN OVERVIEW

Desirable education in the modern American school has been described, in various ways, as *education that will develop the potentials of each individual to the optimum level*. With such an aim as the general goal, educators have written lists of principles, cardinal and otherwise, frameworks, guide lines, and outlines that have served a very useful purpose. The purpose, over a period of time, has been to extend the scope of education outward from the academic to include a concern for the child and his total adjustment.

Concern for the adjustment of the individual is a necessary part of the modern educational pattern. Numerous writers have pointed out the need for adequate adjustment to enable the child to work and play effectively with others. Such authors as Karen Horney[1] and Daniel Schneider[2] have shown the restrictive effects of maladjustment upon performance, and have demonstrated that emotional well-being is a necessary prerequisite to effective leadership or truly creative and original contributions. The modern school in its concern for proper emotional and social growth for the child, as well as for academic learning, is working toward the goal of developing fully the potential of American society.

A more immediate factor than that of eventual social contribution is the problem of classroom learning. The person who is in-

[1] Karen Horney, *Our Inner Conflicts* (W. W. Norton & Company, Inc., 1945), pp. 154-178.
[2] Daniel Schneider, *The Psychoanalyst and the Artist* (Farrar, Straus, and Company, 1950), p. 102.

volved with personal problems is not able to learn efficiently. He spends his time in antisocial behavior, either withdrawn or aggressive, and does not work well with group activities. Until his needs are studied and met, his chances for working at an optimum level are small.

The elementary school is in a uniquely favorable position to provide guidance services for the child and to insure the conservation of learning potential. It has certain advantages and characteristics which facilitate the contributions that planned guidance activities can make.

One factor in favor of a positive guidance program at the elementary level is the age group of the children. The very fact that they are young enables the persons interested in guidance to emphasize a preventive as well as remedial approach. These persons feel that guidance programs pointed toward parent-teacher understanding of children will do much to prevent difficulties, or to erase incipient problems.

Another advantage in elementary guidance is the closeness of association among the parent, child, and teacher. The parent is more willing and more able to work with the school than he may be at the secondary level. He approaches his contacts with school personnel on a positive basis since any existing remedial needs are comparatively recent in origin. The teacher who is in constant contact with the child during the year may work with the parent to meet needs which, if unfulfilled, could become problems of a serious nature. They may use resource persons who will assist them in "catching them young and bringing them up right."

The close personal association between teacher and parent is unique to the elementary school; it decreases at the secondary level, with the advent of departmentalization. At that stage, continuity of contact becomes a problem. The normal increase of independence, too, diminishes the possibility of children working with adults, or of their wanting adults even to be seen together discussing them and their "problems." Elementary school children accept parent-teacher conferences more objectively, with more pleasure, and with much less reserve than the secondary student. A third advantage in favor of the guidance program in the elementary school is related to the remedial problems encountered. The elementary child has developed certain behavior patterns, it is true. The patterns, however, are not of as long duration as those of the adolescent. The elementary child is less likely to have a reputation to live down, or to live up to. He is not involved in groups, especially at the primary level, with the intense peer concerns of the high school groups. With assistance of the proper kind, he may make adjustments in less time than if difficulties are allowed to become aggravated.

A fourth advantage is that of opportunity for contact between the teacher and child. Because the teacher works with the child consistently throughout the school day, she is not limited to the presentation of curriculum materials, but is able to interest herself in his total growth. She is able to see him in many situations and in many relationships. She can plan adjustments for special limitations and capabilities, as needs arise. The advantages of continued contact have led, in some areas, to teacher-child group assignments for longer than one year, so that teachers may develop further their understanding of a particular group's needs.

A final advantage is related to the sensitivity of teachers to children and their needs. Increased training and professionalization of teachers at the elementary level have added to the awareness of needs for special materials, techniques, and resources in guidance. The modern teacher is concerned first with children. She uses the program and all school facilities *for* them, and not *on* them. Because of this primary interest, the teacher is an enthusiastic and highly important partner in the guidance process.

DEFINITION OF
ELEMENTARY GUIDANCE

During the past quarter century the term, *guidance*, has become increasingly a part of the educational vocabulary of the elementary school. The importance of planned guidance programs has been made apparent through the development of scientific child study, and the resultant increase of knowledge concerning the needs of children.

Guidance at the elementary level has meant many things to many people. Depending on the point of view of the individual, *guidance* may have positive or negative connotations. In the thinking of some, it may be extended to include all phases of the school program and all activities. It may be interpreted to involve the work of all adult personnel within the school. To some it may mean the testing program *per se*, to others the remedial program, to others the alleviation of problems, to others the materials and methods that apply to the understanding of children's needs, and to others the total school program. The meaning has been complicated further by such statements as "Guidance is education," or "Guidance is teaching," which tend to imply that the program as we know it today has in reality always been with us, and that the teacher is the sole executor thereof.

Another statement that perhaps has confused some by implication is that "The teacher is the key in the guidance program."

The teacher is the key in the guidance program as she is the key in the health program, the music program, or any aspect of the curriculum. The fact that she is the key to the classroom program does not mean that she does not welcome effective assistance in matters of health, curriculum, or guidance. The teacher who has well-qualified special resources at her call is immeasurably strengthened in her performance with children. This is true in guidance as it is in music, or health, or other areas.

Elementary guidance is defined within the current text as a *planned program involving those materials and procedures that deal* SPECIFICALLY *with the social and emotional welfare of the pupils.* Within the framework of this definition, many persons conceivably make guidance contributions, among them parents, teachers, supervisors, administrators, nurses, and counselors. The extent of all contributions will be governed by two things: (1) the guidance philosophy that has developed within the school, and (2) the special responsibilities of the personnel. With a sound guidance philosophy, the school staff works as a coordinated group in the collection and utilization of guidance information. With the development of specialized responsibilities, it is likely that primary emphases regarding duties will become more and more diverse. The principal will be concerned with administrative duties *and* contribute to guidance; the curriculum supervisor will assist teachers with effective classroom materials and techniques, *and* support the guidance program; and the guidance person will coordinate the guidance program, *and* contribute to curriculum and administrative practices. Similarly, the school nurse, through her health knowledge and contracts with children and their parents, will contribute much guidance information while she carries on her responsibilities. In all cases, special personnel will carry on their primary assignments, according to their training, for one purpose: the best possible adjustment of all children within the school.

The above relates chiefly to those schools that are in areas sufficiently concentrated in population to warrant the employment of specialists. In many parts of the country the teacher may work with no resources other than the principal, or perhaps alone. Regardless of the number of special personnel available in a given school system, the following statements seem appropriate:

1. All functions of a guidance-centered school are pointed toward the best welfare of the child.

2. Guidance activities are carried on through the classroom teacher, or in full cooperation with her.

3. Resource persons, if any are available, apply their special training toward better understanding of children and their needs.

4. Persons directly concerned with the child plan together to make use of all possible knowledge and special skills.

GUIDANCE INVOLVES SPECIAL MATERIALS AND MAY INVOLVE SPECIAL PERSONNEL

A guidance program which is established for the purpose of furthering the social and emotional well-being of the pupils obviously is based on as complete understanding of the children as possible. This means that the effective guidance program is one in which complete personnel records are available. The extent to which guidance materials are used in the school depends upon such factors as time and the training and knowledge of personnel. The more extensive the knowledge of school people concerning child-study procedures and materials, the greater the possibility of efficient record keeping. Special personnel or teachers with special training may be helpful to others in the planning of record materials. The advantage of designated guidance personnel is that of time as well as training: teachers with the best of intentions do not have the time or energy to plan comprehensive, long-range, systematic record programs alone.

The guidance program encompasses all records which pertain to the social and emotional aspects of child growth. Such records may range from a single card to a well-padded folder. The important thing is not the expansiveness of the collection, but the use which is made of it. Interpretation and application of data gleaned from tests, questionnaires, or surveys become the important factor rather than the acquisition of such data. The more specialized the knowledge collected becomes, the greater the need for special personnel to help interpret and apply such knowledge.

GUIDANCE REQUIRES A PLANNED PROGRAM

Good guidance programs do not just happen. They are the result of careful coordinated planning within the school building and school system. Such planning is necessary to use available funds effectively, and to use time to the best advantage.

A planned program eliminates the waste of time and money. It means, for example, that the best tests available are selected systematically, and that administration, scoring, interpretation, and application are all carefully organized. It means, too, that a parent education program in guidance results from careful, cooperative planning based on real needs.

Good guidance programs require planning that is not only careful and coordinated, but also comprehensive. Special functions of a guidance program may be directed to the needs of a limited few—for example, toward the correction of problem behavior and the care of handicapped children. But a planned guidance program, to be comprehensive, aims toward the best adjustment of *all* children within the school system. Such a program, by implication, has the purpose of positive mental health, as well as remediation or correction.

In planning a comprehensive program, the matter of initiation becomes important. There have been many discussions on when a guidance program should be initiated. Some have contended that since the elementary teacher is in close and continual contact with her children, the planned program might be delayed until the secondary level. Others have felt that the need for guidance does not occur at a given age or given grade level, but exists rather throughout life, and therefore throughout the school career of the individual.

The need for guidance varies greatly with persons, but the need exists throughout the grades. If teachers, with or without assistance, can operate in a guidance-centered atmosphere from the time that a child enters school, it may mean that some problems will be eliminated or at least alleviated. Certainly a well-planned guidance program at the elementary level would be of great assistance to the secondary school, and it might even serve to cut some of the costs

4

of guidance at the secondary and adult levels, through early pre-vention.

VALUES OF A PLANNED GUIDANCE PROGRAM

A planned guidance program should make many contributions of value to the child, teacher, school, and community. A child whose needs are known and met intelligently is fortunate. He is able to work positively and efficiently within the school. The teacher who understands him is able to plan effectively for him within the group. She is better able, through understanding, to operate on a mature plane in dealing with difficult situations. The school in which guidance is important is one that works closely and co-operatively. The administrator of a guidance-centered school becomes less of a trouble-shooter, and more of a guide. The community reaps several benefits: closer understanding of their children at all ages, prevention and correction of difficulties which if un-corrected could create serious social problems, and increased un-derstanding of the total school program.

The central goal of the school guidance program and its central value is the adjustment of the pupils, and therefore the increased efficiency of the educational program. Pupils who, as in our defi-nition, have plans made specifically for them with their social and emotional well-being foremost should be those best equipped to take advantage of the school offerings. The result, therefore, should be a saving of (1) time and money, (2) wear and tear on the nervous systems of teachers, and (3) need for intensive future remediation.

summary

The elementary school is in a favorable position to pro-vide valuable guidance services to children. The approach can be positive because of the age of the children. Parents can approach contacts with school personnel optimistically and constructively. Teachers who work with the children on a total-day basis can know their needs better, and make adjustments to provide for optimum growth. The children themselves can change patterns more easily because of their youth and the lessened effect of "typing" by their peer group.

Guidance has many meanings to individuals concerned with the elementary school program. It has been restricted in the thinking of some to the testing program; others conceive of everything in education as guidance. Some consider the teacher the guidance person; others think of guidance as restricted to the specialist. Still others recognize the importance of specialists as resource persons and coordinators of the total program, with all concerned utilizing their particular skills and knowledges in a teamwork approach centered on the welfare of the child. Within the present text guidance is defined as a planned program involving those materials and procedures that deal *specifically* with the social and emotional welfare of the pupils.

In order that the elementary guidance program may be effective, careful planning is necessary. The skills and knowledge of trained personnel must be utilized to plan effective records, test usage, parent-teacher educational programs, and sound mental health for all children. Such a program will provide benefits in the prevention of future cost to the community, and in opportunities for children to utilize their full learning potential.

2

THE DEVELOPMENT
OF ELEMENTARY GUIDANCE

The previous chapter indicated that guidance has many meanings, and that the meanings individuals attach to the term depend somewhat on their own backgrounds of education and experience. The chapter indicated also that many persons are directly associated with the school guidance program, and that a carefully planned program is therefore extremely important. Some of the varied interpretations of guidance, and some of the multiplicity of interests in guidance, may become clear if we examine some of the forces that have led to the current interest in guidance in the elementary school.

The historical sources of guidance are, for many reasons, difficult to trace. Among them are the variety of conflicting opinions regarding scope and definition, the numerous contributory influences from such sciences as psychology, eugenics, sociology, and medicine, and the many persons throughout history who might conceivably be included as contributors to the development of guidance. The fact that educational guidance in this country had its sources in a number of European nations adds to the difficulty. Our purpose, therefore, is to point out briefly some of the important developments that occurred, and some of the leaders who, through their interest in the individual child, pioneered in the guidance movement.

EDUCATORS WHO INFLUENCED
THE GUIDANCE MOVEMENT

If one were to explore the writings of great educators, he very probably would find that most of them made statements of importance to the development of guidance. Prior to the Renaissance, such men as Quintilian, Socrates, and Aristotle might be included among those who provided and advocated guidance for youth. The Renaissance, with its awakening of interest in self-realization, brought forth such educators as Vittorino da Feltre, with his belief in the need for curriculum variations to promote interest on the part of his students.[1]

Three centuries later, Rousseau, in setting the needs and interests of the individual above those of the society of his day, stressed the importance of understanding child nature.[2] Pestalozzi, who also lived during the eighteenth century, is credited with being the first educator to make systematic observations of the growth of children. He studied the past histories of children as well as their present environments in an effort to determine how they might best be taught.[3]

During the nineteenth century, two names are outstanding—those of Herbart and Froebel. Herbart is known primarily for his contributions to the development of modern education as a science based upon psychological knowledge.[4] Froebel emphasized the influence of a faulty environment in childhood difficulties.[5]

G. Stanley Hall and John Dewey are prominent among twentieth century educators in this country who contributed to a scientific interest in education. Hall made a major contribution through his founding of *Pedagogical Seminary*, a journal devoted primarily to articles on child study. The writings of John Dewey are filled

[1] Frederick Eby and Charles Arrowood, *The Development of Modern Education* (New York: Prentice-Hall, Inc., 1942), p. 880.

[2] Jean Jacques Rousseau, *Emile, or Concerning Education* (Boston: D. C. Heath and Company, 1898), pp. 19, 32, 55.

[3] Eby and Arrowood, *The Development of Modern Education*, p. 471.

[4] Johann Friedrich Herbart, *The Science of Education* (Boston: D. C. Heath and Company, 1896), p. 83.

[5] S. S. F. Fletcher and J. Welton, eds., *Froebel's Chief Writings on Education* (New York: Longmans, Green and Company, 1912), p. 77.

with statements that point toward the need for understanding children and for a guidance viewpoint on the part of teachers.

THE CONTRIBUTIONS OF MEASUREMENT TO GUIDANCE

One contribution of science to guidance has been the development of measurement techniques that have made possible objective planning based on individual needs.

Early interest in scientific method was aroused by the studies of Sir Francis Galton. In *Hereditary Genius*, published in 1869, he dealt with the inheritance of mental traits, and advocated the construction of a scale to measure general abilities.[6] The large-scale researches made by Galton and his contemporaries marked the beginning of quantitative psychological studies of human development.

Interest in the needs of individuals began in this country with the recognition of the need for providing for handicapped children. The Psychological Clinic at the University of Pennsylvania, founded by Lightner Witmer in 1896 for the diagnosis of mental deficiency, was an important step in this direction.[7]

Interest in the study of differences among all children received an impetus through the work of James McKeen Cattell during the last decade of the nineteenth century. His sensory-motor tests, given to Columbia University students, were a beginning in the type of experiments that led to intelligence-test development.[8]

Mental measurement as a science was advanced greatly through the work of Alfred Binet, whose extensive experiments in the development of intelligence-test items culminated in the 1905 scale. The importance of his work is indicated by the fact that adaptations of his 1905 scale are found in many scales since developed, and by the widespread use to which the scale has been put in countries throughout the world.

The entry of the United States into World War I gave rise to

[6] Leonard Carmichael, ed., *Manual of Child Psychology*, 2d ed. (New York: Wiley and Sons, 1954), p. 988.

[7] Rudolph Pintner, *Intelligence Testing, Methods and Results* (New York: Henry Holt and Company, 1931), p. 11.

[8] Rudolph Pintner, *op. cit.*, p. 12.

9

the need for measuring the intelligence of large groups of men. Psychologists, working cooperatively, developed tests that proved to be the forerunners of thousands of such tests now in existence. Yearbooks such as Buros' *Mental Measurements Yearbook*, listing thousands of test titles, exemplify the scope of present-day measurement.

CHILD STUDY DEVELOPMENTS

The work of Binet, and the work of the University of Pennsylvania staff, are directed primarily toward the need for identifying and assisting mentally retarded children. Through such efforts, awareness of individual differences in children grew. It was not alone in the area of mental retardation, however, that interest in child needs was centered. Several other influences must be counted, among them the interest in psychoanalysis, the establishment of juvenile clinics, the mental hygiene movement, and the influence of organizations devoted to child study.

Psychoanalysis, a development of the early twentieth century, involved the study of emotional difficulties as outgrowths of happenings and experiences of the past. The study of an individual then came to involve not only diagnosis and classification, but also a detailed and profound research into his personal background. When inquiry centered on past experiences, psychiatric interest was directed toward children for the first time.[9]

The first clinic to be opened after that of the University of Pennsylvania was founded for quite a different purpose—that of assisting juvenile delinquents. This clinic, established in 1909 by Dr. William Healy, created a nationwide interest in child guidance.[10] By 1914 over one hundred clinics had been established to help children in trouble.

In 1921, the Commonwealth Fund became interested in the child guidance movement, and established demonstration clinics in a number of cities throughout the country. By 1927 nearly 500 of these clinics were serving some 40,000 children.[11]

[9] Leo Kanner, *Child Psychiatry*, 2d ed. (Springfield, Ill.: Charles C. Thomas, Publisher, 1948), p. 7.
[10] Ernest Harms, ed., *Handbook of Child Guidance* (New York: Child Care Publications, 1947), p. 22.
[11] Ernest Harms, *op. cit.*, p. 23.

Another factor contributing to the interest in mental health was the founding of the National Committee for Mental Hygiene in 1909 by Clifford Beers. Beers, author of *A Mind That Found Itself*, became interested in problems of mental health as the result of confinement as a mental hospital patient. The Committee, organized to promote improvement in services to the mentally ill, has become nationwide in influence, and through publications and other media has contributed tremendously to public understanding of guidance needs at child and adult levels.

Numerous organizations have contributed to the guidance movement. Some, such as the National Association for Mental Health, have, as their primary purpose, the education of the public in this area. Others, such as the Child Study Association of America, the United States Children's Bureau, the Association for Childhood Education International, the National Congress of Parents and Teachers, and many service organizations, have a broader educational scope, but support the child guidance area extensively through committees and publications. These organizations and others maintain lists of materials for mailing that are directed toward the understanding of children and their needs.

VOCATIONAL GUIDANCE

The interest of educators and scientists in the problem of individual adaptations found practical application in the beginning of the vocational guidance movement in 1908. Earlier, some vocational counseling had been done by interested individuals. Frank Parsons, however, is credited with being the founder of vocational guidance in the United States. On January 13, 1908, the Vocation Bureau of Boston was opened at the Civic Service House, with Parsons as Director and Vocational Counselor.[12] In cooperation with others, he sponsored the first National Conference on Vocational Guidance in 1910, the Boston Employment Managers' Association in 1911, and the Public School Bureau in 1912.[13]

Early courses for vocational counselors included one planned

---

[12] John M. Brewer, *History of Vocational Guidance* (New York: Harper & Brothers, 1942), p. 59.

[13] Anna Y. Reed, *Guidance and Personnel Services in Education* (Ithaca, New York: Cornell University Press, 1944), p. 6.

11

by Parsons which met every two weeks in Boston in 1910. The first university course in vocational counseling was offered by the Harvard University Summer School in 1911. The University of Chicago and Columbia University also pioneered in the vocational guidance movement by offering courses in 1913.[14]

At the present time college and university offerings in guidance are found in every state. The early vocational guidance offerings have been expanded to include other types of guidance as well. Until very recently the emphasis in course offerings in guidance has been on the secondary and adult levels, owing perhaps to the early stress on vocational guidance, and to the resulting expansion of guidance services within the secondary school. It is encouraging to note, however, that general courses in guidance tend increasingly to devote attention to the elementary program, and that a growing number of higher institutions are offering courses in elementary school guidance.

GROWTH OF ELEMENTARY GUIDANCE PROGRAMS

The growth of organized guidance programs in the elementary school has been rapid and extensive. Some of the reasons for the growth have been outlined in the previous chapter, and need not be repeated here. It may be important, however, for all those who work with guidance programs in the elementary school, to review for themselves the recency of the organized guidance movement in schools at this level, and thus understand the flexibility of interpretation of guidance and guidance functions within various school systems.

Two studies point out the recency of organized guidance in the elementary school. One, made in 75 selected cities in the United States in 1928, showed that at that time, only 16 cities reported a definite counseling system in their elementary schools. Only six cities reported counselors in individual schools.[15] Another, involving the guidance practices of 70 cities in the United States with populations over 100,000 (1930 census) revealed that only 23 elementary

---

[14] John M. Brewer, *History of Vocational Guidance*, pp. 184-185.
[15] Lillian G. Gordon, *Summary of Findings of a Questionnaire on Elementary School Counseling*, issued by the Pasadena, California, City Schools on January 31, 1929. (Mimeographed.)

schools of 62 that participated in the study reported any personnel responsible for pupil adjustment work.[16] These schools were in districts that because of their size might logically be expected to provide special services. The figures in Table 2-1 show the tremendous increase in guidance personnel in one county during a recent ten-year period, and attest dramatically to the growing importance of these services at the elementary level.[17]

TABLE 2-1

ELEMENTARY GUIDANCE PERSONNEL

		Directors	Counselors	Psychol-ogists	Psychome-trists	Total
1944	Full Time	4				
	Part Time	1				
	Total	5				5
1954	Full Time	32	71	13	21	
	Part Time	0	1	11	3	
	Total	32	72	24	24	152

The thirty-fold increase in guidance personnel in Los Angeles County elementary schools is significant, too, in view of the fact that a state-wide survey in 1948 served to locate only one hundred such persons throughout the entire State of California.[18]

Growth is indicated further through contrasting the Rosecrance study (page 17) with one published in 1953.[19] The National Association of Guidance Supervisors and Counselor Trainers, in cooperation with state departments of education, surveyed 611 "typical" schools in 19 states and found that approximately one-third had guidance services in some form, although the services, as shown in Table 2-2, were limited. The interest in extension of

[16] Francis Chase Rosecrance, "The Organization and Administration of Personnel and Guidance Services in Large City School Systems" (Doctor of Philosophy dissertation, School of Education, Northwestern University, 1936).
[17] Los Angeles County Superintendent of Schools, Division of Research and Guidance, Mimeographed Bulletin #183, April 30, 1954.
[18] Ruth A. Martinson, "The Elementary School Counselor in California" (Doctor of Education dissertation, School of Education, University of California, Los Angeles, 1949).
[19] National Association of Guidance Supervisors and Counselor Trainers, *A National Study of Existing and Recommended Practices for Assisting Youth Adjustment in Selected Elementary Schools of the United States* (Ann Arbor, Michigan: Ann Arbor Publishers, 1953), pp. 13-14.

13

guidance services is also shown, with 18.9 per cent desiring more visiting teachers, 24.4 per cent more counselors, and 46.2 per cent seeking more services from school psychologists.

TABLE 2-2

PER CENT OF SCHOOLS WITH GUIDANCE PERSONNEL

	Visiting Teacher	Counselor	School Psychologist
Services Available	34.7	32.8	32.8
Full Time	7.3	6	3
Half Time	5	3.6	4.3
Less than Half Time	34	25.1	25.5

PER CENT OF DESIRED INCREASE IN GUIDANCE PERSONNEL

	Visiting Teacher	Counselor	School Psychologist
Services Desired	18.9	24.4	46.2
Full Time	8.1	10.4	7.7
Half Time	8	22.9	9.8
Less than Half Time	10	2	28.7

The brief history of school guidance and its future may be examined from yet another standpoint—that of the length of existence of the vitally essential occupational area of school psychologist. The school psychologist is recognized as an important consultant within the school system fortunate enough to have his services, and the need is expanding rapidly. Yet the school psychologist is a comparatively new person within the school consultant group. The exact date of appointment of the first school psychologist is not known. Some reference is made to their functioning in child study departments and psychological laboratories during the first decade of the century. Arnold Gesell makes this statement about his own professional career:

> In 1915 the Connecticut State Board of Education appointed a school psychologist to make mental examinations of backward and defective children in rural, village, and urban schools, and to devise methods for their better care in the public schools. Connecticut was the first state of the union to create a position of this kind.[20]

The *Journal of Consulting Psychology* for July, 1942, was devoted to the school psychologist. In this issue, the title is described

[20] Norma E. Cutts, ed., *School Psychologists at Mid-Century* (Washington, D.C.: American Psychological Association, 1955), p. 24.

as about twenty years old. The statement is made that the term probably appeared in the published literature in 1923.[21] It seems safe to assume, although exact data are lacking, that school psychologists in any number are within an occupational category that is little more than thirty years old.

The growth of the occupation is shown by a survey in 1953-54, made by the Division of School Psychologists of the American Psychological Association. The survey, which involved members of the Division, identified 1,002 individuals who were serving as psychological personnel in the United States. This figure, on the basis of local surveys, is considered to be conservative.

Although the growth in numbers of school psychologists during thirty years has been great, the demand for more trained psychologists is greater. On the basis of recommended ratios of one psychologist per 3,000 students, the current need is 12,000 within the United States. By the year 1970 the need will be 15,000.[22]

It seems obvious that although the growth of guidance and the increase in guidance personnel during the last three decades has been tremendous, the future growth must be accelerated. At present, needs are being met in some areas, but many parts of the country have yet to make the first steps in the organization of guidance programs and in the hiring of personnel, particularly at the elementary level.

summary

Guidance in the elementary school has grown from many educational sources, and has been influenced by many persons. Noted educators, through their writings, stimulated interest in the needs of children. Scientists, particularly through the development of measurement techniques, underscored the importance of child study. Numerous organizations interested in mental health inevitably became interested in young children and their mental health. The development of vocational guidance and the expansion of the guidance concept at the secondary

---

[21] Norma E. Cutts, *op. cit.*, p. 23.
[22] Norma E. Cutts, *op. cit.*, p. 4.

15

level extended gradually to earlier age levels. The importance of all information concerning an individual, stressed further by the psychoanalytic movement, implied a need for systematic guidance at the elementary school level.

The growth of elementary guidance has been great during the last thirty years. Needs for personnel have become apparent, and school districts have increased greatly the number of guidance resources within their elementary schools. Future needs indicate that growth will be accelerated if increasing demands are met adequately.

3

GUIDANCE
MATERIALS AND COST
IN MODERN EDUCATION

The current chapter is based upon the assumption set forth in Chapter 1: that school guidance logically begins when a child enters school, and that an organized, comprehensive guidance program at the elementary level contributes much to the well-being of all—children, teachers, and parents.

An *organized* guidance program goes beyond good intentions. It requires that some individual or group of individuals coordinate the guidance activities of the school to *insure* an effective program. The organized program requires, too, certain basic materials and facilities.

Our discussion here of necessary materials and cost is centered upon the physical aspects of guidance. Personnel are referred to only in terms of total cost of the program. The relationships of guidance personnel to the educational program, their qualifications and contributions, and possible personnel arrangements are discussed in Chapters 8 and 10.

PHYSICAL FACILITIES

The physical facilities needed for guidance purposes are relatively modest. Primarily they involve storage space for current records and resource materials, and room space for testing, interviewing, and small group conferences. Because of differences between the elementary and secondary school, certain differences exist in these two seemingly simple problems of space.

Storage space for current records at the elementary level can be provided in the classroom. The arrangement for central filing made necessary by departmentalization at the secondary level is not needed in the elementary school. Since the elementary teacher works with the children during the entire day, with few exceptions, and since she may work with the same group for more than one year, she is far more directly and continuously concerned with the welfare of her pupils than any other persons in the school (or outside of the school, with the exception of parents). She has more need than anyone else to refer to records and to add data. It seems logical, therefore, that records should be located in the classroom, and that if records are needed by others for study or for the addition of information, they be requested from the teacher for a specified length of time.

Storage of records in the classroom requires that the confidential nature of records be preserved. Many schools provide small metal files, large enough to hold the folders of a class group. The files are locked except when in use by authorized personnel.

Some persons have questioned the wisdom of keeping records in the classroom. "Can teachers be trusted with the content of records? Won't they gossip and cause trouble for the school?" These questions typify the arguments presented in favor of central locked files. The questions seem to indicate the need for pre-service and in-service training of teachers in professional use of data, more than anything else. If teachers cannot be trusted with records, one might ask whether they can be trusted to carry on discussions with parent groups or to use test results. The writers feel that they can and must be trusted in all areas, and that if questions arise, inservice discussions on effective professional use of records are the real need.

The only exception to the filing of records in the classroom folder would be that of confidential information given to special school personnel that would require interpretation to the teacher, information in which privacy had been requested by the informant, or information that might involve intra-faculty relationships. Ex-

18

amples might be a normally supportive parent who came to school to "blow off steam" to the counselor, or the teacher whose husband became involved in a particularly spicy marital scandal. In the latter case, general interpretation might go to the child's teacher in relation to "difficulties at home" that might affect the child, but the mother's feelings and her future attitudes regarding her group status also would be an important consideration.

Storage facilities need some limited extension beyond the classroom file. Tests, cumulative record blanks, guidance forms in regular use, and library facilities all must be provided for. In some schools, tests and record forms are stored in the administrative offices, or in the counselor's office, if one exists. The important need is for secure storage, with a responsible person in charge, to insure continuous and adequate supplies and professional use of test materials. Library facilities can be provided in either the central administrative office, the counselor's office, or the school library. Library materials for staff and parent use should be classified and located in such a way that they will be used extensively. Whether an attractive display case in the main entrance, with an invitation to check out books and pamphlets with a clerk, or whether a section of the school library is reserved for parents and staff is a matter of local planning and staff cooperation. Attractive, accessible space and publicity will promote use.

In addition to storage facilities, each school should provide some area for individual testing and interviewing. Such a space need not be large, but it should be private. Such a room would provide opportunities for any resource person, whether the local guidance consultant, county consultant, building counselor, principal, or specially trained teacher, to test individual children without interruption, or to confer with children, school personnel, or parents.

Many guidance persons at the elementary level have laughingly referred to the problems of testing in custodians' broom closets (to which the custodians need access) or to testing in nurses' offices (between patches). The multiple use of space is difficult for all concerned and reduces the effectiveness of performance. While the nurse or custodian suffers frustration, the guidance person becomes skeptical about the results of his work. Any worker in the schools needs space, whether he be principal, cook, clerk, teacher, custodian, general supervisor, or guidance worker.

19

The room for guidance should be private and attractive, with space for storage of individual tests and counselor records, and with room for individual and small-group testing. The testing responsibility of counselors at the elementary and secondary levels differs somewhat with regard to the use of group tests. At the elementary level, the classroom teacher more commonly administers group tests. The elementary counselor, however, in addition to individual testing responsibilities, may be asked to test individuals from several groups who were absent at the time of testing, or who are new to the school.

The guidance room might be used for staff conferences, in guidance or in other areas. In addition to providing working space for guidance personnel and guidance committee members, such a room would provide a "home base" for the guidance person or persons, to which teachers and others could come for materials and assistance. Although referrals of children ordinarily are made through the principal, there are occasions when the principal would not function in a liaison capacity. The teacher may wish to talk with the counselor on a confidential basis, and that should be her privilege. Or, she may wish simply to look in and ask to borrow a pamphlet dealing with a topic such as conference techniques. Liaison is important, but so is direct informal contact.

BASIC MATERIALS

The materials that are minimal essentials to any guidance program include *cumulative records* (see Chapter 7 for full discussion), *standardized tests* (Chapter 6), *library materials* for staff use, and any *printed forms* used by the district. Such forms might include, among others, case study forms, transfer forms, and parent conference records. These materials will form the basis for estimations of guidance costs in districts of varying sizes.

COST

Since guidance programs in elementary schools are relatively new and since the organization of such programs varies tremendously, any discussion of cost must be based upon recommendations and their implementation. Although comparison to high school guidance costs is admittedly hazardous because of differences in

20

programs and materials, an application of secondary guidance costs to the elementary school is interesting in consideration of what might be done.

In a survey[1] of approximately eighty nationally known guidance specialists, it was determined that the following items are chargeable to guidance at the secondary level:

(1) salaries paid to directors, counselors, clerks, social workers, and psychologists for performance of guidance functions;

(2) tests and the scoring of tests;

(3) research material for the counselor's library and for the students;

(4) record-keeping devices used for guidance services; and

(5) expenses for follow-up programs.

Of the above items, the first would be equally true at the elementary level; the second would vary only in terms of types of tests and test scoring. Machine-scoring costs would occur only at the upper-grade levels. Research material (item 3) would become materials for the counselor, student, and parent; record-keeping expenses (item 4) would be similar at all levels; and expense for follow-up programs (item 5) would be less at the elementary level, although follow-up programs of individual pupils certainly should be carried on.

Crosby applied the five items listed above to a study of guidance costs in California during the 1947-48 school year. He found that in ten high schools in which he conducted personal surveys, the cost range of guidance services for guidance was from 1.4 per cent of the total expenditures to 5.9 per cent, with an average of 3.4 per cent, and an average annual cost per student of $10.48. In all other high schools of the state, surveyed by means of a questionnaire, he found a percentage of total expenditure ranging from 2.2 per cent to 3.0 per cent of the total budget, with an average cost per student of $9.70. The latter figure is the one with which the costs of an elementary school program will be compared.

Comparison of guidance programs and their costs at the elementary and secondary level should be made only with a full recognition of both similarities and differences. The comparison made is logical

---

[1] Joseph Wallace Crosby, "The Cost of Guidance Services in Selected High Schools," unpublished mimeographed bulletin, Division of Research and Guidance, Los Angeles County Schools.

in one sense because of the following findings by Crosby: (1) the major cost was for personnel, and (2) teachers administered group tests in the majority of schools, as they do at the elementary level. Differences between the guidance programs surveyed and those at the elementary level will occur in the following instances: the smaller high schools utilized homeroom guidance programs; the guidance directors spent all of their time in supervising the guidance program; and much counselor time in all of the schools was devoted to program planning. None of these would be true of the typical elementary program.

One additional word of caution is necessary. The costs of elementary guidance shown in the table that follows (Table 3-1) are less than those of the secondary schools. One should *not* assume that secondary schools should therefore pare their guidance budgets. Thoughtful persons realize that secondary schools do much with vocational guidance, program planning, and with accumulated problems that is not done in elementary guidance.

In Table 3-1, the personnel are listed in the ratio recommended by the California Association of School Administrators.[2] Test costs are taken from the 1954 catalogue of a nationwide test company. The costs of cumulative records are based on an admittedly theoretical 25 cents per folder. However, the allocation for records is more than generous, since the 1955 price list of one publisher indicates that the amount allocated for 2,400 pupils actually would purchase more than 4,000 records in quantity orders.[3] The clerical estimate is based upon the assumption that a psychologist and counselor will use the equivalent of half-time clerical help during the year for test scoring and recording, writeups of case studies, ordering of materials, and keeping records, and the counselor alone will need quarter-time. The salaries of the counselor and psychologist are the writers' estimates of equitable current salaries for positions that require school experience plus one to two years of additional specialized training.

[2] California Association of School Administrators, "Proposed Program of Essential Services for Elementary and Secondary Schools," *Financial Support of the Public Schools in California*, May, 1951, pp. 21-22.

[3] *Listed Prices for California State Cumulative Record Forms, Elementary*, A. Carlisle & Company, 645 Harrison Street, San Francisco, California, Bulletin 23382 (Los Angeles, California: Division of Research and Guidance, Los Angeles County Schools, May, 1955).

TABLE 3-1

ESTIMATED YEAR'S COST OF MINIMUM ELEMENTARY GUIDANCE PROGRAM

	Per 1,200 Pupils				Per 2,400 Pupils			
	Group Int. Tests	*Group Ach. Tests*	*Cum. Records*	*Misc.*	*Group Int. Tests*	*Group Ach. Tests*	*Cum. Records*	*Misc.*
Kindergarten			43.25				86.50	
First		13.84 (Reading Readiness)				27.68 (Reading Readiness)		
Second	13.84				27.68			
Third		22.49				44.98		
Fourth		24.22				48.44		
Fifth	13.84	24.22			27.68	48.44		
Sixth		24.22				48.44		
All Grades:								
Counseling Personnel				(Couns.) 6,000.00				(Couns. & Psychol.) 14,000.00
Library				100.00				200.00
Mimeographed and Individual Test Materials				100.00				200.00
Clerical				(Quarter time) 900.00				(Half time) 1,800.00
Added Cumulative Records for New Pupils or Replacements			43.25				86.50	
Totals	27.68	108.99	86.50	7,100.00	55.36	217.98	173.00	16,200.00

Total per 1,200 pupils: 7,323.17   Total per 2,400 pupils: 16,646.34
Cost per pupil: 6.10   Cost per pupil: 6.94

Although Table 3-1 is admittedly theoretical, it may provide a basis for estimating guidance costs at the elementary level that is somewhat better than pure guess. If one compares the per-pupil cost to the average cost in California high schools during 1947-48, it can be seen that the present elementary program could be planned at a cost that is roughly two-thirds the figure for the high school program. It should be recognized, too, that costs have presumably risen somewhat since that time.

It may be helpful to look also at costs if programs provide for complete and comprehensive guidance activities. Table 3-2 extends

23

TABLE 3-2

ESTIMATED YEAR'S COST OF OPTIMUM ELEMENTARY GUIDANCE PROGRAM

	Group Int. Tests	Group Ach. Tests	Group Personality and Attitude Inventories	Cumulative Records	1,200 Pupils	2,400 Pupils
Kindergarten				X	43.25	86.50
First		(Reading Readiness) X			13.84	27.68
Second	X				13.84	27.68
Third		(Reading) X	X		22.49	44.98
Fourth	X	(General) X			24.22	48.44
Fifth		(General) X	X		24.22	48.44
Sixth	X	(General) X			24.22	48.44

	1,200 Pupils	2,400 Pupils
All Grades: Counseling Personnel	Couns. & Psychol.) 14,000.00	(2 Couns. & 2 Psychol.) 28,000.00
Library	200.00	400.00
Mimeographed and Individual Test Materials	200.00	400.00
Clerical	(1 Full time) 3,600.00	(2 Full time) 7,200.00
Cumulative Records for New Pupils or Replacements	43.25	86.50
Academic Remedial Assistance	(Half time) 3,000.00	(Full time) 6,000.00
Psychiatric and Clinic Resources	1,000.00	2,000.00
Total cost:	22,209.33	44,418.66
Cost per pupil per year:	18.51	18.51

the services and materials suggested in Table 3-1 on minimum costs. The testing program, for example, is extended to include group personality and attitude tests. Guidance personnel are provided in the ratio of one person per 600 children. Library, mimeographed, and testing materials are doubled in cost. The clerical ratio per person is doubled. Funds have been allocated for academic remedial assistance and psychiatric facilities.

Such a program would have many advantages over the minimum. Guidance publications, both commercial and local, could be made available to parents. Counseling and psychological personnel would have time to carry on intensive studies of children who need special help, and plan special educational facilities for them, or arrange for their needs through neighboring facilities. Test materials could be extended to include a variety of clinical tests for use with exceptional children. Assistance could be given to children of normal or superior intelligence who were in need of academic help. Outside resource people could be brought in to work with individual children and to serve as consultants to staff members.

Most important of all, teachers would not face the typical current situation in which they so often recognize the need for help and are unable to summon it. Assistance would be available not only in terms of resource personnel and effective attention to the needs of their pupils, but also in terms of planning their own classroom guidance activities. Further assistance could be available to them in such matters as test scoring and recording of certain basic cumulative record data. With such facilities, certainly the guidance work of the classroom teacher would be easier and more skillfully done, and the adjustment and learning of the children would be improved.

School people may look at Table 3-2 as the content of a never-never land. Organized guidance programs at the elementary level are a new concept in all but a few places. Many school administrators tend to think of guidance personnel for their schools in relation to the use of interested teachers, nurses, or principals. Such use of these individuals is excellent. Their effectiveness is directly related to their time and training, however, and they probably would be the first to welcome trained resource personnel with whom they could work.

Some school people identify the notion of resource personnel at the elementary level with segmentation or departmentalization of the program. Such a notion becomes untenable if one focuses his thinking upon a co-working relationship of all adult personnel, with the efforts of all devoted to the best adjustment of the children. Adults who work together, plan together, and learn together to build the best possible educational program in their schools do not operate in compartments!

The importance of some serious thought concerning organized guidance facilities for elementary schools may become more apparent through the examination of statistics which show that the cost of caring for one child *for one day* in juvenile facilities, including special services, is $6.76 for girls and $6.63 for boys.[4]

The ratio of one resource person per 600 children seems highly conservative, too, when one reads of the counselor-child ratios in correctional facilities. These range from one counselor for every seven boys to others in which one psychologist and four counselors serve 580 boys. Institutions requested six psychologists per 300 boys in one instance, and four psychologists and eight counselors per 580 boys in another.[5]

When we look at the costs and recommendations of institutions, we inspect them with full recognition of their essential nature. We do believe that examination of guidance costs in secondary schools and remedial institutions may cause us to feel that some economies might be effected through allocation of funds on a planned basis for early prevention. Perhaps the need for expansion of custodial facilities might be reduced somewhat through the efforts of adequate and trained personnel when the children are still young and hope still exists! In other words, maybe we need to start at the right end.

summary

Guidance costs in the elementary school are estimated on the basis of an organized program which allows physical space and certain basic materials, such as systematic group tests and records, library materials for staff and parent use, and individual testing materials. Personnel estimates are based upon the recommendations of school administrators.

[4] David Bogen, Executive Secretary, Los Angeles County Probation Committee, *Annual Report* (Los Angeles, 1952), p. 42.

[5] *Los Angeles Times*, July 3, 1955, part 1, p. 2.

In comparing guidance costs at the elementary and secondary levels, it is found that elementary programs can be planned for less. This does *not* imply that existing guidance programs in secondary schools should be altered or curtailed, or that necessary differences between the two levels should be eliminated. The figures simply provide a means for looking at costs. They are offered in the hope that they will show that planned guidance programs in the elementary schools, with personnel who can coordinate the programs and work as resources to the teachers and children, are not prohibitively expensive. Similarly, data from correctional institutions are of interest, to indicate that even highly complete guidance programs would be extremely conservative on a comparative cost basis. Obviously, more attention needs to be directed toward preventive guidance at the early levels.

4

MATERIALS, METHODS, AND ROLES OF PERSONNEL IN INDIVIDUAL CHILD STUDY

Will it not be a glorious day when adults generally look upon bothersome children as individuals who are trying to solve problems instead of individuals who are trying to be problems.[1]

The goal of child study, whether individual, or of individuals within groups, is the promotion of wholesome, normal growth for children. Any separation of child study into study of (1) individuals and (2) groups is, in a sense, artificial, since in the study of any person his social and cultural group is immediately involved.

The separation of this chapter from the following chapter on group study techniques is undertaken for the purpose of discussing materials that are commonly used in the study of one person as opposed to materials that can be used in group situations.

PROBLEMS INVOLVED IN INDIVIDUAL STUDY

Central in child study is the child himself. When the adult centers his attention upon the child, he begins to look at the child

---

[1] James S. Plant, *The Envelope* (New York: Commonwealth Fund, 1950), p. 248.

and his values. He begins to ask, "What things are important *to this child?*" He begins to learn that needs, standards, values,[2] drives (or whatever term is currently in vogue) may differ. What is important to one child may not matter much to another, depending on such variables as the culture of the child, the group with which he happens to be associated during X hour of the day, his chronological, physical, and social ages, and his current ratio of successes and failures. When an adult attempts to reconcile child behavior to his own standards of what behavior ought to be, therefore, he inevitably encounters trouble. The more productive approach centers upon the child and his motivations. Problem One then in the study of the individual is the maintenance of focus upon the child.

A second general problem is that of adequate records and time for teachers to develop them. This problem points toward the need for a dual approach to records in terms of complete data for all children when such data can be easily obtained by group methods, and comprehensive, detailed records only for selected individuals. In other words, teachers need to think of individual child study as *individual,* and not attempt to apply on a wholesale basis individual study techniques to many children, in order to avoid feelings of frustration.

As teachers work with individual child study, a third problem arises—that of organization and correct interpretation of data. In their search to understand individual children (and through them, all children) teachers inevitably encounter the need for study and review of developmental characteristics. Such study is necessary to assure proper utilization of data. Collections of facts need to be checked against the best that is known concerning children.

A fourth general problem is that of the developmental point of view concerning behavior. Adults who work with children on a positive basis recognize the need for time in effecting change. Good teachers have learned to look upon changes in behavior in long-range terms. They have learned that a continuing, mature approach in working with children is necessary, and that magic wands have no part in changes in child behavior.

[2] Dorothy Lee regards *basic values* as a better explanation for the variations and variabilities in culture than *needs.* See Clyde Kluckhohn and Henry A. Murray, eds., *Personality in Nature, Society, and Culture* (New York: Alfred A. Knopf, 1953), pp. 335-41.

OUTCOMES OF INDIVIDUAL STUDY

As teachers work to understand the children and their values, they tend to improve the educational offerings of their classrooms. Their attention becomes increasingly centered upon the human element, and the curriculum becomes a series of materials to be used in the best possible fashion for the benefit of children. As a teacher studies the individual, she learns to use many individual and group materials in order to provide appropriate learning experiences for him.

The study of a child makes the teacher aware of multiple reasons for behavior. She tends to reserve judgment, to deal more intelligently with problems. She is less likely to take misbehavior as a personal affront, and is less likely to punish unfairly. She learns to study the child completely, in all areas of growth, and to make use of many resources in her efforts to understand him. Such study pays dividends for the teacher in two ways—the remediation of any existing needs for the child, and the development of an increasingly mature attitude toward others on her part. In the words of one teacher, "I didn't think it was possible, but I'm actually getting to *like* the child!"

AN APPROACH TO THE STUDY OF INDIVIDUAL CHILDREN

Teachers cannot make complete studies of all of their children. Such studies are neither justified nor necessary. It is important that teachers understand how to study children, and how to work with others in such study. It is important, further, that all persons involved in child study respect one another and assume capability on the other's part to understand findings. The clinician who works with teachers in such an arrangement interprets studies completely to them on the assumption that they are important partners with the same goal as his—the adjustment of the child.

The extent of study, or the depth of study, depends upon the time and training of the participant. The study of the individual, therefore, becomes a cumulative affair, with the teacher as the energizer and executor. The teacher initiates the collection of data, continues with the gathering of pertinent information, collaborates

30

with others who may be of assistance, and works with them in carrying out recommendations. The process becomes one of continuing partnership, with the teacher of the greatest importance so far as the school is concerned. In schools in which consultant services are available, the procedure may resemble the following:

1. The teacher initiates the study, and begins the collection of data.
2. Other persons who have had contact with the child supply requested data. (These may include the school nurse, doctor, principal, other teachers, parents.)
3. If further study is needed, the teacher may request that the principal contact consultants. (These may be counselors, psychometrists, psychologists, school social workers, or others with special training.)
4. If the consultants need assistance, they may contact community agencies.
5. The agencies report action and recommendations to the consultant, who in turn reports to the principal and teacher.
6. The teacher works with the child in terms of the recommendations made.
7. Continuous contact and follow-up is maintained by the consultant with the teacher, through periodic progress conferences or check sheets.

Variations in the above procedure are governed by the resources available, and by the need for the use of such resources. In some instances, only the teacher and principal may work together. In others, a counselor may be the only additional aid. Referrals, too, may be made by persons other than the teacher. In all cases, however, one principle remains constant: that all resources are brought together to assist the teacher in the job she is doing. All agencies, in other words, center their efforts toward the adjustment and increasing maturity of the individual child.

TEACHERS BEGIN TO STUDY THE INDIVIDUAL

In their concern for the individual, teachers may wonder how best to begin the process of understanding him and his needs. They may feel hesitant about their own backgrounds and abilities. The hesitation is natural, and wholesome. Recognition of limitations is important, regardless of the training of the individual concerned. For example, the clinical psychologist without school experience

,ay be a valuable resource to the teacher in terms of her under-
.tanding of a child's potential and needs, but he may not be able to
recommend specific curriculum materials or practices, or even to
talk about general school activities of value. Similarly, the school
doctor may contribute much concerning physical condition and
still learn much concerning abilities. It has been stated many times
that the best-trained teachers are also those who are most cognizant
of children's needs, and the most eager for help. The same is true
of well-trained resource persons, and makes desirable the use of
many facilities when those facilities are available. The responsibility
for seeking help becomes an individual problem, with the attention
centered not upon personal competency, but upon the welfare of
the child.

The logical starting point for child study might be a summary
of what is currently known. The answers to such questions as:
What is he like in the group? What about his ability? What things
does he like to do? How does he compare with others in games?
What is known about his family background? and others will serve
to indicate his present status, and will furnish Step Number One in
the process of understanding the child. The form that is reproduced
here is used in many schools, and may furnish guiding questions to
teachers who are seeking to understand a certain child.

DISTRICT:

TEACHER'S OUTLINE OF PUPIL STUDY*

I. *Identification:*

Name ——————————————— Grade ———

Teacher ———————— School ———————

Birth date ————————— Age ——— Sex —————

Date referred ———— Home address ——————

Phone ————

* *Note to teachers:* To work out a "guidance plan" for a pupil it is necessary to *collect, organize,* and *interpret* information concerning him. The following SOURCES OF INFORMATION are available and valuable:

1. OBSERVE PUPIL'S BEHAVIORS (variety of situations and times).
2. STUDY SCHOOL RECORDS (tests, grades, reports, etc.).
3. TALK WITH PUPIL, PARENTS, AND FORMER TEACHERS.
4. STUDY CREATIVE WORK (oral and written reports, drawings, etc.).

The *Teacher's Journal of Anecdotal Records* may be useful as a record
book in prolonged study.

32

II. *Emotional adjustment:*
   A. In what situations does the pupil most frequently become upset?
   B. What does he do when he is upset or unsuccessful?
   C. What does he say about himself?

III. *Social adjustment:*
   A. What are the most typical activities of the pupil with his friends and classmates?

IV. *Physical maturity and development:*
   A. What is the pupil's physical status in relation to others in his room: appearance, size, speech, vision, hearing, nervous habits, etc.?
   B. What is the pupil's coordination in games and motor activities?

V. *Educational experiences:*
   A. What is your estimate of the pupil's scholastic *ability* in relation to present *achievement*?
   B. What scores has the pupil made on achievement tests and I.Q. tests?
   C. What are the pupil's *interests* and "preferred" activities: outdoor, scientific, mechanical, artistic, musical, social, and academic situations?
   D. What does the pupil say about school and his ability to learn?

VI. *Home background:*
   A. What older or younger brothers or sisters live in the home? What has the pupil said about them?
   B. What "homepressure" is applied to make the pupil "conform" and "achieve"?
   C. What does the pupil say about his family and "his place" in it?

VII. *Statement of problem:* ——————————————————

LACo., R&G
#21010 (T-2a)
8/1/52

The approach that Step Two will take may vary tremendously, depending on the information the teacher needs. The materials that follow are placed by arbitrary choice, and not in any order to be followed. A teacher may want to use any, or part, of them in any order, or may wish to add techniques of her own. The dis-

33

cussion of anecdotal records[3] appears next because it is a popular and valuable approach to further understanding of children.

ANECDOTAL RECORDS

The anecdote is a brief, objective account of an event that seems to be important to the child or to the teacher in understanding the

Varied experiences within the school day increase the possibilities for meaningful observation of individual children. (*Courtesy Division of Elementary Education, Office of the Los Angeles County Superintendent of Schools.*)

child. It is used by the teacher in conjunction with her regular teaching duties, and may accumulate without set limit to add to her

[3] For those who wish additional information about the use of anecdotal records, and particularly about the group approach to the use of anecdotal records in studying children, many fine books are available. Two well-known sources are *Helping Teacher Understand Children* (American Council on Education, 1945), and the Association for Supervision and Curriculum Development, *Fostering Mental Health in Our Schools*, 1950 Yearbook (National Education Association, 1950).

background of knowledge about the child. The criteria for use of the anecdote are simple. They may be stated as follows:

1. Describe those incidents that seem important TO THE CHILD. Child and adult values differ. Look at his behavior from his point of view.

2. Use clear, exact descriptions of exactly what the child does. If possible, include the names of others involved.

3. Avoid personal reaction to behavior. (Lazy, sweet, etc.)

4. Write about a variety of behaviors and a variety of situations.

5. Reserve final judgment. Regard the child as worthy and different in some respect from all others in his group. Use the developmental approach.

6. Keep the anecdotes brief and to the point. Literary style is a minor factor. Abbreviate or use partial sentences if the meaning can be kept clear.

7. Give the place, date, and situation for all anecdotes.

A teacher may initiate the use of anecdotal records by choosing any child of interest to her. It is important that the teacher start the use of anecdotes through the study of one child to prevent diffusion of effort. As the teacher works with one child, she will find that she is learning about others as well, and she may transfer her study to another child at any time.

No set method for recording anecdotes is necessary. It is necessary primarily that they be readable and usable by persons other than the immediate teacher. Anecdotes properly written can be of tremendous value to counselors, psychologists, and future teachers of the child. The anecdote may be written on a card, in a notebook, on a simple prepared form, or on a pad. The important factor is recording the anecdote accurately and as completely as possible, which means as soon as feasible after the occurrence. This cannot always be done immediately; the teacher may be working with a group, and may have to rely on her memory until recess time or after school.

The following anecdote illustrates one form that may be used:

Name of Child _____ Charles K., 2nd Grade _____

Observer: _____ Miss Merrill _____

Description of Behavior	Time, Place Date
Charles stood on the sidelines with me during baseball game. He said, "I make a horse picture this morning. Did you see it?" Went on to tell that he often painted at home; that he painted scenery; that he painted from top of roof; that he put board on chimney and sat there. Then he could see *whole* world!	10:30 Recess 12/2/54

As the anecdotes about a given child accumulate, so does information. The teacher begins to see patterns of behaviors, attitudes, interests, and abilities. She begins to see the need for added information, so that the record becomes again a part of the cumulative continuing approach.

In many parts of the country, teachers have worked together in child study groups which have used the anecdotal record as a point of departure.[4] The study groups have the advantage of teachers carrying on in-service study of children together, with meetings in which they discuss and check each other's understandings of children. The discussions serve to point out the need for study and for consultation with experts as the teachers go along, in order that they have the opportunity to check the validity of their hypotheses concerning a given child.

The following anecdotes illustrate events of importance to children, or reveal attitudes, learnings, and needs that are important to the teacher in her understanding of the child.

Name of Child	Dennis V., 4th Grade
Observer:	S. G., Teacher

Description of Behavior	Time, Place Date
Talked out of turn when I was explaining something. I told him that if he had anything to say he should raise his hand. He said, "Oh, no one ever listens to me anyway."	10/20 11:45 Spelling
A visiting photographer selected several students for a picture to be taken indoors. D. was working outdoors	10/21 9:45

[4] *Helping Teachers Understand Children* (Washington, D.C.: The American Council on Education, 1945).

36

with the group. He was not chosen and said, "It's a damn gyp!" (He mumbled this several times to the other students.)

The adult observing Dennis would begin to wonder what Dennis thought of himself as a group member, and whether the feelings expressed here would be borne out in subsequent anecdotes.

The following anecdote reveals poignantly the differences between child and adult values:

| Name of Child | Peter A., Kindergarten |
| Observer: | M. C. D., Teacher |

Description of Behavior	Time, Place Date
During sharing time Peter rose and volunteered the following: "My Mommy didn't want a dog and my daddy didn't want the dog, but I did, but they asked a friend of theirs if they would like to have the dog, and they said they would, so they took it, and I won't have a dog to play with no more."	*5/5/55* Sharing

This anecdote, though brief, illustrates dramatically the attitudes of a group toward one of its members, and suggests certainly the need for further study:

| Name of Child | Ben J., 4th Grade |
| Observer: | D. T., Teacher |

Description of Behavior	Time, Place Date
The class was choosing an inspector for lunch tables. Henry suggested Ben. I asked how many wanted him. No one raised his hand.	11:30 Classroom 10/31/54

Positive attributes of children, as well as their problems or needs, should be recorded. The goal should be a wide sampling of be-

37

haviors, characteristics, and interests. The following illustration reveals how a boy demonstrated positive group behavior, and furthered both group fellowship and his own popularity:

| Name of Child | Kiyoshi H., 5th Grade |
| Observer: | F. G., Playground Director |

Description of Behavior	Time, Place Date
It was mid-afternoon and the playground was filled with many children. Kiyoshi was captain of a baseball team and was arguing that his team should be up. "The champions are up at bat, not the bad-luckers," Kiyoshi stated. His rival team captain conceded that his team had lost the last two games. As Kiyoshi took his team up to bat, he suddenly changed his mind and placed his team out in the field, letting the rival team be up to bat. "Why did you let them have your ups?" I asked. "Some guys don't ever have a chance to be at bat, Coach," K. said. "We'll give them a break."	3:35 Playground 9/25

Another example of positive attitudes that might be recorded appears below. The anecdote, though brief, illustrates well the sensitivity that children often show toward the needs of others:

| Name of Child | Peggy S., 7th Grade |
| Observer: | H. S. H., Vice-principal |

Description of Behavior	Time, Place Date
P: "We had an election in homeroom today. It didn't go so well except for one thing." "What was that?" P: "Jimmy won sergeant. All of us were glad, because none of the boys will play with him or talk with him on account of his braces. All of the girls like Jimmy, even though he does wear braces. He's cute!"	3:30 Office 2/8/55

38

One might speculate that the above anecdote contributes data not only on the sensitivity toward others, but also on the developmental level of the individual!

The two groups of anecdotes that follow are written about two kindergarten boys, in different groups and schools. Both boys were under great pressure from their parents to "behave," be "good," and in general to grow up with unreasonable speed. In both instances, the teachers kept detailed records of the children, consulted with the psychologist, and worked directly with the parents themselves. In the case of Jamie, the psychologist's time did not permit the needed continuity of contact, and in the case of Bobby, the mother did not want to confer with a psychologist, because she felt that such a conference would indicate that something was wrong with her son. The contribution of the psychologists, then, was behind the scenes, and consisted of suggestions to the teachers, who used parent observations at school and at home, conferences, and pamphlet literature to help the parents and children.

Name of Child	Jamie N., Kindergarten
Observer:	J. H., Teacher

September 29:	Came into rest. Running and dancing. Went to toilet. While having tomato juice he hit Elizabeth. Elizabeth: "Jim hit me!" Jim: "I like to hurt people." I told him that we keep our hands to ourselves. He fought the air with his hands and then hit Elizabeth again, saying "I like to hurt people." He noisily danced to his cot. During rest there were periodic times of scratching on the bottom of the cot and making vocal noises. These stopped when I sat by him, but he didn't seem to really rest much easier.
October 3:	Jamie came up to rabbit cage where the children were looking at the new rabbit. He banged on the cage and said, "I like to scare animals."
October 6:	Herbie: "You know what I did last night? I went to the circus." Jamie: "I can't go to the circus until I learn to sit still in church."

Name of Child	Bobby W., Kindergarten
Observer:	Mrs. F., Teacher

September 23:	In sand, saw toy being used by boy and decided that he wanted it. Said, "Give it here," grabbed it and pulled. Other child resisted. B: "Give it to me! Do you want to grow up to be a mean, selfish little boy?"
September 28:	Was working on puzzle and said to Ronny, "You ought to have a knock on the head, you dummy!" I interrupted and said that it wasn't necessary to hit people on the head, just because puzzles are hard for them. B: "My mother hits me when I don't do right."
October 11:	In social studies we were talking about goats. Everyone told about an experience. I finally called on Bobby, who told the following: "My mother and dad bought me a goat yesterday. I keep it in my backyard. It ran at me and butted me. I butted it right back and then jumped the fence. I'm tough, I am!"
October 22:	Bobby was absent five days. Upon his return he got up and told the group he had the mumps. (His mother had told me that he had a cold.) During play, overheard remark to Bruce: "Let's play. You be the good boy and I'll be the bad boy."

Both teachers approached the study of the children on a positive basis. Their work with the parents, the continued study of the children, the adjustments that followed, all provided satisfaction and learning to them. Their own professional growth and understanding undoubtedly contributed to the welfare of other children as well.

The practical possibility for the use of observational records in studying children is proved very well in the case of Bobby. His teacher found time to keep records, and to work with the parents, despite the fact that she worked also with 53 other kindergarten children in two sessions during the day, and had a family of her own.

The final set of illustrative anecdotes was kept by a teacher who was concerned about the evidences of immaturity in a boy whose ability she felt was greater than sometimes was indicated by his behavior. These materials were collected, along with work samples, for the school psychologist.

Name of Child	Freeman T., 2nd Grade
Observer:	D. T., Teacher

October 24:	During play (1:30) asked if there was any equipment he could carry. Later during science, said the flowers grew "cause they got the vitamins from the earth."
October 25:	Helped with dramatic play setup. Said he liked to do it. Fixed boxes. We needed more than we had, so he asked if he could go to the first grade area and swipe some for our group. Talking to peers playing in house environment during dramatic play: "I'll be the father and my job will be the delivery truck." Went to store. "I need some baby food." Abandoned truck and walked as if truck were moving and delivered food to homes. Went to store, "Here's your money. I want some salt and butter." Later: "Here's my money. Now give me the pie."
October 26:	Asked to measure our wheat.
October 27:	Absent
October 28:	Helped get equipment from shed. Was in group outside circle. Asked to play game again so he would get chance on inside. Halloween party: Paraded through classroom with others, made faces as if had mask on. Showed me his hat with pride.
October 31:	Took my hand when we lined up to go to games. Wouldn't play follow leader with other boys. Sat by self. Finally joined circle game. Slipped while running. Cried and sat outside of game. Continued to cry and wouldn't line up. I had jump rope in my hand. Called his name and told him to catch rope and take it in for me. Immediately got up, stopped crying, took rope and was at head of line, walking beside me.
November 1:	Cried when told me he left play lizard in Miss R.'s car after trip to round house. Told him I'd see Miss R. at staff meeting. Wanted to go to her then. Had bought lizard with all money he had saved. At games said he'd "stick" by me so the other children wouldn't bother him and then he wouldn't get into any trouble. When we reached sand pile and I dismissed children he remained. Told me his mother

was back from hospital. "She feels much better than when she left." After this he played on slide.

November 2: When I told children about Mothers' meetings, said his mother couldn't come, just out of hospital.

November 3: Art lesson. While making clay turkey, said he couldn't get hole underneath so he could hold on to it. After I showed him, he did rest by self. I was quite surprised when I saw what lovely work he can do at times, when he concentrates upon it.

November 4: Painted turkey with slip. Enjoyed his work of art. Going to games, said John just hugged him and kissed him on cheek. Laughed about it and told each child individually. (This was the first evidence of affection toward him I have seen from the other children.) While in play yard told me he couldn't take off shoes in rhythms because had athlete's foot. Pronounced rhythms badly and asked me to pronounce it correctly. I told him. Laughed and said he always had trouble with it. (Pronounced like "ribbons.")

In talking with Freeman's mother, the psychologist learned that Freeman was the "spitting image" of her adult brother, who was feebleminded and in an institution. Freeman had attained an I.Q. score of 109 on the Stanford-Binet Scale, Form L, and the psychologist was able, in interpreting Freeman's ability level, to help the mother tremendously in changing her attitudes toward her son.

In all situations in which anecdotes are used, whether to learn how to write them objectively, whether to supply information for the teacher's own use, or whether to use them as part of a more extensive study of a child, the teacher is the usual initiator of interest in the study. She may or may not consult others, depending on the kind of help that is needed.

As we have indicated, the paper on which the anecdotes are recorded is not particularly important; neither is the form that they take, as long as they are written objectively, clearly, and as completely as possible. They do serve a valuable function in centering the interest of the teacher on a particular child and his needs.

TIME SAMPLE AND RUNNING ACCOUNT

The observer who uses time samples and running accounts in the study of individuals departs somewhat from the form of the

42

anecdote, but utilizes the same principles in recording his information.

The *time sample* is simply a series of anecdotes written at definite selected intervals during the day or week. For example, the teacher may wish to record observations about a child during certain specific times during the day. She may wish to accumulate data concerning his contacts, behavior, and interests during social studies, physical education, and music. Or, she may wish to record his behavior during one selected activity for a period of time. The selection of time is usually governed by the teacher's desire to learn more of the child's reactions to a specific activity and to his group during that activity.

Through the time sample, she may learn that a given activity may be used to further a child's status, as in the case of a child who performs poorly in structured academic areas, but shows tremendous interest in collecting and classifying materials for a terrarium. She may gain clues to ways in which she may assist a child to gain acceptance. (Does she need to play more closely with her second graders for playground activities to help the child who goes out and dawdles in a swing day after day?) The time sample supplements the anecdotal record in directing the teacher's observation to single activity periods on an intensive basis. It follows, therefore, that the time sample comes after general observation, and is taken for the purpose of confirming or denying previous "hunches" about the child.

The *running account* again is described by its title, as is the case with the anecdote and time sample. The running account consists of a recording of all possible behavior during a set period of time. The teacher may elect to write a running account about a child during a two-hour period of a given day. Her account might appear like this one in part:

8:55   Pete came into the room and slapped Barry on the back. (Not too hard.) He went over to the current events map, ran his finger over it, looked at one or two spots, then to his desk. Said to Joan, "What are you wearing earrings to school

9:00   for?" Opened his desk, rearranged some papers, picked up his library book, changed his mind, closed desk. Started to get up, stopped when room chairman called group to order.

9:05   Looked around at others when chairman asked if anyone had

9:08   anything to share. Made no move to volunteer. Yawned

43

several times, mussed hair. Tommy gave short description of weekend camping trip. Pete sat up, leaned forward, lis-
9:10 tened closely. Then offered the following: "We're going on a camping trip this weekend. My mom doesn't want to go, but she's going anyway. We have a tent with aluminum poles that my dad borrowed. It cost $200, and is big enough for six people. We're going down the coast, and are going to do surf fishing. It's lots of fun." To question, "Do you ever catch
9:12 anything?" P. replied indignantly, "What do you think we go for?" Sat down, scratched side vigorously, stretched out in seat, stuck out tongue briefly at Joan.

Obviously, the chief problem involved in the use of the time sample is that of teacher time. It is written, therefore, either at a time when the teacher is relatively free, such as during noon or on the playground when another teacher is in charge, by another observer, or by the teacher who is in a situation with more than one adult in the classroom so that responsibilities are shared. Such a situation might be a cooperative nursery or kindergarten, or a classroom with a student teacher. The regular classroom teacher who plans to write time samples or running accounts must plan in advance for her group so that she may be free to record information.

CHILDREN'S WORK

Since a child is not generally too satisfying to the adult who seats him and attempts a direct, questioning approach in his desire to "understand," skilled observation remains one of the important avenues to working satisfactorily with him. In addition to written observations about the child and his performance, the teacher may wish to use other means toward knowledge about him. These means may be found in the everyday school life of the child. They may evolve from the curriculum or from somewhat casual contacts with the individual. They do not involve verbal boring into what makes the child operate as he does. In the words of Leo Kanner:

> Direct inquiry is usually not very productive. A sustained discussion of himself is not a part of a child's way of living. The necessity of answering pointed questions about his feelings tends to create an awkward situation for which there has been no precedence in his experience. He may find it difficult to relate even those things about which he knows. . . .[5]

[5] Kanner, *Child Psychiatry*, p. 220.

The approach of the teacher who is interested in her pupils is the use of her best observational skills in a school environment that furnishes many means to children to express their feeling spontaneously. A highly structured, adult-directed environment furnishes fewer such means than one in which children work creatively in areas of real interest to them. In a child-centered, active environment even the busy teacher has many opportunities to observe the individual with others.

Art products furnish one such possibility for observation. The finished product, either by itself, or through the child's discussion of it with the group, may be intensely revealing. The two drawings below, done by members of a third grade group, illustrate the potential study value of children's art work. The group did a picture of themselves and their friends within the class. The first shows Dennis, an accepted, popular member of the group. His picture of himself, complete with freckles, smile, blue eyes and brown hair, is a reasonable facsimile. His position in the group is accurate.

The second picture was done by a girl who was in constant conflict with her peers. Both she and her mother had been under periodic psychiatric care. She was new to the group, and her at-

tention from the others consisted of comments to the effect that
Susan couldn't help acting like she did. Susan is alone in her group
picture. The violent scribbles and decapitated drawing are elo-
quent testimonials to her need for additional help.

The third illustration appears to be commonplace—a mother, a
father, a little boy, and a dog. It appears so until one learns that it
was done by Sammy, a second grader, who told about it thus:

"This is my mother, and my father, and my little brother, and
the dog."

In answer to the teacher's question, "Where are you?" Sammy
replied, "I don't belong in the picture."

The picture had been done in response to the teacher's suggestion
that they make pictures of their families. Sammy had accurately
indicated his problem.

Continuous observation of children and their art work may reveal
deviations that, along with other observations, indicate a need for
help. Children with extremely immature coordination or erratic
coordination, children who regress from the use of form to mass,
children beyond the kindergarten who persistently use a single
color, or children who are excessive either in neatness or in dis-

organization, may be children who need to be referred for additional study.

Art work is not confined to drawings of the type pictured, but may extend to finger painting, clay, easel painting, design, and many other areas. In addition to the values in content of the finished product and discussion of it, the teacher may gain many clues from comments made during the creative process itself.

Children who are at work in classroom play situations reveal many things of importance concerning themselves. A child who is hard at work in the kitchen may indicate many of the feelings that exist in her own household. Children in any informal group relationship reveal very quickly their own ability to work with others cooperatively.

INFORMAL INTERVIEWS

As stated earlier, a wise adult does not seat the child and begin a verbal probe. The adult may, however, through casual questions, or conversation with small groups, learn much about the individual. Discussions of such topics as What did you do on Sunday? What do you like to do most? What are you going to do when you grow up? Brothers and sisters? Money? Wishes? What do you like most

47

in school? may take place on the corner of the playground, before recess, after school, or during construction. A friendly adult who does not pry can learn much.

TEACHER'S DESCRIPTION

If teachers desire assistance in the study of a child, they contribute greatly in supplying information concerning him. Some teachers find that simple forms such as the one reproduced here are of help in guiding them toward complete descriptions.

DISTRICT:

TEACHER'S DESCRIPTION OF CHILD

Child's name ——————— Birth date ——— School ———

Grade — Sex — Nationality ——— Language in home ———

Teacher ————————————— Date ————

Please jot down *your impressions* of the child. Use additional sheets if you wish.

Physical conditions (i.e., size, strength, energy, "looks," health, coordination, etc.):

Ability to communicate orally:

Relations with other children:

Achievements in school:

Interests:

Mental abilities:

Emotional behavior (i.e., which feelings seem usual for him, which unusual, etc.):

Home situation:

Statement of problem: ———————————————

LACo., R&G
#21010 (T-2)
12/16/53 Revised

(If further space is necessary, use other side of sheet.)

48

ROLES OF PERSONNEL

As has been indicated throughout this chapter, the teacher has a very important role in child study, as the day-to-day observer of the child, and as the adult in continuing contact with him. The extent and depth of study in which the teacher engages depends on her time, ability, and training. The kinds of materials used and the values in their use depend upon the skill behind them. Since most teachers do not have the time or training for intensive study, they rely on resource personnel. When the efforts of all resource personnel are directed toward the collection and synthesis of data concerning a child, *child study* becomes *case study*. The tenet on which the case study is built is an assembling and synthesizing of facts, for proper interpretation by the psychologist. In addition to the teacher, various individuals contribute to the case study, among them the nurse, doctor, parent, guidance person, other teachers, principal, and other adults such as scout leaders or school librarians.

Health areas are the responsibility of the school nurse and doctor. The contributions that can be made toward understanding the needs of a child through home interviews and examinations are great, and may form the principal content of studies that involve physically handicapped children. All children should have access to regular examinations, and special examinations should be a service to any child for whom such studies are recommended. Sample forms for regular examinations and special examinations are shown on the following pages. Special examinations are usually required prior to placement in special education groups for the visually, aurally, mentally, or emotionally handicapped.

Psychological study is carried on by the appropriately trained counselor. Such study may include home conferences, classroom observations, observation of the child in other situations, study of records, conferences with school personnel, interviews with the child, and individual testing.

Tests may be given in the areas of intelligence, achievement, or personality, or in any combination of these three, depending on need. Individual testing presupposes careful training, through college or university courses, and clinical training to insure proper diagnosis.

49

MATERIALS, METHODS, AND ROLES OF PERSONNEL

DISTRICT:

NURSE FINDINGS AND RECOMMENDATIONS

Child's name _____ Birth date _____ School_____

Grade __ Sex __ Nationality _____ Language in home_____

Height-weight: _____ inches _____ pounds   Date _____

_____ inches _____ pounds   Date _____

Vision: Date _____ Right eye _____ Left eye _____

Corrected: Right eye _____ Left eye _____

Hearing: Date _____ Right ear _____ Left ear _____

Hearing defect _____

Speech: _____

Teeth: _____

Nutritional condition: _____

Health history: What illnesses, accidents, operations, birth injuries
has the child had?

Age   Type of illness, etc.

_____   _____

_____   _____

_____   _____

_____   _____

Developmental history: Are there any evidences of late development of walking, talking, bladder control, etc.?

_____

_____

General physical appearance: _____

Recommendations: _____

_____

Date: _____   Nurse _____

LACo., R&G
#21010 (1-2)
8/1/52

50

DISTRICT:

REPORT OF PHYSICIAN'S EXAMINATION

Child's name _____ Birth date _____ School_____

Grade ___ Sex ___ Nationality _____ Language in home_____

This information is to be recorded by the physician when he examines the child.

Vision: Right eye: _____ Left eye: _____

        Corrected: Right eye: _____ Left eye: _____

Hearing: Right ear: _____ Left ear: _____

        Hearing defect: _____

Condition of teeth: _____

Heart and circulatory system: _____

Nose, throat, lungs, and respiratory system: _____

_____

Neuromuscular system: _____

Gastro-intestinal system: _____

Genito-urinary system: _____

Orthopedic observations: _____

Glandular disorders: _____

What are the major health problems of this child?

Physician's recommendations:

                    Signature of physician: _____

                         Date: _____

LACo., R&G
#21010 (1-3)
8/1/52

EYE EXAMINATION REPORT

This child has been referred for possible defective vision and placement in a sight-saving or braille class. The information which you give is necessary before a final decision can be made.

Child's name ——————— Address ——————— Date ————

School ————— Grade —— Birth date ——— Vision R. —— L. ——

Reason for referral: _____
                        History of eye condition, date of onset, etc.

_____

(School Should Complete to Here)
. . . .

Eligibility for Admission:

Eye conditions necessary to be eligible for SIGHT-SAVING CLASS. (These may vary according to the eye specialist's recommendation.)

1. Children whose visual acuity ranges between 20/70 and 20/200 in the better eye after correction and treatment.
2. Children with progressive eye conditions.
3. Children with non-communicable diseases of the eye or body that affect the sight and require care to conserve the remaining vision.
4. Children might be enrolled in the special class temporarily because of:
   a. Operations on the eyes.
   b. Crossed eyes or other muscle anomalies.
   c. Effects of such diseases as measles and diabetes.

Eye conditions to be eligible for BRAILLE. (This may vary according to the eye specialist's recommendation.)

1. Children whose visual acuity is 20/200 or less in the better eye after correction and treatment.
2. Children whose peripheral field is contracted to such an extent that the widest diameter subtends an angle no greater than 20 degrees.
3. Children whose vision shows an equally handicapping visual defect.
4. Those diagnosed by a specialist as being blind or having a condition leading to early blindness.

THE FORM ON THE REVERSE SIDE HAS BEEN PRO-
VIDED FOR YOUR CONVENIENCE IN MAKING YOUR
RECOMMENDATIONS.   (*Reverse side follows.*)

LACo., R&G
#21010 (1-4)
8/1/52

Child's Name _____

	Right	Left	Both

Visual acuity without glasses _____ _____ _____

Visual acuity with present glasses _____ _____ _____

Visual acuity with Rx recommended _____ _____ _____

Type of refractive error _____

Prescription for glasses _____

Other ocular defect or disease _____

Etiology _____

Prognosis _____

Recommendations: (See reverse side for description of class and eligibility for admission.)

Class Placement: Regular _____ Sight-Saving _____ Braille _____

Restrictions: *Close eye work _____ Physical activity _____

Use of glasses: None _____ Close work only _____ Constantly _____

Other examinations needed (specify) _____

Further treatment needed (specify) _____

Symptoms to watch for _____

Other recommendations _____

_____

Date for next examination _____

Signature of Examiner

_____   _____
Date of examination   Title

*(If sight-saving placement is recommended it is assumed that re-
strictions on close eye work are based on the use of visual materials
planned for sight-saving class pupils, e.g., Large clear type.)

53

I hereby give my consent for this information to be released to school personnel.

_____   _____
Date   Parent or Guardian

LACo., R&G
#21010 (1-4)
8/1/52

Cⱻ

DISTRICT:

EAR EXAMINATION REPORT

This child has been referred for possible defective hearing and placement in a hard-of-hearing or deaf class. The information that you give is necessary before a final decision can be made.

Child's name _____ Address _____ Date _____

School _____ Grade _____ Birth date _____

Reason for referral: _____
                        History of ear condition, date of onset, etc.

_____
            (School Should Complete to Here)
. . . .

Eligibility for Admission:

Ear conditions necessary to be eligible for HARD-OF-HEARING CLASS. (These may vary according to the examining specialist's recommendations.)

    1. Children whose auditory acuity indicates a loss of 20 decibels or more in one or both ears in any two (2) frequencies in the speech range.
    2. Loss of 30 decibels or more in one ear at any one (1) frequency in the speech range.
    3. Children with a mild hearing deficiency with accompanying signs of pathological conditions that might result in progressive loss of hearing.

Ear conditions necessary to be eligible for DEAF CLASS. (These may vary according to the examining specialist's recommendations.)

    1. Children whose hearing losses range from 70 decibels in the speech range to inability to distinguish more than one or two frequencies at the highest measurable level of intensity in the better ear.

54

2. Children whose hearing losses average 50 or more decibels in the speech range in the better ear and have not learned language and speech through the unaided ear.

3. Children diagnosed by a hearing specialist as being deaf.

THE FORM ON THE REVERSE SIDE HAS BEEN PROVIDED FOR YOUR CONVENIENCE IN MAKING YOUR RECOMMENDATIONS. (*Reverse side follows.*)

LACo., R&G
#21010 (1-5)
8/1/52

OTOLOGICAL DIAGNOSIS

Child's name ————————————— Age ————— Date—————————

Audiogram

RIGHT EAR

Frequency in Cycles per Second

128	256	512	1024	2048	4096	8192

0——————————————————————
10——————————————————————
20——————————————————————
30——————————————————————
40——————————————————————
50——————————————————————
60——————————————————————
70——————————————————————
80——————————————————————
90——————————————————————
100——————————————————————
110——————————————————————
120——————————————————————

Blue—Air Conduction
Red—Bone Conduction

NOTE: The forms entitled Eye Examination Report, page 52, Ear Examination Report, page 54, and Orthopaedic Examination Report, page 57, were prepared by the Bay Area Psychologists' Group of Los Angeles County, composed of Miss Clarice Bennett, Director of Elementary Guidance, Culver City; Mrs. Corabelle Clark, School Psychologist, Compton; Robert Dunlap, formerly School Psychologist, Manhattan Beach; Mrs. Margaret Lund, Coordinator of Guidance and Special Education, Manhattan Beach; Mr. James Gladhill, formerly Director of Guidance, Hermosa Beach; Mrs. Ruth Wolfe, Director, Pupil Personnel Services, Paramount; Harrison Daigh, formerly Director of Guidance and Special Education, Redondo Beach; with Dr. Beatrice Lantz, Consultant in Research and Guidance, Office of Los Angeles County Superintendent of Schools, as Consultant.

LEFT EAR
Frequency in Cycles per Second

128   256   512   1024   2048   4096   8192

0
10
20
30
40
50
60
70
80
90
100
110
120

Blue—Air Conduction
Red—Bone Conduction

_____ Examining Audiometrist

POSITIVE PHYSICAL FINDINGS:

Mouth and Throat:
Nasal Pharynx:
Nose and Sinuses:
Ears: Right
      Left
Neck:

Additional Findings:

Causes of the hearing impairment:
Recommended class placement: Regular __ Hard-of-Hearing __

Deaf __

Date _____ _____ Examining Otologist

I hereby give my consent for this information to be released to school personnel.

_____   _____
Date   Parent or Guardian

LACo., R&G
#21010 (1-5)
8/1/52

DISTRICT:

ORTHOPAEDIC EXAMINATION REPORT

This child has been referred as being orthopaedically handicapped and for possible placement in a special class. The information that you give is necessary before a final decision can be made.

Child's name ———————— Address ———————— Date ————

School ————————————— Grade ———— Birth date ————

Reason for referral: ————————————————————————
History of handicap, date of onset, etc.

———

(School Should Complete to Here)

. . . .

Eligibility for Admission:

1. Children, diagnosed by a specialist, whose locomotion has been seriously impaired by crippling due to:
   a. infection, such as bone and joint tuberculosis, osteomyelitis, etc.
   b. birth injury, such as Erb's Palsy, bone fractures, etc.
   c. congenital anomalies, such as congenital amputation, club foot, congenital dislocations, spina bifida, etc.
   d. traumatic, such as amputations, burns, fractures, etc.
   e. tumors, such as bone tumors, bone cysts, etc.
   f. developmental diseases, such as coxa plana, spinal osteo-chondritis, etc.
   g. other conditions, such as fragile bones, muscular atrophy, muscular dystrophy, Perthes disease, etc.
2. The condition should be sufficiently severe to require enroll-ment in special schools or classes and transportation to such special schools or classes.

THE FORM ON THE REVERSE SIDE HAS BEEN PRO-VIDED FOR YOUR CONVENIENCE IN MAKING YOUR RECOMMENDATIONS.   (*Reverse side follows.*)

LACo., R&G
#21010 (1-6)
8/1/52

57

MATERIALS, METHODS, AND ROLES OF PERSONNEL

Child's name _____

Diagnosis _____

_____

Location and extent of orthopaedic handicap: _____

_____

_____

_____

What special mechanical aids should be used? _____

_____

Suggested activity restrictions including recommendations for rest:

_____

_____

_____

Other recommendations: _____

_____

_____

Date of next examination: _____

_____   _____
Date   Signature of Examiner

                                         _____
                                                 Title

I hereby give my consent for this information to be released to school personnel.

_____   _____
Date   Parent or Guardian

LACo., R&G
#21010 (1-6)
8/1/52

58

DISTRICT:

REPORT OF NEED FOR HEALTH ADJUSTMENT

This child has been referred for a restricted activity class designed to meet the needs of children with low vitality. The information you give is necessary before a final decision can be made.

Child's name _____ Address _____ Date_____

School _____ Grade _____ Birth date _____

Reason for referral: _____

History of handicap, etc.

_____

(School Should Complete to Here)

· ·

Eligibility for Admission:

1. The intent of this class is to include those children who would profit from a modified school program, but are physically unable to benefit from regular class activities. These children must be able to take care of their own physical needs and be ambulatory.
   a. In general, these include those children who need:
      (1) Supervised rest period.
      (2) Restricted physical activity.
      (3) Special nutrition.
   b. Accepted handicaps may be cardiac defects, extreme malnutrition, arrested tuberculosis, severe allergies, certain diabetic conditions, petit mal, nephritis, non-contagious febrile conditions, hemophilia, other weakening conditions, etc.
   c. A flexibility of placement is expected in this class. As the physical condition of the child changes, recommendations for transfer to a regular class, a home teacher, or other placement should be made by the parent, health consultant or school personnel.

THE FORM ON THE REVERSE SIDE HAS BEEN PRO-VIDED FOR YOUR CONVENIENCE IN MAKING YOUR RECOMMENDATIONS. *(Reverse side follows.)*

LACo., R&G
#21010 (1-7)
8/1/52

MATERIALS, METHODS, AND ROLES OF PERSONNEL

Child's name: _____

Diagnosis: _____

_____

Extent of handicap: _____

_____

Are there any special effects of the treatment given this child that the school should know about and for which provisions should be made? _____

_____

Suggested activity restrictions including recommendations for rest:

_____

_____

_____

Other recommendations: _____

_____

Date for next examination: _____

_____   _____
Date   Signature of Examiner

                                       _____
                                       Title

I hereby give my consent for this information to be released to school personnel.

_____   _____
Date   Parent or Guardian

LACo., R&G
#21010 (1-7)
8/1/52

Individual intelligence tests are used in relation to two factors: (1) previous knowledge of the child and his potential for performing adequately on a given test, and (2) the reason for which the test is given. For example, a child from an "average" English-speaking environment may be given the Revised Stanford-Binet Scale, while a child from a bilingual background may be given a performance scale such as the Grace Arthur, or the Goodenough

A well-trained guidance worker can learn much about a child during an individual testing session. (*Courtesy Division of Elementary Education, Office of the Los Angeles County Superintendent of Schools.*)

Draw-A-Man Test, as a check. In working with exceptional children, the psychologist may choose to administer the Nebraska Test of Learning Aptitude or the Leiter International Performance Scale to children with severe hearing loss, or the Bender-Gestalt to children with suspected neural involvement. The use of any one of the above scales, which are but a few selected from many possibilities, presupposes careful training in both use and interpretation on the part of the examiner.

61

In academic areas, the examiner may use group tests with individual children, or may use diagnostic tests in one specific area, such as the Gates Reading Diagnostic Tests, Gray Oral Reading Paragraphs, the Durrell-Sullivan Reading Capacity and Achievement Tests, or the Iowa Tests of Basic Skills in Reading, in assessing strengths and weaknesses. In the use of both academic and intelligence tests, the trained examiner often gains valuable insights into social or personal problems.

Some of the better known individual personality measures are the Rorschach Test, the Children's Apperception Test, the Rosenzweig Picture Frustration Study, and the World Test. These tests are used and interpreted by adequately trained psychologists.

Other methods used in the intensive study of personal adjustment are story completion, play, puppetry, and finger painting. The use of these techniques or those above is determined by the need of the child.

Numerous other persons may have contributions to make toward the study of individual children. The following partial listing suggests some of the individuals and groups who may be contacted in the process of a study:

> Parents.
> Child welfare and attendance supervisor.
> General curriculum supervisor.
> Other teachers.
> Vice-principal.
> Principal.
> PTA officer.
> Service clubs.
> City or county health office.
> Community Chest agencies and clinics.
> Juvenile Probation departments.
> Scout leader (or leader of other youth group).

This listing could be extended greatly. It is given here merely to indicate the possible scope of an individual study.

CASE CONFERENCE

When all of the facts are in, and when the study is properly interpreted, the planning for the child begins. This process, known as the *case conference*, is necessarily a cooperative affair. The medical recommendations are best interpreted by the medical representative; the psychological data and psychological or intellectual needs are best presented by the psychologist or appropriately trained counselor; specific academic planning becomes a shared responsibility in which the teacher and general curriculum supervisor play important roles. Other individuals, notably the principal, who know the child well, participate and offer suggestions.

Usually the responsibility for conduct of case conferences is delegated to the psychologist, or to the counselor, if the district has no psychologist. There are several advantages in this:

1. The person who arranges the conferences needs time to contact others and to organize group meetings. Conferences may be repeated periodically, and contact with the child should be continuous.

2. The special training of guidance personnel is utilized directly in formulating plans for the child.

3. The guidance person may use the case conference not only to help individual children, but for in-service training of teachers.

4. The responsibility is assigned in relation to the primary responsibility of the school personnel.

Through the group conferences, the persons concerned with the child are able to talk together, formulate plans, and in the conference process, to learn much from one another.

It may be well to state here that recommendations and reports, either written or oral, should be made in non-technical terms, for the use of the teacher. She is not concerned with abstractions, but with the child. Recommendations should not carry an air of finality, but should reflect the dynamics of growth itself. In other words, the tenor of the conference might be this: A group of adults have studied this child as completely as possible. The study seems to indicate that certain factors are true. In the light of what is known at the present time, certain recommendations seem logical. The hope is that they will contribute to his better adjustment, but the group recognizes the need to get together from time to time in order to evaluate him in relation to his psychological and environmental changes.

With this attitude on the part of the conference participants, the

63

child study becomes a longitudinal process, and group conferences concerning children become a professional team activity.

INDIVIDUAL THERAPY

Some school districts provide for intensive therapy and treatment of children with severe emotional problems. Such provisions are unusual, and the more common practice is that of referral to private or community agencies. The question becomes one of best use of available funds. Although individual treatment facilities unquestionably are needed, proper balance of resources must be considered. School districts use referral in dentistry and medicine, and rarely assume treatment obligations, because of limitations that would then be imposed upon the general health program. The same facts would be true in guidance. Individual therapy should not be provided at the expense of adequate guidance resources for the entire school. If therapy can be given without curtailment of these resources, that is another story, and a promising one.

FOLLOW-UP

Study of individual children cannot be dismissed without follow-up. Unless someone is responsible for long-range planning, tremendous wastes of time and money occur. Children for whom detailed studies are necessary have spent time getting that way, and logically need time and assistance in making adjustments. Teachers new to the child need help in understanding his needs and the progress he is making (or his periodic regressions). Counselors may arrange for follow-up case conferences in which teachers who have worked with a child for several years take an important part. When a child leaves the district or goes to junior high school within the district, they may indicate on transfer materials that study data are available to the proper persons in the new school. Through follow-up studies, counselors may check and guide the progress of a child to the point at which further study and contact is unnecessary. The form reproduced here may serve as a follow-up guide.

64

DISTRICT:

PROGRESS REVIEW AND FOLLOW-UP

Name _____ Birth date _____

School _____ Grade _____ Sex _____

Age _____

Significant new data:

Further recommendations:

Need for further study:

Signature _____ Date _____

Title and Position _____

LACo., R&G
#21010 (7-1)
1-29-54

summary

Individual child study begins with the classroom teacher, and is implemented by the efforts and skills of resource personnel. Observation in many areas contributes much to the teacher's understanding. Her observation may be supplemented by the use of descriptive forms, informal interviews, and individual tests. The latter require special training, and are usually the responsibility of the guidance person. The case conference becomes a means for assisting the child on a continuing basis, and provides means for in-service training of all personnel. Child study to be adequate requires constant follow-up and evaluation. Children and situations change, as well as knowledge and techniques of understanding children.

5

INFORMAL
METHODS OF
GROUP STUDY

From the time of birth, a child is necessarily a member of society. He is a unique member because of the effects of his own individual perception of social forces and happenings, but he is a group member, nevertheless. Understanding involves not only understanding him as an individual, but also understanding him as a social being. The effort at understanding must be directed toward the attitudes of others, the effects of those attitudes, and his feelings about himself and his position in the group.

The individual cannot be studied as an entity. What he is or thinks he is has been determined in large measure by the impact of others. His personality and behavior are affected by the period of history in which he lives, as well as the rules and regulations that govern his social group. The futility of separating the individual from his group in study is stated well by Murphy:

> Exactly as the Gestalt psychologist shows in the study of perception that the value of a color or a tone depends upon its context, so the individual personality can be understood only if membership character which it sustains in society at large is made clear. Personalities are not independent building stones of society; they are interdependent. Their interaction makes

the social world, and the social world acting on the young makes new personalities.[1]

The problem of group study is complex. Any teacher of experience knows that a "classroom group" consists of many subgroups at different times and in different situations, and that these subgroups are fluid. She knows, too, that Classroom X may differ greatly from Classroom Y, not only across town, but also next door. Her group in the same room varies from year to year. Each member of each group has had experiences that are different from those of other members, and from those of the teacher. The age of the teacher, even if she is a young teachers' college graduate in her first year, operates as a barrier to her efforts at understanding why the five-year-olds or ten-year-olds behave as they do. Add to this the wide variation of each individual's reactions to others in the total group or in its subgroups, and the complexity increases.

Teachers and others who study groups need to study them from a base of knowledge concerning children. We know that group behavior is related to growth change in individuals, and that age, developing insights, and outside impacts all serve to alter groupings as children grow. Teachers who work for satisfactory group relations, therefore, need to keep in mind those learnings that they have accumulated concerning children at various ages. A teacher who applies child-development knowledge to her work with young children will accept frequent change in groups and small groupings, and will avoid attempts to "socialize" large numbers. She will recognize the need for very young, immature, or new children to have time to attain group membership, and will provide environmental opportunities of interest, rather than adult pushes. She will need to work from the standpoint of her own importance to the young child, and the influence that her own warmth and acceptance have on his learnings about others. The teacher of upper-primary children knows that her children can work together in groups, but that they still need adult help in planning. They are becoming increasingly less dependent upon adults, and attach more importance to their peer associations. They do need help in working out group problems, because of imperfectly formed concepts of game rules, and because of their inability to plan complete projects. The

[1] Gardner Murphy, *Personality, A Bisocial Approach to Origins and Structure* (New York: Harper & Brothers, 1947), p. 767.

teacher of fifth and sixth grade children adjusts her group sights to the strength of the peer group, to single, intense friendships, secrets, codes, unwillingness to rely on teachers as much as formerly, and to outward separation of the sexes. She provides many opportunities for the children to work and play with others in their class group, but does so again within the context of her knowledge of children.[2]

We have learned, in the study of children and their groups, that still another important variable exists—that of individual differences in sociability. Because of varied circumstances, including interests, abilities, and past experiences, some children may show marked tendencies toward gregariousness, others not. The surface conclusion that the non-gregarious child is maladjusted is not always justified. The observer needs to evaluate the child's attitudes when he does contact others, to obtain clues to his real relationships with them. We may have, for example, a bright child who is intensely interested in science. He may spend a good share of his free time at the edge of the grounds, collecting specimens while his classmates play Run, Sheep, Run. He may still feel perfectly secure in making contributions during sharing time, in working with others, and in participating in rhythms. We cannot assess adjustment to the group solely on the basis of frequency of contact. We need to look at the child, his attitudes toward himself, and his feelings about others, to approach adequacy in our judgments.

VALUES IN GROUP STUDY

The teacher who focuses attention upon the children in her group finds that they grow and develop as interesting individuals in direct relation to her knowledge about them. She may plan specific curriculum experiences to meet the needs of individuals as she learns about their backgrounds. Angelo, for example, may gain much-needed prestige from the visit of his father, with whom the teacher has planned an illustrated discussion of harbor activities. Or Katie may gain her first peer recognition through the visit of her mother, who describes her childhood in Switzerland to a

---

[2] The teacher who wishes to review some of her learning concerning the social development of the children in her group may find the resources listed in the bibliography helpful.

fascinated class group. As children tell about themselves, teachers get cues to special interests and talents which may be used to enrich the experiences of all.

A final satisfaction may be found in the professional growth that the teacher experiences. Instead of manipulating the children to fit a prescribed curriculum, she finds that she is using the curriculum for the children. A teacher who learns about her children acquires information that is used frequently as she selects materials, or arranges activities with her group. The more she learns, the more interesting and diversified her occupation becomes. In planning and discussing group study with her professional associates, she constantly extends her informational background.

MATERIALS FOR GROUP STUDY

The materials that appear in the following sections have been placed within this chapter because they can be used with a group of children as well as with individuals. Those who examine them will find that they may be utilized with one child as well.

The materials are placed here rather than in the following chapters because they are informal, and can be adapted by teachers or guidance workers for teacher use. Teachers should, in fact, feel free to adapt and revise any group study materials to fit their own needs.

CRITERIA FOR USE OF GROUP STUDY MATERIALS

The following questions may be of help to individuals who are using or developing materials for the study of classroom groups:

1. *What is the purpose that the materials will serve?* A difference exists between using certain devices for the study of children, or using them because they seem to be interesting and the teacher hasn't seen them in this particular form before. Anyone who uses group study techniques, or suggests them to teachers, should weigh the values against the time that will be required to develop and use them.

2. *Is the material in the best possible form for efficient teacher use?* The answer to this question is governed by the answer to Question One. If a teacher is using a questionnaire to gain clues to attitudes within a small group, she may not

need as complete a form as if she were planning to tabulate responses for use in a teacher study group. Forms should be planned carefully so that they do not become burdens to busy teachers.

3. *Is the content appropriate for the age group involved?* The materials should be selected so that they have the under-standing and interest of the child who is responding to them. Reaction stories should have content appeal for the audience. Questionnaires for elementary children should not be filled with items concerning vocational plans, employment, and college choices. Nor should elementary children be expected to respond to items that may seem infantile to them!

4. *Is the material appropriate in length?* A single-page sheet may pose tremendous obstacles to third graders, who have not had great experience with writing and spelling.

5. *Is the vocabulary appropriate?* Children's responses and the teacher's calm may suffer if this is not the case. Entertainers have capitalized on the limitations of children's vocabularies. For example: "Has your dog a pedigree? No, he has brown spots." This type of discussion provides entertainment—not always information.

6. *Is the method of response well planned?* This is best clarified by several additional questions: Are necessary materials available? Has sufficient time been planned, free from interruption? Has the primary teacher planned for her group so that children may respond orally to her with reasonable effective-ness?

7. *Is the material acceptable to the student?* The student should feel free to respond to the material without embarrassment or reservations. Motivation to respond should be such that he will participate willingly, without feeling that the answers requested are "None of your business." Questions that are highly personal or that invade the feeling sphere directly should be avoided.

QUESTIONNAIRES AND INTEREST SURVEYS

Surveys that are used with elementary school children should be planned carefully for ease of response. Such seemingly simple questions as *Where were you born?* or *Of what church are you a member?* may present grave problems to children who were born in Albuquerque or Winnemucca and who are Presbyterians, while the Mormon who was born on Rib Hill may respond with ease. Similarly, the child of Tajudin Senanayake may have difficulty in listing his *father's name*—far more than the son of Bob Jones. The wording of questions is important, as is the choice of questions. The person who constructs the questionnaire needs to consider first whether the question is necessary, or whether the answer is available through other, more efficient means. In most elementary schools, the child who responded to the items above would be duplicating data that could be found in the cumulative record.

If data such as those requested above are needed, the wording of items is an important consideration. We well know the variety of responses available to the question, *Where were you born?* or the item, *Father's nationality!* Items should be stated in such a way that the response sought will be obtained. Otherwise, questionnaires that have been formulated at the cost of considerable time may not be particularly informative.

QUESTIONNAIRES FOR CHILDREN

In general, questionnaires that require pupil viewpoint or reaction are the best type to use with elementary children. They are probably best at fifth grade level, or above. The general criteria stated on pages 69-70 would, of course, apply. The person who uses written forms for response needs to assess their value in relation to the many informal opportunities to discuss topics, such as sharing time, and in relation to the possibility of parents supplying information. Forms that list vital statistics or health data are often more accurately completed by the parents. Forms that explore interests, out-of-school activities, attitudes toward others, or attitudes toward self, are of great value in understanding children. Such forms should be fairly specific and brief.

The following questions illustrate the kinds of items used by a sixth grade teacher to investigate the television habits of her pupils:

1. Do you have a television set in your home?
2. If you do not, do you watch television anywhere else?
   Where?
   How often?
3. Name the programs that you watch every week:
   Monday:
   Tuesday:
   Wednesday:
   Thursday:
   Friday:

Saturday:
Sunday:
4. List your five favorite programs in order.
5. In what room is your television set?
6. Does anyone watch television with you?
   Who?
7. What do you like best about television?
8. Is there anything you do not like about television?
9. What rules do you have at home about television?

Television guides were collected by the teacher and brought in to assist the pupils in making their responses to item three. The guides were helpful with spelling, and, in the teacher's opinion, curtailed the use of others' ideas by individuals.

The purposes of the teacher in using the television survey were to learn:

1. What are the favorite programs? (And with which programs, therefore, should the teacher become acquainted?)
2. How important is television in the total recreational pattern of the child? [3]
3. How late does he stay up?
4. What is the pattern of selection for the group? For individuals?
5. Is any home evaluation of programs apparent?

The chief general purpose of the study was to learn which programs might form the bases for group discussions of an important area of communication, and to develop selection and evaluation skills on the part of the pupils.

Other questionnaire forms may be devised for use of individual teachers or groups of teachers on such subjects as these: Present family and home composition, home responsibilities, hobbies, reading habits, radio program choices, movie habits, participation in organized activities out of school, or a variety of other topics. The forms that follow are partial examples of areas that might be informative to teachers.

[3] Harrison McClung, Consultant to the National Citizens' Committee on Educational Television, stated, in an address at the UCLA Conference on Improving School-Community Relations (August, 1954), that children average 22 hours a week in watching television and during this time see an average of 77 murders and kidnappings.

OUTSIDE ACTIVITIES

Name ———————————————————— *Date* ———————————

Grade ——————————————

The questions below are asked to help your teacher know and help you. Knowing what you do outside of school helps us plan in school, too. Answer all of the questions, please. Do not worry about spelling. No one but your teacher will see your answers.

1. What are your favorite radio programs?
2. Do you attend Sunday School?
3. What pets do you own?
4. What is your favorite game?
5. What is your hobby?
6. How often do you go to the movies?
7. What kind of movies do you like best?
8. What regular jobs do you have around home?
9. Do you have any collections? If so, what?
10. What kind of books do you like to read?
11. Do you play a musical instrument?
12. About how much time do you spend each day in practicing?
13. Do you take any other kinds of lessons? If so, what?
14. What are your favorite comic books?
15. What are your favorite television programs?
16. What do you like to do best in your spare time?
17. What groups or clubs do you belong to, such as Scouts?
18. What do you and your family do when you have fun together?
19. What interesting trips have you taken?

The following form may reveal much to a teacher concerning outside responsibilities of children. A teacher who is annoyed by a boy who regularly goes to sleep at 2:30 in the afternoon will be less annoyed when she sees his daily schedule. The form will require some introduction. The following statement will help to establish interest and willingness to participate:

It's always interesting to us to take a little time, and see what we do during a school day. We know our schedule here in school, but many of us do different things away from school. This sheet will help us look at the things we do during the day. Put down only the things that others may see. The teacher will be the only one to see your paper, but some of you may want to talk about the things you put down. We'll start very

73

early in the morning, when most of you are asleep, and go on until the time you went to bed.

This is the schedule of the boy referred to above:

DAILY SCHEDULE

Name   Joe Anderson

Morning:

Time of Day	*What I Did*
3:30 to 4:00	Slept
4:00 to 4:30	Got up to peddle papers
4:30 to 5:00	Peddled papers
5:00 to 5:30	" "
5:30 to 6:00	" "
6:00 to 6:30	" "
6:30 to 7:00	" "
7:00 to 7:30	Went home, ate breakfast
7:30 to 8:00	Washed dishes
8:00 to 8:30	Went to school

Time at School

3:30 to 4:00	Played baseball
4:00 to 4:30	Played baseball, went home
4:30 to 5:00	Went to store for mother
5:00 to 5:30	Looked at TV
5:30 to 6:00	" " "
6:00 to 6:30	Ate supper
6:30 to 7:00	Played catch with Bill H.
7:00 to 7:30	" " " " "
7:30 to 8:00	Watched TV
8:00 to 8:30	" "
8:30 to 9:00	" "
9:00 to 9:30	Went to bed
9:30 to 10:00	Asleep
10:00 to — —	"

Such heavy work responsibilities are not usual for elementary school children. However, it is possible that a child of an economically privileged family will indicate heavy responsibilities of another sort—namely a schedule that is so loaded with "opportunities" that he lacks time to breathe freely. This is the child whose parents do not want him to miss a thing; therefore, his after-school hours are filled to bursting with such activities as piano lessons, art lessons, Scouts, riding lessons, or swimming lessons to the point at which he has no time to choose activities, be inventive, play with others, or just "loaf." A schedule of this sort would not be evident unless the form above were used for a week.

QUESTIONNAIRES FOR PARENTS

The contribution that the parents of elementary school children make to school information is tremendous. The parents usually are highly interested in facilitating their child's adjustment to school, and cooperate willingly in supplying information that will assist school personnel in planning for him. Parents should be assured that the information sought will be used only by professional staff members, and that it is confidential. The usual information that is given on forms filled out by parents deals with developmental history, or health status.

Two complete forms that could be filled out by parents enrolling their children in kindergarten are reproduced here. Such forms could be filled out by mothers who bring their children to visit school in small groups prior to the opening of the term, or they could be completed at the time of the first "roundup" in the spring. It is important that the teacher explain the purposes of the forms prior to submitting them to parents.

NURSERY SCHOOL[4]

University of California at Los Angeles

Name of Child _____ Age _____ Date _____

Date of Birth _____ Place of Birth _____

Name of Parents _____

Address _____ Telephone _____
       Street   Zone

[4] Permission to use these forms has been granted by Dr. Helen Christianson, Director of the University Nursery School, University of California at Los Angeles (retired). A few minor changes (mostly omissions) have been made to adapt them for public school use.

75

DEVELOPMENTAL HISTORY:

At what age did child begin to talk? _____

What was the first word he used meaningfully? _____

At what age did he begin to use sentences? _____

Does he have any speech difficulties? _____

If so, what corrective methods used, if any? _____

_____

At what age did he cut his first tooth? _____

At what age did child first sit without support? _____

Begin to climb stairs? _____ Take first step unassisted?

_____ Walk freely and easily? _____

Does he show marked preference for right hand? _____

Left hand? _____

HABITS AND ATTITUDES AT PRESENT:

Dressing habits:
Does child dress himself: Completely _____ partially

_____ not at all? _____

If he needs assistance, how is he helped? _____

_____

Describe any arrangements for self help in getting and putting

away articles of clothing used most frequently. _____

_____

Washing habits:
Does he take such responsibilities as flushing toilet? _____

taking care of his own clothing (assistance given if necessary?)

_____ washing hands after using toilet? _____ drying

hands? _____

Eating habits:
At what regular hours does the child eat? _____

76

Does child eat at any other time? _____ If so, what?_____

Does the child eat alone? _____ With others? _____
If so, with whom? _____
What foods does the child especially like? _____
What foods does the child especially dislike? _____

Any problem connected with eating at present? _____
Guidance with reference to problem _____

Elimination habits:
Is daytime bladder control established? _____ If so, at what age was it established? _____
Does child usually stay dry at night? _____ Is child taken up at night? _____
Is bowel control established? _____ If so, at what age was it established? _____
Can he use the toilet independently or does he need assistance with his clothing? _____
Any problems connected with eliminative habits at present?

Sleeping habits:
At what time does child usually: go to bed? _____ fall asleep? _____ get up? _____
Does child take a nap? _____ If so, he naps from _____ to _____ P.M.
Does child sleep alone? _____ In room alone? _____
With whom? _____
Describe the child's routine of going to bed _____

Any problems connected with sleeping at present? _____

_____

Guidance with reference to problem _____

_____

Emotional life:

Is your child usually happy? _____ Does he laugh and smile

easily? _____

How does he show a sense of humor? _____

Is he friendly with other children? _____ With adults?

_____

Does he prefer associations with adults? _____

How does child meet new situations? _____

_____

Has child shown marked fears? _____

Guidance in such instances? _____

Does child show anger easily? _____ Does he have anger

outbursts or temper tantrums? _____ If so, on what oc-

casions? _____

Guidance in such instances _____

_____

Does child have any nervous habits? _____

Special emotional problems _____

_____

Guidance with reference to problems _____

_____

Family relationships:

Who is responsible for child's discipline: Father? _____

Mother? _____ Both? _____

Type of control most often used? _____

_____

78

Do other members of the household (relatives, servants) discipline child? _____ How? _____

Is child usually cooperative with father? _____ mother? _____ with other children in family? _____ with other members of household? _____

What points are most often at issue between parent and child?

_____

In what part of the child's daily play or routine does the father participate? _____

the mother? _____

What occasional opportunities for family fun or enjoyment are planned to which the child looks forward? _____

_____

How does the child share in housekeeping tasks in the home?

_____

Interests and play activities:
What special provision, if any, have you made in your home for your child's play? _____

_____

_____

Room of his own? _____ Alcove? _____ Patio? _____

Play yard? _____

Are arrangements such that it is easy for child to share responsibility in getting out and putting away his playthings?

_____

_____

Is an adult always present during the child's play time or does he play alone part of the time? _____

What opportunities, if any, are provided for play with other children? _____

State sex and age of each _____

_____

What are the child's special interests or toys at present? _____

_____

What pets does the child have, if any? _____

_____

Education:

Has the child attended any school? _____ List schools and

length of attendance at each _____

_____

Further data:

Note anything that may contribute to a better understanding

of your child and his needs _____

_____

THE HOME AND FAMILY

Father: Place of birth _____ Age ____
Education:

High school: name and location _____

Dates attended: _____

College or university: name and location _____

_____

Dates attended: _____

Vocational school: name and location _____

_____

Dates attended: _____

Present occupation _____

Place of business _____

Previous experience, business or professional _____

_____

Religious affiliation _____

Hobbies or interests _____

Could he be reached by phone in an emergency if no one

were at home? _____ Phone number? _____

Mother: Place of birth _____ Age ____
 Education:
 High school: name and location _____

 Dates attended: _____

 College or university: name and location _____

 _____

 Dates attended: _____

 Vocational school: name and location _____

 _____

 Dates attended: _____

 Occupation before marriage _____

 Occupation after marriage _____

 Religious affiliation _____

 Hobbies or interests _____

 _____

Children: List all children in family, including this child, in
order of birth.

Name	Sex	Age	Birth date

Other members of the household: List other adults in the home (relatives, employees, etc.)

Name	Sex	Relationship to Child	Comments
_____	_____	_____	_____
_____	_____	_____	_____
_____	_____	_____	_____
_____	_____	_____	_____

Household routine: Who is responsible for the daily routine of the child in the home? _____

When the parents are away the child is cared for:

    a. In his own home _____ By _____

    b. In the home of _____ By _____

Is he usually cared for by the same person? _____

Has he been accustomed to accept care from various people?

_____

Group experience: Has the child had any previous group experience with his peers? (Such as Sunday school or neighborhood play groups.) *Describe:* _____

_____

_____

_____

_____

In case of an emergency in which neither mother nor father can be reached, the school is authorized to call _____

at _____

☞

82

MEDICAL HISTORY

Name _____ Age ____ Date _____

Birthday _____ Pediatrician _____

Name of Parents _____

Address _____

Personal Health History

Physical and mental health of mother during pregnancy _____

Pregnancy: Full term _____ Premature
_____

Birth
Conditions

Weight at birth _____

Labor: Normal _____ Instrumental

_____ Duration _____

Caesarean _____

Condition of baby immediately following birth

_____

Injuries and malformation _____

_____

Breast feeding _____ Bottle feeding _____

Cod liver oil: When begun? _____ Amount

Nutrition   _____ Is he still receiving it? _____

Amount _____ Type _____

Nutritional disturbances: As infant? _____

Nutritional upsets at present? _____

Check diseases child has had by giving age at which he had them.

Chicken Pox _____ Whooping cough _____

Diphtheria _____

83

Other illnesses:

Respiratory: Frequent colds _____ Head colds _____ Chest colds _____

Diseases

Heart _____

Gastro-intestinal: Vomiting attacks _____

Diarrhea _____

Skin _____

Kidney _____

Operations: _____ Tonsils:_____

Immunization: Age: Smallpox _____

Diphtheria _____

Whooping cough _____

Mother: _____

Father: _____

Brothers: Number ___ Health conditions _____

Family Health History

Sisters: Number ___ Health conditions _____

Constitutional diseases in family: (Underline and give relationship of person to child.)

Tuberculosis _____ Blood disease

_____ Hay fever _____

Asthma _____ Eczema _____

Nervous _____

Has child any allergic tendencies? _____

Type of allergy: Skin _____

Nose _____ Bronchial _____

Allergic
History

What has been done to control it? _____

_____

_____

_____

_____

_____

_____

PANELS AND DISCUSSIONS BY PUPILS

Many informal opportunities for discussions by pupils present themselves in the elementary school. The teacher who capitalizes on these opportunities can do much in group guidance and can learn about the feelings and attitudes of her pupils. Informal discussions relate to classroom behavior and usually take the form of group planning sessions. The panel may be used as an outgrowth of pupil discussion, and may serve as the basis for further group participation. After the group discussion of a topic, certain children may be selected by the others to think about the subject further and these children may then present their views, to be followed by group reaction.

Topics that have been found interesting to children include these:

Is it the substitute teacher's job to keep the room quiet?
Whose job is it to keep the grounds clean?
Should the little children imitate the big ones?
Who makes the classroom a good place?
How do we make visitors like our school?
What do you like most about your friends?
What can teachers do to make the school better?

Panel discussions by pupils may be used effectively with pupil groups in other classrooms and with parent groups. Parents find discussions by children informative and stimulating. The presentations involve views that are not always considered, and form excellent bases for adult group discussions after the children have contributed their ideas and are no longer members of the group. Adult study groups have invited groups of children to discuss sub-

85

jects like those listed below, and have found the discussions extremely enlightening:

> How can families have fun together?
> How can parents help children?
> Things that make me mad.
> Television in the home.
> Things we do that are fun.
> Should children have jobs at home?
> Spending money.
> Pets.

MEASURES OF SOCIAL RELATIONS

The feelings of a child concerning his acceptability to his classmates affect profoundly his performance within the group. If he has friends and is accepted, he is free to work with others. If he is unable to gain group status, he lacks a basis for group performance. He then indulges typically in either withdrawn or aggressive behavior.

Such behavior is not always easy to classify; this fact makes the study of group relations necessary. The child who is in frequent contact with others, even in ways that are acceptable to adults, is not always accepted by other children. He may indulge in much verbal maneuvering within the group, with resultant polite response and little actual status. The verbal aggression becomes an unsatisfactory means toward solution of his problem, and diminishes only when means for developing social acceptability are found.

Teachers can recite endless examples of children who have worked hard to achieve group status. Their accounts will include stories of children who employ fawning, bribery, cajolery, annoying, and teasing, as well as the more obvious scuffling and hitting or pushing. They can describe also children who were so painfully shy that until something was done to help them attain status they performed on such a poor level that the teachers thought them to have considerably less ability than they actually possessed.

It is through the measurement of group status that the teacher can determine a child's rating with his peers. Although the teacher may feel that observation provides an adequate avenue to her understanding of group status, teachers who have experimented with the prediction of relations prior to the actual measurement know that this is not the case. Teachers may be right many times, but also may achieve a surprising number of errors.

The *sociogram* is perhaps the best known means for studying the classroom social structure. The procedure is relatively simple, and the possibilities for use are numerous.

The first criterion in the use of a sociogram is that of legitimate purpose. The question toward which the sociogram is directed should be real, and the follow-up should be immediate. If a teacher asks the children about friendships, with the promise that seating arrangements will be based upon their wishes, then the wishes should form the bases for rearrangement as far as possible. The same would be true of working arrangements, committee assignments, trip partnerships, or any other purpose.

Possible reasons for the construction of a sociogram might include these:

> A trip, where a child needed to indicate three choices for seat partners on the school bus. Such trips are taken to a wide variety of places, including the fire station, airport, bakery, dairy, museum, or zoo.
> Social studies committees. Such groupings might include children in planning, research, construction, writing, or seating.
> Room care committees.
> Science projects.
> Partners for regularly scheduled trips, such as to the school library.
> Planning dramatizations.

In presenting the question, the teacher may use her own techniques, certainly. It is important that she think out the presentation procedure carefully so that the children will understand clearly the purposes of the question. The wording may resemble the following:

> By next Thursday we are going to be ready to start work on the culmination projects for social studies. Before I talk with each of you about the particular work you want to do, I need to know something also about the working arrangement you would like. Therefore, I am going to ask you to put your name at the top of this card, and below it the numbers 1, 2, and 3. Beside the number 1, place the name of the person you would most like to work with; beside the 2, your second choice, and

87

SOCIOMETRIC TABULATION FORM

Chosen → / Chooser ↓	Ruth Allis	Irene Brown					Joseph Gold											John Smith	
Ruth Allis	•																		
Irene Brown		•																	
			•																
				•															
					•														
						•													
							•												
Joseph Gold	2	3					•											1	
								•											
									•										
										•									
											•								
												•							
													•						
														•					
															•				
																•			
John Smith																		•	
																		•	
																			•
Chosen as																			
1st choice																		1	
2nd choice	1																		
3rd choice		1																	
TOTAL																			

Sociometric tabulation form. List names in the same order vertically and horizontally. Insert a "1," "2," "3" in the proper squares to indicate the order of choices. Note example in the form: Joseph Gold chooses John Smith first, Ruth Allis second, and Irene Brown third.

beside the 3, your third choice. You may choose either boys or girls. Keep your choices secret. I am the only one who will see your cards.

The simplest method for tabulating responses is that developed by Helen Hall Jennings[5] which is shown on page 88.

To follow the charting a step further, the teacher constructs a sociogram, which portrays the group relationships more clearly to her than a chart can. To make the sociogram, she scans the chart to indentify the most popular and least popular children. These she places on the chart at the center and at the fringes, locating other children in relation to their choices. Symbols such as triangles and circles are used to designate boys and girls. (Neither sex wants to be placed in the "square" category these days!) The sociogram is first made on a sketch, trial basis, in pencil, so that alterations can be made in positions if necessary. Any clear method for showing level and direction of choice is valid. Some persons have used colors to differentiate choice, such as a red line for a first choice, green for second, and black for third. Arrows have been used for direction of choice, with a small vertical line on the arrow indicating mutual choice.

SOCIAL STRUCTURE OF A SIXTH GRADE

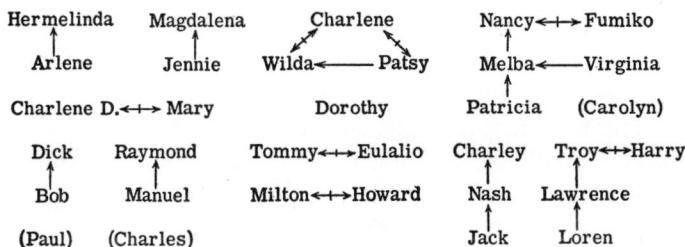

Hermelinda	Magdalena	Charlene	Nancy◄─┼─► Fumiko
Arlene	Jennie	Wilda◄────Patsy	Melba◄────Virginia
Charlene D.◄─┼─► Mary		Dorothy	Patricia (Carolyn)
Dick	Raymond	Tommy◄─┼─►Eulalio	Charley Troy◄─┼─►Harry
Bob	Manuel	Milton◄─┼─►Howard	Nash Lawrence
(Paul)	(Charles)		Jack Loren

In using the sociogram, the teacher should attempt to follow the choices of the pupils, starting with the choices of the unchosen pupils. She will need to plan all groupings as much as possible in relation to actual choices, checking the distribution so that the unchosen and chosen are not placed into distinct groups, or so that there are no cleavages of race, sex, economic groups, or social

---

[5] Helen Hall Jennings, *Sociometry in Group Relations* (Washington, D.C.: American Council on Education, 1951), p. 18.

cliques. This can be accomplished by working from second and third choices as well as first choices. The aim will be to set up working groups that will be harmonious in their relationships, and in which all group members will have an opportunity to benefit from their associations.

Teachers can use sociograms as a starting point to study status roles of children. They may use interviews to ask how one child happened to choose another, and what he likes about a particular person. They may use interest surveys to learn of talents, and use those talents as status builders. They may, through their own demonstrated appreciation of an individual, enhance his status with his peers, especially at the primary-grade level. This appreciation should be sincere at all levels and used sparingly at the upper-elementary level. Well-accepted children can assume group leadership roles, and can be asked to help less well-adjusted children.

The sociogram can be used as a basis for examining classroom procedures, opportunities for children to work with many others, to experience leadership, and to participate in purposeful group planning. The teacher will use the sociogram in evaluating her total program, the opportunities the children have for developing desirable social relationships, in and out of the classroom. She will work to break down some of the socially imposed cleavages through group games, dancing, mixed-sex groups and lines, and will maintain fluid groups so that non-accepted children may contact others in small groupings where they can work well together. She will strive, through the maintenance of high interest levels in her working groups, to keep motivation and self-direction up, and bickering down. Above all, she will use the sociogram as a *starting point*, and will realize that all planning must be evaluated through another sociogram, used several months after the first.

For the teacher who wishes to measure more than the acceptability of children in friendship, work, or play, adaptations of *social distance scales* are helpful. The social distance scale, first devised by Bogardus in 1925, has appeared in numerous forms since then. The typical form, used with children in upper-elementary grades and above, lists items that indicate degree of choice as well as the choices themselves. The type of question used by the Horace Mann-Lincoln Institute of School Experimentation at Teachers College, Columbia University, enables the child to react to his peers, and estimate their evaluation of him on a self-social distance scale. As is true with the sociogram, the social distance scale requires respect of the children's confidences on the teacher's part, and high rapport between the children and teacher.

SOCIAL DISTANCE SCALE[6]

Names of Pupils

1. Would like to have him as one of my best friends.

_____

2. Would like to have him in my group, but not as a close friend.

_____

3. Would like to be with him once in a while but not often or for long at a time.

_____

4. Don't mind his being in our room, but I don't want to have anything to do with him.

_____

5. Wish he weren't in our room.

_____

Social distance scores may be obtained by assigning values of one to five to the items. The children scoring the lowest number of points would rate highest in acceptability.

Teachers may use completion sheets of the type that follows to check pupils' attitudes toward their classmates in a variety of group contacts. The instructions may be so phrased that the teacher gets a first reaction of one individual who is the child's first choice for each category, or she may ask them to list three choices, if she wishes their reaction to more than one child. The

[6] Ruth Cunningham and Associates, *Understanding Group Behavior of Boys and Girls* (New York: Bureau of Publication, Teachers College, Columbia University, 1951), p. 406.

91

single choice is probably preferable, since relative ranking of more than one choice is necessary when the children are asked to list several children, and spontaneity decreases.

COMPLETION SHEET

Name _____ Grade _____ Date _____

1. Who always keeps his place in line? _____

2. Who always pushes and shoves in line? _____

3. Who always runs to the head of the line? _____

4. Who always enters the room quietly? _____

5. Who criticizes others for not coming into the room quietly?
   _____

6. Who always touches someone or something while entering the room? _____

7. Who always does his work when asked to do so? _____

8. Who has to be told a second time to do his work? _____

9. Who usually plays with children younger than himself at school? _____

10. Who usually plays with children older than himself at school?
    _____

11. Which boy (or boys) would rather play girls' games? _____

12. Who always likes to play alone? _____

13. Who always shares the equipment? _____

14. Who always enjoys square dancing? _____

15. Who would rather take care of the records than dance? _____

16. Who always says "excuse me," "thank you," or "I'm sorry"?
    _____

17. Who seldom says "excuse me," "thank you," or "I'm sorry"?
    _____

18. Who figures things out for himself during reading? _____

19. Who usually needs help from his neighbors during reading?

_____

20. Who is usually a leader in the group? _____

21. Who enjoys being a part of the group without taking the lead?

_____

22. Who always thinks his ideas are best? _____

23. Who usually helps others who are having difficulty in spelling?

_____

24. Who is usually willing to listen to the ideas of others? _____

25. Who seldom helps anyone? _____

26. Who usually works hard during construction? _____

27. Who usually wastes time during construction? _____

28. Who is popular with all his classmates? _____

29. Who usually tells on the children who break the class or school rules? _____

30. Who always keeps his desk neat and clean? _____

31. Who usually has to be reminded about keeping his desk neat and clean? _____

32. Who seldom forgets his room duty? _____

33. Who always has to be reminded of his room duty? _____

34. Who always wants to do another's room duty? _____

35. Who usually remembers to raise his hand? _____

36. Who usually talks out of turn? _____

37. Who usually shares with the group? _____

38. Who would rather listen than share with the group? _____

39. Who is often chosen to have a room duty? _____

40. Who is seldom chosen to have a room duty? _____

41. Who always looks neat and clean? _____

42. Who seldom looks neat and clean? _____

43. Who always plays fair during game time? _____

44. Who seldom plays fair during game time? _____

45. Who would you most like to be like? _____

BIOGRAPHICAL DATA

All data that supply information about an individual are in a sense biographical. But in this section we shall discuss specific biographical tools and their place in the elementary guidance program. These tools include data that are supplied by the individual (autobiographical) and data that are supplied by other individuals (biographical).

Usually the autobiography is confined to the upper grades of the elementary school, since skill in writing is an essential prerequisite. In some schools children work with the autobiography as part of their language arts experience. They may decide to write "The Story of My Life" and present it in booklet form. The story can be structured or unstructured, although if it is unstructured, it may be helpful to discuss informally what some of the pupil plans for content are. If an outline is used, it is well to keep it fairly simple and general, so that the response of the pupil will be free. Illustrations through drawings or photographs have been used by children and add to their interest in the process.

An outline for the pupil autobiography usually includes topics like the following:

Places I Have Lived
My Home
My First Memory
Places I Have Visited
My Family
My Hobbies
What I Do for Fun
My Favorite Friend
My Favorite Grownup
The Most Exciting Thing That Ever Happened to Me
Things That Scare Me
What I Like Best About School
What I Like Least About School
My Wishes
My Life Ambition

If teachers use the autobiography rather than other methods to gain insight into their pupils' backgrounds and attitudes, the primary purpose of the writing must remain uppermost. The emphasis should be placed on the interest of the content and on freedom of expression rather than on structure, spelling, or penmanship. Indeed, if the emphasis that should be maintained for the writing of the autobiography were the emphasis in all writing activities, more refreshing, creative products would be the result!

The diary is a much more limited approach to biographical information, in the time sense, than the autobiography. It can be highly revealing of outside activities and interests, however, as the two accounts of weekend activities below indicate:

M _____ M _____   (boy)

Monday, March 20

First I finished school. Then went home. Now's when the fun began. First a friend of mine came over. Then she asked what was in a little box I had on my workbench? "I said," a frog! "Then she said "let's make it a bigger house! "Allright!" I said "let's do it. Well first we found a big box. Then we filled the box with dirt, weeds and a dish of water and put the frog in the box, that finished. Then I ate dinner went over to my freind's house to see telivision. Then home to bed.

                    .   .   .

O _____ B _____   (girl)

I was at P_____ on the weekend and came home Monday in the car. I arrived at 15 after 3 and didn't think it was necessary to come to school because it takes 10 min. to get to school. After school I played cowboy and indians and I scalped Melinda after that I brushed my theek and took a bath and went to bed.

Young children cannot furnish autobiographical data except verbally; however, the teacher who enjoys rapport and close contact with her parent group may enlist their aid in the study of her children. One teacher experimented with this means of collecting data through asking some of her parents to write the story of their child's life up to the kindergarten stage in which the child was. The requests were made during individual conferences and were based on the teacher's desire to know each person in her group as completely as possible. The teacher used both free response and an outline, and found both approaches informative. The parents expressed interest in and approval of the teacher's request, and stated that the writing helped them to assess their

95

relations with the child. The two biographies that follow are presented in detail to indicate the wealth of information available to the teacher who works closely with her children's parents. The headings and italicized items in the first represent outline items that were given to the parent. Other data were items taken from baby records and memory that the mother felt important. Anyone who reads the biographies will be as impressed as the writers were with the wealth of developmental data given

BIOGRAPHY OF K_____ _____ _____

GENERAL BACKGROUND

On July 19, 1949, a warm and pleasant night, at about 2:00 A.M. in the morning, the first child of R_____ ____. (20 yrs.) and L_____ _____ (22 Yrs.), decided it was time that she start her journey into the world. After eight hours and twenty-four minutes of hard work and impatience a tiny bundle of joy was held by one ankle and patted on the behind until in indignation at such treatment she let out a cry and yet it was one of the most beautiful sounds I will ever hear (I had been administered a "saddle-block" anesthetic and was conscious all during her birth). The delivery was easy and fear was not present, only love and expectation. K_____ weighed in at 7 pounds, 15 ounces, and was 20½ long; health at birth —excellent!

After four days at the hospital daddy brought mother and daughter home, what a proud day! K_____ was breast fed until she was eight months old. She drank little water during her first seven months even when sweetened with Karo. She gained well on my milk and when six weeks old weighed eleven pounds. At this time orange juice was offered, but was not accepted until she was able to drink it from a glass.

K_____ was kept on a demand schedule and soon worked out a schedule of every four hours for a feeding. She only cried when hungry, wet, or uncomfortable.

MENTAL DEVELOPMENT	*Six weeks to four months*
Noticed light at	5 weeks
Followed bright object with eyes at	7 weeks
Held head up when placed on abdomen	5 weeks
Turned head in direction of a sound at	9 weeks
Reached for an object at	5½ months
Smiled at	3 months
Further comments: unusually perceptive, very good baby.	

K—— slept in a bassinette in our room until she was almost six months old. I played with her and held her at every opportunity; the fact that I had produced this tiny individual and that her future lay in our hands, was a marvel that I could hardly believe and I thanked God often for such a wonderful blessing.

I was the "frantic" type mother with K—— as far as cleanliness and letting people near the baby, or hold her. It paid large dividends though. K—— never had an illness of any sort until she was about eighteen months old (and that was a cold).

MENTAL DEVELOPMENT   *Four to six months*

Laughed out loud at   4½ months
Held toy at   4 months
Held head up well at   4½ months
Rolled over at   5½ months
Giggled at   5 months
Coughed artificially at   5 months
Pulled self forward in an attempt to
  sit up at   4½ months

Further comments: went without 10:00 P.M. feeding at six months, four days. Likes to be played with, cries when lonely. Talks to self quite a bit, says da-da-da.

(The house in which we lived when K—— was born had cement floors.) I laid K—— on our bed for periods of time during the day when she was tiny and she only fell off the bed three times, after that even though she was tiny, whenever she had squirmed her way to the edge of the bed she would stop wiggling and hold onto the spread until I would move her back to the center. It seemed to me she had a lot of common sense and has more than proved that to me during the years.

K—— was started on solid foods at three months, three weeks. Her first food was carrots offered by spoon, and she didn't like it too well. Second solid food given was pudding, offered at four months, refused to eat it. Third solid food given was cereal, offered at four months, reaction was lukewarm.

MENTAL DEVELOPMENT AND HABIT
TRAINING   *Six to twelve months*

Bowel training begun at   7 months 29 days
Reasonably complete at   9 months 14 days
Cup feedings begun at   5 months 14 days
Accepted reasonably well at   7 months 23 days
Baby's comprehension is now in-
  creasing rapidly.

97

Give examples by conduct:

Accepts food given by spoon at	5 months 2 weeks
Holds and eats cookies well at	7 months 3 weeks
Knows what no-no means at	10½ months
Waves and says bye-bye at	12 months 2 weeks
First words spoken at	5 months 1 week (they were da-day
	10 months (babee)

PHYSICAL DEVELOPMENT	*Six to twelve months*
Sat up alone at	9 months
Weaning begun at	7 months
Completed at	8 months
Began creeping at	9 months
Pulled self up at	11 months

K—— didn't crawl like most children; she had a little scooting habit of putting her left foot in front of her and dragging her right foot.

MENTAL DEVELOPMENT AND HABIT TRAINING	*One to two years*
Showed preference for right hand in reaching at	12 months
Held cup to drink at	13 months
Daytime bladder training begun at	15 months
Reasonably completed at	23 months
Night bladder training begun at	22 months
Reasonably completed at	24 months
Used spoon with good control at	18 months
Pointed to eyes, nose, or hair at	18 months
First tantrum at	19 months
First said "I won't!" (no) at	20 months (Beginning of negativism)
Began to feed self at	17 months
Used sentences at	22 months
Snipped with scissors at	24 months
Identified pictures at	20 months

PHYSICAL DEVELOPMENT	*One to two years*
Walked with help at	12 months
Stood up without help at	15 months
Lowered self from standing to sitting position at	11 months
Walked alone at	15 months
Threw a ball at	15 months

PHYSICAL DEVELOPMENT | *One to two years*

Climbed stairs with help at	18 months (No stairs until then)
Climbed stairs unaided at	20 months
Climbed into chair unaided at	12 months 3 weeks
Ran with confidence at	20 months
Jumped down at	23 months

Further comments: at 22 months started identifying things in connection with their owners, Mommy's dress, Daddy's trousers, K⎯⎯'s shoes.

K⎯⎯'s daytime bladder training was very easy to accomplish and night bladder training even more so!

At about 13 months or so K⎯⎯ was in her stroller keeping me company while I hung clothes. I stopped to chat with a neighbor and K⎯⎯ unnoticed for the moment, found a pail and paint brush full of green paint (left outside by her dad) and proceeded to paint her face, shirt, chest and stroller. Imagine my shock to turn and find a little green face with two big eyes and bright smile exposing pink tongue and white teeth looking at me. Paint remover on the stroller and Dreft (detergent) on the baby soon cleaned the matter up.

At 14 months K⎯⎯ fell out of her crib, over the foot end, while trying to climb out. She lit on her forehead and the sound on that cement floor was horrifying. She lost all the color in her face and later had a black eye, but other than that there seemed to be no ill effects.

K⎯⎯ loved to get in my powder and one day I found her looking at herself in the dressing table mirror patting large amounts of powder on her face and purring "pre-e-e-e" the closest she could come to pretty.

She is a complete extrovert. She loved to play with us and entertain us with her antics. One of her favorites was playing catch with her slip. She would start by throwing it to daddy or me, but it was soon reduced to her throwing it over her shoulder with nonchalance and then a funny face at us and scurrying to get it before we could.

MENTAL DEVELOPMENT AND HABIT
TRAINING | *Two to three years*

Vocabulary at 2 years 500 words

List several typical sentences or sayings:

"Home, again. Go see bampa, maa-maw. Go home, Mickey. Hush Duchess."

Fed self whole meal unaided at	20 months
Began to dress self at	23 months
Began to wash self at	30 months

99

List favorite songs and stories:

"The Right Somebody to Love"
"Jesus Loves Me," "Animal
   Crackers"

First memorized song or poem at
Carried tune at

PHYSICAL DEVELOPMENT

*List new physical skills and ages at
which acquired:*

Tried to clean mud off shoes at
Jumped down off steps at
Played ring around the rosie at
Jumped off floor with both feet at

*List favorite indoor toys
and amusements:*

Pencil and paper, books
   and magazines
Pounding block, blocks
Purse, powder, and lip-
   stick
25 months
25 months

Two to three years

25 months
23 months
24 months
25 months

Further comments: loves to sing and dance (we gave her dancing lessons for nine months, ages 39-48 months, but she never showed much interest or special talent for it. She preferred to talk to other children and watch them.)

K_____'s ability to talk still astounds me, even at this age she spoke very clearly and at 22 months she was using three-word sentences.

At about 30 months she saw for the first time her daddy kill and dress a rabbit. It worried her until we explained away her questions. She's always been around animals, rabbits, chickens, dogs, and I believe having played with rabbits on the lawn caused this concern over killing one for food. Even today she doesn't care too much for cooked rabbit or chicken (she has, also, seen these killed and dressed).

When I became pregnant with our second child I told K_____ as much about it as I thought she would understand and tried to answer any questions she asked. When I felt life, I would take her hand and put it on my abdomen and let her feel this life inside me. At my showers she opened the presents for the new baby and so by the time the baby was ready to be born she was anticipating the new baby with joy. The night C_____ was born I began my labor early in the morning and without my waking her she came into our bedroom and found me packing my suitcase and said "Is the new baby coming?"

K_____ stayed with my parents while I was at the hospital and the evening we came home from the hospital K_____ was there to ride home with us. She was very quiet and so sweet around C_____, but she somehow knew things would be different now. The second

100

day home I started to nurse the baby and K_____ had been sitting by me on the bed, she slipped off the bed and with tears in her eyes started to leave the room, closing the door behind her saying "I know, the baby is going to eat and you want me to leave you alone" (on previous feeding I had admonished K_____ to leave us alone), but when I saw the heartbreak in her eyes, the expression of the outsider, I decided it was better for the baby to get a few germs and a little rough handling, than to shut K_____ out of this new grand experience our family was having. So I immediately invited her to come back to her perch on my bed and the look in her eyes was a rich reward!

MENTAL AND SOCIAL DEVELOPMENT   *Three to five years*

Vocabulary at three years contained 1000 words.
List typical comments: "You hear me."
Attitudes toward other children: friendly toward all. Takes lead in social relationship.

Describe special traits and skills, favorite indoor play materials, stories, and songs:

3 years—dries dishes, talks very intelligently; colors, dolls. Likes me to recite "The Little Bisque Doll." Songs—"Jesus Loves Me," "Little Red Wagon Painted Blue."
4 years—songs, "The Crooked Man," "Give a Little Whistle," "Everybody's Got a Laughing Place."

PHYSICAL DEVELOPMENT   *Three to five years*

List favorite outdoor play apparatus and special physical abilities at:

Three years—swing, spring horse. K_____ started skating at 3 years.
Four years—swings, tricycle.

At 41 months I started taking K_____ to pre-school for two hours, one day a week. She loved to go and took part in everything. The most interesting thing I learned about her was that she was more concerned about others having a good time than she was about her own good times. When painting she would take time out to tell some other child painting at the same time how good his or her picture was.

At 4 years 11 months K_____ always would say "How do you know?" when I answered a "Did you know?" question.

At 38 months K_____ had a tendency to urinate more than ordinary. We took her to the doctor and after an examination we made an appointment at Children's Hospital for a glucose tolerance test. K_____ was very good through all of it, didn't cry, but was reluctant after the first test was taken. The results were uncertain and fearing she might have diabetes the doctor put her on a sugar restricted diet. She has cooperated, always, excellently and together we have succeeded in doing as the doctor requested.

At five years during her kindergarten physical examination sugar was found in the urine, and having a new doctor he wanted us to have another test made, we complied and the results showed her to have "renal glycosuria," again, a restricted diet (not as rigid as the first one) was given in hopes that by working together we can help her from getting diabetes at a later age, we pray this will come true.

MENTAL, PERSONALITY, AND CHARACTER DEVELOPMENT *Five years*

Describe reactions at entering kindergarten, any adjustments required, how worked out.

K‑‑‑‑‑ wanted me to go with her the first day of school and after registration I left, she didn't cry and was completely enthralled by the whole experience. She enjoys taking part in the sharing time with the class and takes great pride in showing us her paintings and the things she has made in school. Sometimes she will volunteer information on what she is doing at school and at other times has to be asked about it. She loves her teacher and considers her a friend of the family. She walks to school and follows a certain route and when they were working on the road it upset her to have to go another way to cross the street. She walks with Sam and cries if he runs off and leaves her.

List favorite indoor games and play materials; special skills; favorite books, songs, and stories.

Games: School (she likes to be the teacher and pretends she is Mrs. M‑‑‑‑‑), store, house, dolls, office.

Materials: My discarded envelopes and papers, pencil and paper, crayons, paints, dolls and doll clothes, dress-up clothes, purse, comb, mirror, pretend powder and lipstick.

Special skills: Colors and paints with artistry, is able to comb her doll's hair in varied and nice styles, washes dishes expertly and can straighten her room very neatly. Uses her hands with skill and artistry in creating things. She enjoys talking and will talk to imaginary people and will do commercials and demonstrations for imaginary audiences.

Favorite books: "Timothy," the story of a little boy whose grandmother comes to visit (K‑‑‑‑‑ has a wonderful companionship with both sets of grandparents). "Humpty Dumpty" a monthly magazine. Books of any kind are greatly enjoyed and after they have been read to her, she will read them to her sister from memory quite accurately.

Favorite story: "The Three Bears" if dramatized is even more delightful and enjoyed.

102

K―――― loves responsibility and is delighted when I allow her to do the dishes and clean up the kitchen in her own way and time. On vacation last year she washed all the dishes at every meal except one and helped to straighten up our camp site.

K―――― minds much better than the average child; one day she had been punished for being noisy outside her sister's window while she was napping; it consisted of making her sit on the front steps and not allowing her to have any friends to keep her company. I forgot about her and forty minutes later when I thought of it I went to the front porch and there she sat, her friends playing next door, waiting for me to come and dismiss the punishment, which I did with a loving gesture.

K―――― receives 25¢ a week allowance and loves to go shopping; however, she usually ends up buying some kind of sweets or pads of paper to play with in her "school."

K―――― was happy when her second sister was born and I would show her pictures of the development of a baby within the mother and would tell her the story of her own birth and the time we spent at the hospital and other little stories about her babyhood; she loved every minute of it. She is very helpful in caring for the baby and gets along pretty well with her first sister, but resents having to take her with her to play and likes her to take naps.

GENERAL INFORMATION

We moved to ――――― ――――― when K―――― was 21½ months and never having had any other children around her to play with she was really happy about the whole thing. Unfortunately, she has never had a little girl her own age to play with, but her closest companion is a girl about two years her senior. She lives next door and while being bossy she has never been mean to her and I am thankful for this quality in her. Another close companion has been a boy six months her senior who has been like a brother to her. He says that he's going to marry K―――― and she in return says that she's going to marry Sam, maybe. At about three years of age while swimming together in the wading pool they got to acting silly and took off their suits and they found out the physical differences between a boy and a girl. They had a natural curiosity about this, but after asking his mother and me many questions they were satisfied and continued their swim without any self-consciousness. I have always tried to create a natural and normal air about sex and the differences between an adult body and a child's, while at the same time I have tried to teach modesty, in this, as in all things concerning our family. Her father cooperated to the fullest.

K―――― has always been a clean child and doesn't like to get really dirty while playing. Perhaps this was due to previous training and it used to worry me, and I encouraged her playing and getting dirty, but she still likes to stay clean and I have stopped worrying about it.

103

She loves to talk to people and is able to carry on a very intelligent conversation. At about three years she loved to entertain my parents by sitting at the piano and pretending to play and would sing and talk to them for sometimes as long as an hour. They never said a word for she carried on their part of the conversation for them.

She has an excellent memory and is able to learn songs, prayers, poems rapidly. She often is able to refresh my memory about things that I'm hazy about.

K_____ loves to play school (this was a favorite past-time when she first entered school), office, or any game that has lots of papers and "business things" to do. She likes to play dolls and combs her doll's hair and dresses her often. However, this interest didn't fully develop until she was about five.

Until she was two and a half years old, K_____ went almost everywhere with us. As a baby she went in her bassinette and we took her to church, choir practice, parties, visiting, everywhere and we went quite a bit. When her sister was about four months old we found it impractical to take both of them and so started the era of a babysitter in our family. She is particular about whom we have sit and we try to please her as best we can.

K_____ has attended church since she was six weeks old and she feels very much at home inside one. We attend regularly and attend various activities during the week; our life revolves around the church and K_____ accepts this and her religious training here at home as a perfectly normal activity. To her it's just part of growing up.

K_____ has been around animals always and has seen the birth of puppies and the hatching of pheasant eggs. (She held one egg in her hand that had started to crack until the chick had pecked it open and the little wet thing fell into her hands.) She thought it was a wonderful experience. Life in any form is of great interest to her. This includes flowers and trees, etc. Ever since she was able to walk and be outside she derives great enjoyment from picking a flower and bringing the beauty of it to me to share.

She loves beautiful clothes. She has worn a tee shirt and overalls (corduroy) most of her life. I felt they were warmer than dresses and offered more protection against scratches and bruises. Sundays she always wears a dress and to school and when she goes out, and she likes to pick the dress she is to wear. She prefers a dress with a full skirt that swirls out when she pivots and everytime she puts one on she has to dance in it just to get the feel of it. Whenever we go out or have company she has me comb her hair and as she puts it, "I want to look pretty, too."

Parents

K——'s father and I are of Protestant faith and attend church regularly. L—— was raised in the church, but I didn't join the church until I was sixteen, at which time I was baptized. We both have high school diplomas and have attended college for eighteen months or more. L—— has had only one serious contagious illness. That was scarlet fever at the age of seven years. He was hospitalized with it. When he had been in the service for about a year (19 years of age) it was discovered that he had renal glycosuria. It has never been determined if it was inherited. I have had only two serious illnesses, whooping cough and the measles at the same time. I was not hospitalized (I was three years of age). Our income is moderate; our tastes are similar and we love each other and our family.

In conclusion

K—— has been a pleasure to us. It is a great thing to us to watch this new life unfold before our eyes. From the time we first held her in our arms and then through the steps of growing into a small young lady that is quite grown up in her understanding and abilities. With God's help we will guide her through the years until she stands a young woman at life's threshold, ready, willing, and able to accept the future as it lies before her.

CHARTS

Weight:

Birth	7 lbs. 15 oz.	15 months	. . . .	22 lbs.
1 month	9 lbs. 2 oz.	24 months	. . . .	26 lbs.
2 months	12 lbs.	39 months	. . . .	31 lbs.
5½ months	17 lbs. 8 oz.	48 months	. . . .	34 lbs.
7 months	19 lbs. 8 oz.	54 months	. . . .	38 lbs.
8 months	19 lbs. 14 oz.	60 months	. . . .	38 lbs.
11 months	21 lbs.	68 months	. . . .	41 lbs.

Height:

Birth	20½ inches	11 months	29½ inches
1 month	21¼ inches	15 months	30½ inches
5 months	26 inches	33 months	36¾ inches
7 months	27 inches	60 months	43½ inches

Appearance of Teeth:

Upper Teeth		Lower Teeth	
Right	Left	Right	Left
1. 10 mos.	10 mos.	1. 7 mos.	8 mos.
2. 12 mos.	13 mos.	2.	
3.	14 mos.	3.	15 mos.
		4.	
		5.	24 mos.

105

Record of Shots:

D.P.T.

1. 5½ mos.   1st booster   30 mos.
2. 6½ mos.   2nd booster   61 mos.
3. 8   mos.   Vaccination for smallpox taken at 8 months

⊂⊨

BIOGRAPHY OF P____ __ _____

This is the story of a five-year-old girl named P____ __ _____.
She lives in ____ _____, _____ with her mother, father,
and sister. P____'s mother and father are both of Scotch-Irish
descent. Her mother devotes her time to keeping the house and to
teaching her children. Her father makes his livelihood as a mechanical engineer, and works long hours away from home. As it happens,
there were twins on both sides of the family. So it was then that
P____ and her sister ____ were born at the _____ Hospital, in
_____, _____, on June 29, 1949. If it had not been for the
capable hands of Dr. P____ H__, P____ might not have lived.
The mother and father were grateful to Dr. H__ and named the
second born P____.

Being a twin is not an easy thing to be, particularly for an identical twin. To begin with, you have to be lucky because the odds are
about 400 to 1 that you will not be an identical twin. Although alike
in looks, the girls have very different personalities.

It seems as though P____'s sister, ____ was the more active even
before birth. In fact, in their 5 years ____ has always been the
leader. P____ has always been more inward in her feelings and
therefore she doesn't make friends as easily as ____. P____ has
proved the more studious. She doesn't learn quite as fast as her
sister, but once she does get it she doesn't forget. P____ is more
apt to stay home and color, sew or pretend she is washing dishes
than go out to play. ____ is more aggressive in every way and
may "outshine" her sister when they are together.

The _____ family lived in many rented houses. The first was a
one-bedroom cottage in _____, which needless to say became too
small all too soon. The twins were healthy infants and continued
to be so under the watchful care and feeding of their parents. Although small in stature, the girls had a lot of energy and sometimes
wore their parents as well as grandparents out.

When the girls were four years old, the family moved into their
own home in ____ _____, _____. The whole family shared
in the yard work, and the girls took great delight and pride when
their daddy bought them their first plants. P____ and ____ had a

106

room of their own and were good housekeepers. The family also shared pleasant vacations camping in the woods. Every year a new spot was picked and they all set out for a wonderful time.

When the girls started Kindergarten in September, 1954, they were placed in separate rooms. This did make a difference in P_____. She seemed more sure of herself, but still held back somewhat around her sister.

From here on only time will tell. P_____ _____ will have a full lifetime to prove to herself and family that she has a very definite place in this world. In June of this year, 1955, the girls will be six years old. So you see there is lots of time.

RATING SCALES AND CHECK LISTS

Rating scales and check lists may be used by the teacher to study individual children's general group progress, by children to assess their classmates, or by children to assess themselves.

The following form is one that combines a check list with questions concerning the individual. It is of value to the classroom teacher in evaluating a child's adjustment.

PUPIL BEHAVIOR OBSERVATION RECORD*

To understand any pupil's behavior it is important to observe his reactions in the classroom, on the playground, at school, in the neighborhood and at home. The following items are aids in reporting observations of young people. Underline *any* and *all* words or phrases that describe the behavior of the pupil as you have observed it. If no phrase seems appropriate, write in an answer. Please feel free to individualize the report as much as possible. If you know of reasons for the conditions you underline, please jot them down at the right of your answers.

Is this pupil as strong physically as others?

Is exceptionally strong and active
Seldom tires
Has ordinary endurance
Is seriously handicapped and weak
Is very sluggish, easily exhausted

Does he have purpose and persistence?

Keeps goal constantly in mind
Completes what he starts

* Adapted from form developed by Division of Research and Guidance, Los Angeles County Schools.

Is able to evaluate his work
Prefers to do own planning
Works without outside stimulation
Has long interest span
Usually tries
Needs urging to stay with a task
Has short interest span
Is easily discouraged
Seldom completes the job

How does he get along with other people?

Is a successful leader and organizer
Works well with others
Earns recognition of the group
Is considerate of others
Works against group interests
Prefers to work by himself
Is destructive of property
Has bad temper when thwarted
Is quarrelsome
Is over-aggressive; wants own way
Is easily led, a follower
Is given to lying to get out of difficulties
Is continuously disobedient to parents, teachers and others
Is inclined to bully others
Has few friends, alone much of the time

What is his usual disposition?

Cheerful, full of life
Kind and sympathetic
Self-controlled, calm
More quiet than most
Responsive to humor
Irritable, selfish
Changeable, sometimes moody
Impulsive, given to tantrums
Stubborn, cruel, very destructive

Are there indications of nervousness?

Is inclined to be startled and upset by unexpected occurrences
Is extremely irritable; unduly annoyed by noise
Is readily and unexpectedly moved to tears by apparent trifles
Reports frequent digestive upsets
Is extremely restless and endlessly active
Stutters; speech is often blocked or garbled
Constantly complains about his health
Bites nails, fidgets, picks at self, masturbates

Has a variable appetite; is finicky or nauseated frequently
Has episodes of disturbed breathing; allergy and asthmatic attacks
Has apparent tremors, spasms, tics
Reports disturbed sleep; has nightmares, talks out, walks in sleep
Loses bowel or bladder control
Complains of headaches, dizziness, fainting

Does the pupil behavior indicate self-confidence and assurance?

Meets new people and situations easily
Recites in class and talks freely in a group
Is willing to play games though unskilled
Faces problems or trouble without seeking aid
Is not easily discouraged by others
Is proud of appearance or physique
Is a good competitor; easily accepts success or failure
Participates freely in activities
Is inclined to worry unduly about school success, family prob-
lems, personal popularity
Hesitates to enter a competitive situation
Makes continuous excuses for personal failures
Is very sensitive to limitations of appearance or physique
Exaggerates minor illnesses or physical difficulties
Blames others for own failures
Has great difficulty in making a decision
Is easily discouraged by criticism or failure
Seems to daydream a great deal of the time
Is boastful about self and accomplishments
Is shy and timid, afraid to take part in life situations

What are the pupil's special interests and abilities?

What forms of discipline have been used? How often? How does
he respond?

How much is he praised and for what?

What way have you found to be the most satisfactory manner of
guiding this pupil?

How does he respond to success?

How does he respond to failure?

What is the attitude of others toward him? What are his friends
like?

Is he satisfied with his progress in school? Does he like school?

What persistent mannerisms or behaviors are characteristic of him?

What type of situations seem most often to precipitate his behavior
difficulties?

To what extent do you think the pupil's problem is due to his physical condition, previous school experience, conditions at home, or his ability to get along with others?

.   .   .

The form as it appears here is a rather comprehensive rating schedule designed to serve as an individual behavior check list for a given time in a child's development. Such a schedule becomes cumulative and permanent through the selection and listing of traits alongside a check grid that indicates the year of school attendance. For example:

	K	1	2	3	4	5	6
Is this pupil as strong physically as others?							
Is exceptionally strong and active							
Seldom tires							
Has ordinary endurance							
Is seriously handicapped and weak							
Is very sluggish, easily exhausted							

At times it is helpful to the teacher to examine the progress and behavior of her entire group through the use of a check sheet. The questions that follow are of help to the teacher who wishes to evaluate this area:[7]

	Yes	Need Improvement
1. The children are responsible for classroom routines.		
2. The children are polite and considerate of one another.		
3. The children make suggestions for room arrangements and operations.		
4. The children take responsibility for cleanup.		
5. The children go from one activity to another with reasonable independence.		
6. The children are helpful to each other.		

[7] Adapted from form developed by J. Richard Harsh, Consultant in Elementary Research and Guidance, Los Angeles County Schools (Bulletin 23163) *What Are the Children Doing?*

110

Need
Yes Improve-
ment

7. The children assume leadership for group activities.
8. The children have a businesslike attitude in their approach to class work.
9. The children are interested in their work.
10. The children follow directions well.
11. The children assume responsibility for the completion of projects.
12. The children make use of resource materials.
13. The materials are appropriate to their level of maturity.
14. The working atmosphere is conducive to achievement.
15. The children are at ease with one another.
16. The children are using their own experience and life situations in their work.
17. The children are stimulated to develop individual interests and creative activity.

A check sheet of the above type is of value to the teacher not only in examining various aspects of her group's behavior, but in examining aspects of the curriculum and classroom organization. Teachers may use check sheets like this in discussions with the guidance resource person and curriculum consultant or principal. The check list then becomes a means for identifying group needs and a starting point for plans for improvement.

Self-ratings by pupils may be either oral, as conferences with the teacher, or written. They may be used with the group and in individual conferences between the pupil and teacher. They are of value when they help the pupil to evaluate himself in relation to his daily progress as a successful group member.

Self-ratings may be used by the teacher to help pupils grow in desirable group relationships and to assess the pupils' attitudes toward themselves. The way in which a pupil periodically reacts to his success and failure in the group tells a teacher much about his feelings of adequacy or inadequacy with others.

Self-ratings are used best in connection with the daily life of

111

the classroom. They should evolve from the needs of the group and should be used periodically to gauge progress in group living. The self-rating scale for the elementary school child should be much more specific and brief than that employed with secondary students and adults. Rating scales that list "responsibility" or "co-operation" or "initiative" do not have much meaning to elementary children, although the children may attempt response willingly. If rating scales are to be used as learning devices for the children, they must be related to the learning activities and needs of the group on a "here-and-now" basis, with simple, understandable vocabulary. A brief rating scale, used several times during a two-weeks period, or during a month, has much more meaning to the elementary child than the semi-annual or quarterly report on which the child rates himself on "cooperation" and "respect for the rights of others."

Because rating scales are specific and related to group needs, no prescribed forms that will meet the needs of teachers can be offered. However, the evolution and use of a rating scale may suggest ideas to those who wish to use this form of group evaluation.

A group of children, during the evaluation of their construction period, may discuss the question, "Did we work well together today?" (The teacher and pupils know full well that they didn't!) In a discussion of "What things do we need to do to work well together?" the children may make suggestions like the following which are listed on the chalk board:

Take turns in talking
Share materials with others
Listen to others' ideas
Help others
Do my share of the work
Keep the room neat

These and other suggestions may form the basis for a rating sheet related to group working situations to which the children may react at specified periods of time, such as twice a week, or every Friday, depending upon need and the age.

The items above might appear on this form:

Directions: If the statement is true about you, put a 1 beside it. If you are improving on what is said, put a 2 beside it. If you need much improvement, put a 3 beside it.

Name _____   Date Date Date Date

Take turns in talking				
Share materials with others				
Listen to others' ideas				
Help others				
Do my share of the work				
Keep the room neat				

The items above can be varied by the use of graphs or of colors.

Rating scales may be used at any level at which the child has attained sufficient reading skill to use them easily. They should relate to the maturity of the group, and therefore should be planned as brief, simple forms that will meet changing needs within a group. The form above, for example, might be usable with third-grade children for a one-week period; after that time, the effectiveness of the form could diminish rapidly, in comparison to its effectiveness with a group of sixth graders. The younger the child, the more important it is that the form be brief, used frequently, and used for a short total period of time.

Self-ratings by pupils have been commonly used in pupil-teacher conferences based upon report-card listings of behavior traits. Such conferences are planned to assist the child in self-evaluation and to clarify to him the meaning of teacher evaluations. In preparing for individual conferences with each pupil, the teacher may hold a group discussion of the traits listed on the report form. Terms such as "cooperation" or statements such as "works well with others" may be clarified through group illustrations of meaning. The pupil-teacher discussion then may be based upon independent ratings of the pupil and on a comparison and discussion of the ratings. The discussion should be centered upon plans that can be utilized by the pupil. If he needs to be more considerate of the umpire on the ball field, for example, this fact might be one listed under the category, "works well with others," on a conference summary sheet. This sheet could be kept in his

113

cumulative record folder for use as a guide during the next conference.

The self-ratings are useful also in conferences with parents. The recommendations that the children make for themselves help parents understand child interpretations of terms that adults often take for granted. The ratings may reveal also areas in which parents may be of help, such as punctuality, or self-esteem.

REACTION FORMS AND DRAMATIZATIONS

A popular approach to the study of children has been through the use of informal projective devices such as the sentence completion test, unfinished story, creative writing, reaction story, and sociodrama. The objective of this approach is the acquisition of information that is not obtained easily through other means. Instead of non-productive quizzing, the teacher may use novel and entertaining means for studying the reactions of her children and thereby build a basis for helping them. Young children are not hesitant about expressing themselves if rapport is good, and the techniques above, properly used, may reveal much helpful information.

Teachers who use these means for group study need to evaluate their use not only in relation to the criteria for group study listed on pages 69-70 of this chapter, but also in relation to the following questions:

> 1. Is the material palatable to the children, and *would it be palatable to parents*? Teachers need to consider the reactions of parents to highly personal questions and situations.
> 2. Can the material be used without danger of emotional upset? Topics or items that deal with individual, emotional subjects are best used by the trained clinician, with individuals, and for specific reasons.

The *sentence completion* form is one in wide and popular usage. Sentence completion items cover such topics as wishes, school likes and dislikes, home responsibilities, classmates, and ambitions, to name but a few. The completion of such forms can be extremely informative to teachers. Teachers do need to evaluate carefully the items to which they expect children's reactions. Perhaps the best means for such evaluation is a preliminary self-test of the completion type. A teacher who takes the following test should be impressed with the importance of using items that can be handled comfortably in the classroom situation.

⊂≑

SELF-IDEA COMPLETION TEST

Complete these sentences to express your real feelings. Write down the first idea that comes in your mind. There is no "right" answer. Each person's answers will be different. Write—do not "think"!

1. At home _____

2. The best _____

3. At bedtime _____

4. What annoys me _____

5. If my mother _____

6. I feel _____

7. Other people usually _____

8. All children _____

9. I regret _____

10. If I had my way _____

11. When I was a child _____

12. The most dangerous _____

13. My nerves _____

14. A husband _____

15. What puzzles me _____

16. My ambition _____

17. My father used to _____

18. I miss _____

19. My greatest fear _____

20. The happiest time _____

21. The men around here ⸺⸺⸺⸺⸺⸺⸺⸺

22. I am best when ⸺⸺⸺⸺⸺⸺⸺⸺⸺

23. I hate ⸺⸺⸺⸺⸺⸺⸺⸺⸺⸺

24. The future ⸺⸺⸺⸺⸺⸺⸺⸺⸺

25. My greatest hope ⸺⸺⸺⸺⸺⸺⸺

26. My mind ⸺⸺⸺⸺⸺⸺⸺⸺⸺

27. My education ⸺⸺⸺⸺⸺⸺⸺⸺

28. I failed ⸺⸺⸺⸺⸺⸺⸺⸺⸺⸺

29. My job ⸺⸺⸺⸺⸺⸺⸺⸺⸺⸺

30. I secretly ⸺⸺⸺⸺⸺⸺⸺⸺⸺

Please check: Male ⸺ Female ⸺ Married ⸺ Single⸺

⸺⸺⸺⸺ Total years taught

⸺⸺⸺⸺ Age

Completion forms that tap children's feelings about group performance and their own attitudes are found with numerous variations. The following illustrates items found in many:

OUR CLASS

Here are some unfinished sentences about our class. Finish each sentence with any thought you have. Just say whatever comes to your mind. There is no right or wrong answer. Just say whatever you think first.

1. I like our class when
2. The thing I'll remember most about this class is
3. Other teachers
4. We need to
5. We have fun when
6. Our work
7. The thing we need to improve most is
8. Other persons in her think that I
9. Our teacher feels that the class
10. The most interesting thing we do is
11. Sometimes I wish that the teacher
12. Sometimes I wish that the others
13. Our class is
14. Our teacher
15. I wish

116

Creative writing may be used as a means to learn about children. Topics must have appeal and be of such a nature that children can work with them easily. Some stories will be informative to the teacher; she may find some that require assistance in interpretation. The teacher who uses writing by the pupils as a means for study will need to select the topics carefully and use them in such a way that the children will respond with interest. Teachers should use topics sparingly, and only after proper motivation. The topics below suggest some that have been used successfully:

> A Dream I Remember Well
> My Family
> When I Grow Up
> The Best Things About Me
> My Biggest Problems
> Coming Back to School
> The Kind of Person I Would Like to Be
> My School
> If I Had Three Wishes
> The Most Fun I Ever Had

Writing topics, as is true with any other device, are selected by the teacher. They cannot be listed or prescribed for her successfully. Those above are illustrations only and should be looked upon only as suggestions.

Reaction stories and *unfinished stories* may be used to aid children in the evaluation of their beliefs and standards. The stories should be written so that they fit into the regular school program, and should be so constructed that they appeal to children.[8] Stories should be read to the children without comment, expression of emotion, or opinion by the teacher. Following the reading, the story may be discussed and sometimes dramatized by the children. The reactions of the children provide a learning situation for them without preachment, and provide insight for the teacher into their feelings and values.

The use of stories and classroom situations that provide opportunity for dramatization is commonly called *role-playing* or *sociodrama*. In the sociodrama children have an opportunity to work out spontaneously, through drama, problems that are of con-

---

[8] Ruth Drewes, "Finders Keepers?" *Pi Lambda Theta Journal,* Spring, 1952, pp. 255-257.

cern to them as a group. Jennings defines sociodrama as an "intensive vivid, *living through* of experiences of common concern to the group members—experiences which may have been cut short in life and blocked from full expression, leaving unresolved, buried emotional impact." [9] Moreno terms it "a deep action method dealing with group relations and collective ideologies." [10]

Reaction stories, unfinished stories, and role-playing are discussed together here because several criteria for successful use apply to all. In order to provide for spontaneity and successful, emotionally healthful learning these factors should be considered:

1. The teacher and her total attitude must be accepting, permissive, and non-critical. The children must be able to be themselves without adults' judgment. Correction of the children's grammar or choices, or the expression of personal opinion should be avoided by the teacher. This acceptance of the children's actions and ideas is one of the teacher's most difficult problems. Children should be allowed to make wrong choices and work out the proper solutions themselves.

2. The situation must be a representative problem of the group. It should appeal to the majority without singling out individuals in the group with intense emotional impact.

3. Participation in the discussion or dramatization should be voluntary. Participants should be encouraged to act and speak with complete freedom. The teacher should not push for insights, but be willing to wait.

4. All members in the group should be encouraged to participate through role-playing, through reenactment, or through group evaluation of the process and solutions. The summary and final recommendations should evolve from the group members.

The following steps and procedures have been listed by Jennings, Moreno, Shaftel,[11] and others:

1. Study needs of the group and choose situation applicable to needs.

[9] Helen Hall Jennings, "Sociodrama as Educative Process," in *Fostering Mental Health in Our Schools* (Washington, D.C.: National Education Association, 1950), p. 260.

[10] J. L. Moreno, *Who Shall Survive?* (Beacon, New York: Beacon House, 1953), p. 87.

[11] Fanny and George Shaftel, *Role-Playing the Problem Story* (New York: National Conference of Christians and Jews, 1952).

2. Through vivid discussion, through curtailing a story at a crucial point, or through a dramatic incident, stimulate the group so that they want to learn the best ways of coping with a situation.

3. Sensitize the children to their roles by telling them that they will be asked to take parts.

4. Clearly define the problem. The class members speak of their own experiences and add to the dramatic possibilities.

5. Select children to play roles. Little time is involved in planning so that the action remains spontaneous and uninhibited. *The dialogue is never planned.*

6. Prepare the audience to observe intelligently and alertly. Remind the children that they will have opportunities to replay the situation, and that they are looking only at the roles, not at the child personally. They should understand that mistakes can be made, and accepted, that more than one answer is possible.

7. During the discussion, have the children define the problem, consider alternative action, weigh the consequences of each choice, choose new possibilities, gain deeper insights.

8. Follow through with new enactment and new planning if needed.

Sociodrama, properly used, is a valuable supplement to other techniques of working with group behavior. If correctly managed, it fosters desirable behavior far better than any rules can. It gives children an opportunity to examine motives, behaviors, and emotions without threat, and helps them to realize that many alternatives to a given course of action may be utilized. They are able to face developmental tasks, examine group relationships, gain information, resolve prejudices, and learn to communicate effectively. Their insights into the feelings of others deepen as they identify with different roles.

The dangers in sociodrama lie in its use within emotionally charged situations, in which the private feelings of individuals within the group are spotlighted. It is necessary, therefore, that the teacher center the problems upon *social, group needs, within the areas of daily living.* The teacher needs to consider carefully the need for the sociodrama or the reaction story), plan the warm-up and procedure carefully, and use skill in directing the proceedings.

Some situations in which children may use reaction stories or drama with profit are illustrated below:

Planning a trip to the museum, bakery, fire station, etc., so that all can see and hear.

Helping the doctor during the classroom checkup.

Helping the substitute teacher who will be with the group tomorrow.

Taking turns on the playground equipment (before and after).

Preparing for a party with another class group.

Serving as hosts at a tea.

Welcoming a new student to the group.

Working together during dramatic play.

Taking turns in sharing.

Helping a child who is poor at baseball.

The following illustrations of reaction stories and sociodrama were used by students and friends of the authors. They are included here to show the reader more concretely the type of material used by teachers who have found this approach useful. They were, of course, developed by the teachers to meet specific needs within their own groups, and would be of value to the reader on an illustrative basis only. Their use without real need would predetermine artificiality in another classroom group.[12]

I

The teacher had been concerned because of the behavior of the children as they took tools from the toolrack during construction period. The children had evaluated the problem, discussed it, set up standards, all to no avail. Still a few children were rushing and grabbing for tools. The teacher decided to try sociodrama to help the children work out the problem.

The warm-up consisted of questions:

What did the children do when the tools were brought into the room?

What did they say?

Show us how they looked when they were fighting over the tools?

What happened when more than one person wanted a clamp?

[12] The writers are indebted to Virginia Armfield and Beatrice Armstrong, Pasadena; Jane Sevy, Bellflower; and Phyllis Strange of the Orange County School, California, for these materials.

By this time the children were eager to have the play. They re-enacted with gusto the undesirable work situation, evaluated, made suggestions, and in three brief sessions, resolved the conflict.

The value of the play to the group, according to the teacher, was that the problem was presented and acted out, with the audience and actors alike then working to find a solution. In this activity the children discovered factors that were contributing to their feelings of frustration. At the same time they were discovering satisfactory ways of overcoming the problems involved. One important generalization that came from these third graders was that there was no one right way of behaving, but many ways.

II

The following reaction story was used by a teacher whose group had had some problems because of their indefinitely defined sense of property rights. The children had indulged in some "horse-trading," with resultant difficulties and negative reactions from one parent. She hoped, through the story, to have some carry-over regarding belongings.

Cheryl is a very pleasant, sparkling little girl whom all of the first graders loved to have around because she made their games so much fun. She had wonderful ideas for things to do and usually played with a large group of children. Cheryl liked to play games with her friends, but she wanted, sometimes, to play with just one person and to feel that one child really liked her best. On Cheryl's sixth birthday her grandmother gave her a lovely gold bracelet with flowers on it. The next week when Cheryl wanted Mary to come away from the game and play with her alone, Mary wanted to stay with the others. So that Mary would come and play with her, Cheryl gave her the new gold bracelet.

That night when Grandmother came to visit, Cheryl and her friend, Mary, were playing in the yard and Mary showed Grandmother the bracelet Cheryl had given her.

What do you think happened then?

After a number of reactions, the teacher chose the children who had commented on the feelings voiced by Cheryl, Mary, the Mother, and Grandmother. The first dramatization found Cheryl isolated in her room by her mother, Grandmother feeling sad,

121

Mary giving back the bracelet in a huff, and departing for home. The teacher prepared for a follow-up by asking these questions:

> Is that what you think really happened?
> Why did Grandmother feel sad?
> Do you think that Mary really liked Cheryl?
> Did she like her more because she gave her the bracelet?
> Who has a different idea about what happened?

In the second dramatization Mother scolded Cheryl, but Grandmother told Cheryl she gave her the bracelet because she loved her, and that she could give it away if she wanted to. Mary said that she would not give it back because Cheryl gave it to her. Cheryl suggested giving her another bracelet she had. When Mary refused, Cheryl told her that she had made a mistake, and suggested letting Mary wear it a few days, and then returning it. Mary agreed.

In the discussion that followed, the children decided that Mary liked Cheryl better because she gave her the bracelet, that Cheryl probably would have been put in her room, that she shouldn't have given the bracelet away, and that she should have thought about how Grandmother would feel. The teacher had not anticipated the solution, which was a good one. She had hoped that the children would verbalize the possibility that people liked Cheryl even if she didn't give them presents, but felt in retrospect that such a reaction would demand an excessively high level of maturity from six-year-olds.

III

The two stories that follow were written by a fifth-grade teacher who used them in working with her class on problems of sportsmanship and honesty. She felt that the real values derived from this approach far exceeded any listing of rules or discussion. Indeed, one of the problems that upper elementary teachers face is the fact that their pupils have gazed upon lists of rules for classroom and personal behavior so frequently, in many instances, that they cease to have meaning.

> Jim was an only child and often felt lonely and left out of things. This was caused perhaps because his parents moved two or three times and he didn't have very many friends. But finally they moved to _____ _____ and Dad had

a job that was permanent and so Jim felt that now things would be all right. They were in a way. He liked school, could do the work well, but it seemed hard to get to feel just right during play time.

Above all things Jim liked to play baseball. He got along fine during Physical Education when the teacher was umpire but at noon recess he had a hard time ever getting his "ups" in work-up.

He stood in the field day after day waiting for a fly to come his way and when one did there was always a big boy to jump up and get it.

Once by great luck he did manage to tag second and so got his up—he hit a pretty good one but sure enough he was out at first and had to go last man. He told his father about it that night and said he felt pretty sure he was safe but everyone yelled "Out! Out!", so of course he had to be out. Then father told him that sometimes umpires have trouble deciding too but they often listen for the sound of the foot hitting the base and the ball meeting the glove.

Jim felt very smart to know this so he began to watch. Day after day he noticed the boys just called "Out! Out!" whether the boy was out or not. If one of the well-liked boys was making first, a few weak "outs" would be heard. If the boy would say he was safe, they would accept it.

After a week or two of watching, Jim became quite expert deciding outs in his own mind. Not that the boys paid one bit of attention to him.

One day luck was with him. He caught a fly and was up. The first time in days. Wham went the ball over the base—he missed but braced himself for the next hit. He wanted to stay more than anything. Here came the next ball which was too low. "Aw thatz a good one, why don't you hit at it," yelled a boy whose fly he caught. The third ball came over a bit high but he hit it hard and raced toward first base. His foot hit first base, the ball followed with a whine into the mitt of the first baseman. "Out, out, out" rang out a chorus of boys.

Jim opened his mouth to say - - - - - - - -

.   .   .

Sharon and Vickie talked about the party on their way home from school. Valentine's Day was just two days away, but tomorrow was the day when they were going to get ready for it. Today they had planned the menu, and tomorrow the whole class would go to the big market and shop for the food. Then they would come back to school and make cookies and jello.

Sharon was worried, though. Almost everyone else in the whole class had brought their ten cents to pay for the party.

123

Sharon had asked Mother for her ten cents, but Mother had said that she would have to take it out of her allowance. But she had spent her allowance last Saturday, the day she got it. She had explained all this to Mother, but it hadn't seemed to make a bit of difference. Sharon still did not have her ten cents, and tomorrow was the last day they could bring it.

That evening at home she examined her piggy bank carefully, but found nothing in it. She even tried to borrow a dime from her brother, Bill, but he either didn't have any money or he didn't want to let her have it. Sharon was still thinking and worrying about it when she went to bed that night.

Sharon arrived at school early the next morning. She had a wonderful idea. She would go to the office, tell the lady at the desk that she had lost a dime the day before, and see if a dime had been turned in.

"Can I help you?" asked Mrs. Lyon, after Sharon had waited a few minutes.

"Yes," replied Sharon, "I lost a dime in the sand pile yesterday, and I want to know if it has been turned in."

"I'll look," said Mrs. Lyon, and Sharon held her breath until she returned.

"Yes, here's a dime that was turned in yesterday, and it was found near the sand pile," said Mrs. Lyon.

She handed the dime over the counter to Sharon, and just as she did so, Mrs. Weston, Sharon's teacher, walked into the office.

.   .   .

ROLES OF PERSONNEL IN GROUP STUDY

Any group work with a classroom full of children is ordinarily carried on by the classroom teacher. The only exception to this would be a demonstration, or a group survey made by a person very well known to them. It is usually desirable that the teacher carry on group study activities, since the presence of another person causes children to attach more than ordinary importance to the occasion and may cause apprehension in some.

Teachers need opportunities to work together in formulating and evaluating materials. The principal can assist them by scheduling time for them, by working with them, and by keeping them informed of other teachers' activities in group understanding. The guidance person can assist teachers and administrators by helping them devise materials that they need, by providing them with

124

forms for specific purposes, and by helping them interpret the results of their work. Any persons—teacher, administrators, or guidance workers—who have particular skill and knowledge in any phase of group work can assist their colleagues by carrying on meetings and demonstrations. On a building basis, such meetings could be arranged by the principal, in collaboration with the teacher(s) concerned, and the guidance person; on a district-wide basis, coordination of meetings devoted to the study of child groups probably would be the responsibility of the guidance resource.

summary

Children must be studied as group members as well as individuals, in order to be understood adequately. The study of groups should be based upon a knowledge of children's growth characteristics and needs. The materials themselves should meet the criteria of *useful purpose, efficient format, appropriate content, appropriate length, appropriate vocabulary, adequate method of resonse,* and *acceptable content.*

Many approaches to group study are described and illustrated within the chapter. The illustrations are given so that teachers may make adaptations for their own purposes, rather than to furnish specified materials for classroom use. It is hoped by the writers that the forms may furnish ideas concretely enough so that teachers and others working with them may gain some ideas of value to them in their constant quest to better understand their pupils.

TESTING PROGRAM

The testing program in elementary schools forms an important part of the total guidance program. Its broad purpose is that of other aspects of the guidance program—to provide teachers with understandings and knowledge concerning their class groups that may be used in the planning of appropriate experiences. Standardized tests, intelligently and systematically used, can do much to improve teacher insights into group needs. Careful organization of the total program is necessary to insure adequate study of readiness for academic work, to evaluate academic needs, and to assess children's ability and personal adjustment. These factors concerning children cannot, of course, be evaluated with definite and final assurance through the testing program alone. Nevertheless, tests of intelligence, readiness, achievement, and personality, used properly with other materials, are of great value in the task of understanding children's needs. Tests are an important tool in the planning of effective and realistic learning activities, which are basic to a good learning climate in the classroom.

VALUES

In addition to helping teachers in the difficult task of understanding the capabilities and needs of their children, the testing program serves several other functions. It provides a basis for the selection of materials for classroom groups. It aids teachers in identifying children with special needs who need further study. Through the

126

use of tests with other study devices, teachers are able to make longitudinal studies of children's growth and progress in learning.

Group test results are used by teachers as basic information in making more detailed studies of the entire groups. Such group studies form the bases for in-service discussions and planning, with good group adjustment the goal for all children.

Test results may be used with adults other than teachers to promote understanding of modern educational procedures. Group intelligence test results, for example, serve to indicate to parents the need for many materials of varying levels of difficulty. Achievement test results for a period of years may be used to demonstrate to school boards or study groups the achievement growth of a school. Summaries of test results for such purposes are always used without the identification of individual children.

CRITERIA FOR USE

Test results are used best as guides rather than absolutes. If school personnel become concerned with specific scores rather than general areas of performance, skepticism regarding tests is inevitable. Tests at best are limited samplings of various behaviors, and the accuracy of results is affected by many factors, among them the skill of the examiner, the attitude of the child, and testing conditions. If, during the course of a child's school career, several samplings of ability result in intelligence quotients of 94, 101, and 106, and the scores are consistent with performance, the school may feel fairly certain that the child is of average ability. Similarly, consistent scores in the 80's, checked by daily performance, indicate a slow-learning child in need of a modified program.

It is important that samplings of ability, adjustment, or achievement not be restricted to single measures. Periodic samplings are necessary to evaluate the variability or consistency of growth patterns. The planned program should include enough measures during the elementary years so that patterns may emerge.

Tests should be selected and used by qualified persons. The matter of test selection is of utmost importance. Tests of all varieties now published number in the thousands, and the selling of tests to schools is a large-scale business. Careful evaluation of reliability, validity, and usability is essential. Persons charged with test selection should be thoroughly versed in criteria for test selection. Measurement texts, such as Torgerson and Adams' *Measurement and Evaluation for the Elementary School Teacher*,[1] or Anastasi's *Psychological Testing*[2] are among the many excellent general sources on testing that discuss in detail specific areas in which tests should be evaluated. These books are invaluable to individuals who wish to acquire background or review their knowledge in the field of tests and measurement.

Another resource indispensable to those who select tests in Buros' *Mental Measurements Yearbook*.[3] The purposes of the fourth *Yearbook*, stated in the introduction, reveal the contribution that the editor hopes to make to its users:

1. To make readily available comprehensive and up-to-date bibliographies of recent tests published in all English-speaking countries.

2. To make readily available hundreds of frankly critical test reviews, written by persons of outstanding ability representing various viewpoints, which will assist test users to make more discriminating selections of the standard tests which will best meet their needs.

3. To make readily available comprehensive and accurate bibliographies of references on the construction, validation, use and limitations of specific tests.

4. To impel authors and publishers to place fewer but better tests on the market and to provide test users with detailed and accurate information on the construction, validation, uses, and limitations of their tests at the time that they are first placed on the market.

5. To suggest to test users better methods of arriving at their own appraisals of both standard and non-standard tests in light of their particular values and needs.

6. To stimulate cooperating reviewers—and others to a less extent—to reconsider and think through more carefully their beliefs and values relevant to testing.

7. To inculcate upon test users a keener awareness of both the values and dangers which may accompany the use of standard tests.

[1] Theodore L. Torgerson and Georgia Sachs Adams, *Measurement and Evaluation for the Elementary-School Teacher* (New York: The Dryden Press, 1954).

[2] Anne Anastasi, *Psychological Testing* (New York: The Macmillan Company, 1954).

[3] Oscar Krisen Buros, ed., *The Fourth Mental Measurements Yearbook* (Highland Park, New Jersey: The Gryphon Press, 1953).

8. To impress test users with the desirability of suspecting all standard tests—even though prepared by well-known authorities—unaccompanied by detailed data on their construction, validation, use and limitations.

In addition to reviews by several outstanding authorities of each of 793 tests, which represent all of those commercially available from 1948 to 1951, the fourth *Yearbook* is useful in two other ways: It lists 429 books on measurement and closely related fields, and supplies cross-references to other reviews of the tests evaluated. Thus the person seeking appropriate tests may easily locate additional information if he should so desire.

Finally, the entire school staff should understand and interpret to others the fact that tests provide just one way of studying a child. Good schools go beyond the notion that the testing program is the guidance program. The teacher who has administered, scored, and summarized the test results has not done her guidance work for the year. She has, rather, a basis for beginning her guidance activities.

A PLANNED PROGRAM

One of the concerns of school administrators and guidance personnel, in addition to the selection of tests, is that of scheduling appropriate tests. The kind of test to use at a given grade level, an effective testing schedule, and a suitable over-all pattern of group testing, are all problems. The philosophy of education within the school district affects directly the uses made of tests throughout the grades.

The modern elementary school is designed to meet the needs of children through appropriate experiences. In terms of academic learnings, this means that the greatest effort is made to plan experiences in the three *R*'s and other areas in such ways that the child is ready and able to work with them successfully. Since educators have learned that average children who have passed the age of six and one-half years are ready to *begin* reading experiences, they have planned the kindergarten year as a *pre*-academic experience. A good share of the first grade is devoted to readiness activities for many children. This means that reading readiness tests are better given at the beginning of first grade, after the child has been in school for a few weeks, than at the end of kindergarten. Giving the tests at the beginning of the first grade serves to take away all reading emphasis from kindergarten, which should be true for all but those who are extremely mature and extremely bright, and eliminates the span of time during summer vacation, which serves to reduce the predictive value of the test.

Careful consideration also should be given to the timing of other tests at the primary level. We have learned that the ability to read is not turned on like a faucet at a given age, but that the entire primary school is devoted to teaching beginners to read. The first and second grade teachers are both working with many beginners. It would seem, therefore, that at the beginning of the third year and standardized test in reading might be used to help the teacher of that level assess the reading needs of her group.

A reading test rather than a general achievement battery is suggested for beginning third graders because of the variations between modern primary programs and standardized test content. Spelling is an experience that is based upon an established reading vocabulary and considerable writing, as well as on a need for writing. Arithmetic in the abstract form, which is necessarily a part of standardized instruments, is not employed appreciably by the modern first or second grade teacher. The disparity in test content and educational program is reflected in the test norms themselves; a child may succeed on very few items within a subtest and still attain the national norm for his grade, with only slight sampling of his actual performance. General achievement batteries, therefore, may furnish better information to the teacher at the beginning of fourth grade and after.

Group intelligence tests are difficult to use with young children who are accustomed to working together informally. The whole problem for a young child of becoming a working member of a group is one that needs careful thought in the scheduling of tests. Because tests are expensive and time-consuming, they should be used when the child is old enough to adjust to group work under controlled, standardized directions. A group intelligence test given to second graders in small groups of ten-to-fifteen, after they had been in school for a month or more, should produce more reliable results than one given to kindergartners.

A school testing program might be planned somewhat like that listed below. It is planned to eliminate repetition of testing in all

130

grades but one in the first six grades, and all but two in an eight-grade school, if intelligence and achievement tests are used. If personality and attitude tests are used the overlap of testing necessarily increases.

GROUP TESTING PROGRAM

	Achievement	Intelligence	Attitude and Personality
Kindergarten			
First	x (readiness)		
Second		x	
Third	x (reading)		
Fourth	x (general)		x
Fifth	x "	x	
Sixth	x "		x
Seventh	x "	x	
Eighth	x "		

A testing program like the one above might be enlarged to provide testing in all areas each year. In the usual elementary school however, testing and scoring are the responsibility of the teacher and the program should be scheduled in such a way that the burden to the teacher is as light as possible. Some duplication of testing is needed if tests are to serve one of their purposes—that of evaluating growth patterns.

The time of year when tests should be given is another aspect of the scheduling problem. Questions are raised most frequently regarding the fall versus spring scheduling of achievement tests. If the testing program is to be used to study children's needs and thereby plan their educational experiences, the fall of the year would seem to be a better time. Test data accumulated in the fall rather than during the previous spring are recent and can be used with more assurance of accuracy. The problem of modern social mobility, too, seems to favor fall testing. In many communities, a teacher may send spring test results to another teacher who learns that the group composition has been altered radically by summer moves. Although children move away at all times of the year, the teacher who tests in the fall of the year has at least initial assurance of complete data.

Some persons have favored end-of-the-year testing on the grounds that growth in achievement during the school year can be better evaluated. If achievement testing is done periodically, teachers are

131

able to study the results of several tests and determine patterns of growth so that single tests are used within a frame of reference. Because of the limited areas of content within achievement tests, it is difficult to state that they adequately measure total achievement in any area. If teachers know that they will test in the spring of the year, they may stress academic learnings in the types of skills that will be measured on the tests. Rare is the teacher who can approach with complete objectivity the spring testing of a group that she has taught all year! It is much easier to be completely objective and ethical when one's performance and reputation are not involved. School-wide testing in achievement areas during the spring of the year is perhaps less threatening to teachers if individual class summaries are the only ones prepared, and if all school personnel assiduously avoid any comparison of groups within the school.

PREPARATION FOR THE USE OF TESTS

Group tests are designed so that they may be administered by the classroom teacher. Good test manuals include clear, specific instructions on preparation for the testing situation and on administration, scoring, and use of the results. The commercial materials often are supplemented by district bulletins and pre-testing discussions of test procedures. Thorough preparation through group discussion and individual study is essential before tests are used. The extent of preparation necessary is governed by the previous experience of the teacher in the use of a given test, but even veterans need some individual review of materials and procedures. A teacher should go through the procedure of administering the test to someone individually prior to using the test with a class group.

The following items may serve as a check for the teacher in testing procedures:

1. Thorough study of test manual and the test itself.
2. Check on physical arrangements: lighting, temperature, ventilation, spaced seating.
3. Check on needed materials specified in manual: markers, extra pencils, stop watch, etc.
4. Arrangement for uninterrupted testing through sign on door: TESTING, PLEASE DO NOT ENTER.
5. Arrangements for uninterrupted testing through check with office to avoid phone calls and visits.

6. Scheduling test at desirable time of day: avoiding conflict with recess, lunch periods.

7. Arrangements with other teacher to take part of group if small group for testing is desirable.

8. Planning for efficient distribution of materials.

9. Development of a calm, normal working relationship to encourage good work.

10. Strict adherence to exact directions and timing.

11. Utilizing a pad for notations of any deviations in performance, such as fatigue, lost time, emotional upset, copying or misunderstanding of directions.

12. Constant check on test performance.

Group tests often are designed for either hand or maching scoring. Hand scoring is usually done by teachers or by specially trained clerks. If clerks are employed, it is important that test booklets be returned to the teachers concerned so that they may study the performance of individual children. Whether teachers or clerks score tests, careful training should be given, and responsibility for accuracy and professional attitudes should be charged to those doing the work.

Machine-scored tests are best used with children who have had experience in taking tests, and are sufficiently mature to transfer responses to the correct spot on an answer sheet. The problem of recording correctly on answer sheets may cause anxiety in children who are young and unaccustomed to working under standardized testing conditions. It is questionable whether answer sheets and machine scoring of tests should be used below the fifth grade level.

USE OF TEST RESULTS

The systematic use of group tests serves to aid the teacher in the identification of group variations, group similarities and individual needs. She learns, for example, that within her fourth grade the achievement range may be from second to sixth grades, and that the children tend to group differently in the various academic areas.

Some teachers, to personalize test results, use numbers that correspond to the rank order of the children, and record the numbers in the appropriate columns to show both group range and individual range, as in the chart reproduced here.

Through the inspection of the chart, or others similar to it, the

133

GRADE 4

	1.5–1.9	2.0–2.4	2.5–2.9	3.0–3.4	3.5–3.9	4.0–4.4	4.5–4.9	5.0–5.4	5.5–5.9	6.0
CHRONOLOGICAL AGE GRADE PLACEMENT		3, 10, 14	4, 8, 18	15, 24	1, 4, 5, 10, 11, 12, 21, 22	6, 7, 13, 18, 19, 20	2, 3, 8, 9, 14, 17	16, 23		
MENTAL AGE GRADE PLACEMENT	6		2, 8	1, 2, 15	11	17, 21	19	9, 13, 23		7, 20
READING GRADE PLACEMENT		1, 3, 18, 23		10, 12, 14, 16, 22	9, 17, 19	4, 5, 6, 7, 11, 15, 21, 24	20	13		

(This chart may, of course, be extended to include other test areas, such as arithmetic and spelling.)

teacher may begin to ask questions that relate to a need for adjustments for individual children, or to further study to determine needs. She may, for example, identify one or two children whose abilities and achievement are considerably higher than those of the group, for whom special enrichment materials and individualized activities should be planned.

A child of high potential who is underachieving may create another problem. In this case, planning would be related to the age and experiential background of the individual. The younger child may need time, or may be one whose growth and interest in a given academic area will accelerate at a later time. Teachers occasionally have contact with underachievers who create problems for them by not reading or doing arithmetic according to expectation until they are third or fourth graders, at which time they may show remarkable progress. Underachievement requires special study, not only in relation to the total academic growth pattern, but in relation to such factors as language background, possible emotional problems, types of past experiences, the child's reactions to the curriculum, his special interests, or needs for special materials. The relationships between all growth factors and academic achievement need study. Several modern students of child growth, notable among them Olson,[4] have pointed out that comparisons of individuals on the basis of test scores and chronological age are inadequate. Longitudinal studies of individuals have shown significant relationships among such factors as social maturity, emotional maturity, height, weight, carpal development, grip, age of menstruation, intelligence, and academic performance. A child with slow growth patterns may have intelligence equal to that of another child, yet take longer to attain a given academic level. The comforting fact in this realization is that the child has the potential and, with proper pacing rather than pressure, will perform according to growth expectations. We need to study bright underachievers with all facilities at our command before planning programs for them.

Another concern of the teacher may be a child who is developmentally mature, of average or better intelligence, and who is retarded in one area, such as reading. The retardation may be due to previous illness, changes in schools, or other factors. The term

[4] Willard C. Olson, *Child Development* (Boston: D. C. Heath and Company, 1949).

remedial implies potential for remediation. Children for whom special assistance is planned should have been in school longer than the learning period of the primary grades, should be more than a year retarded, and should have the ability and general maturity to profit from help.

Occasionally children may perform inconsistently on tests and daily work. For example, a child may be one of the better students in a group, and yet may indicate only mediocre ability and achievement on group tests. Such a pattern would require further testing to determine whether a child has an unrealistic level of aspiration that is interfering with his normal adjustment. Or, a student may be one who has coasted along as an average student, although test scores indicate high capacity and achievement. Any test results that are inconsistent with daily performance should be checked by further testing and observation.

Children of yet another type may be identified for further study through the use of group tests. These are the pupils with abilities and performance levels sufficiently low that they are in need of special attention to insure ultimate social and economic usefulness. The group tests usually serve to select children for complete psychological study prior to special placement.

Finally, test results charted on a summary sheet may serve to indicate that certain children need grade adjustments. Children who are too old for the group, who are mature socially and physically, may need to be moved to older groups. School entrance standards and promotional practices vary, and modern social mobility requires periodic checks to be sure that groupings are sound.

In addition to surveying and identifying individual needs, the teacher may use the class summary sheet to plan groupings within the classroom. Grouping can be planned not only from the standpoint of several levels of reading ability, spelling ability, or arithmetic ability, but also from the standpoint of flexible groups based upon specific needs, such as the need for help with simple combinations, the need for help with problems involving the use of zero, or the need for skills in word analysis. To plan for specific needs, the teacher would make diagnostic studies of the test booklets of certain children. It is important that she assess the types of difficulties in relation to the curriculum for her grade, so that assistance is given within the level of expectation for her group.

The problem of interpreting test results to parents is one of concern to many educators. Questions often center around the need to make test results meaningful in a constructive way.

The answer is not in the quotation of test results. Teachers who have had the usual two-unit course in tests and measurement can testify to the limitation of their real knowledge concerning various tests and their true validity. Yet those who have had even a single course have had thirty to forty hours of training, which most parents have not experienced. Most persons would question the adequacy of a single course in training individuals to interpret tests.

Test scores, even achievement test scores, have a finality to many parents. The parent cannot be "objective" about his child's performance. Reaction is inevitable. The task of the school is to assist the parent to react positively for the sake of the child.

Achievement tests are best interpreted in terms of samples of work—what the child is reading, and the kinds of problems he is working successfully. Teachers may discuss progress over a period of several years, and point out to parents the growth a child is experiencing, where he still needs help, and what they are doing to eliminate difficulties. Such discussions are more positive and more meaningful to parents than "Your son scored 8.5 in arithmetic reasoning."

Intelligence tests vary sharply in the types of learning aptitudes they measure. The scores of tests may have widely different meanings. Scores of any tests must be interpreted not only in terms of test content, but also in terms of testing conditions, complete knowledge of the child, his background and attitudes. If teachers quote scores to laymen, they inevitably receive comments like these: "How could he score only 95 when he scored 100 last year and he was a year younger?" or, by a mother at a bridge party: "I'm so proud of Susan! She took an I.Q. test at school and made 99, which is practically a perfect score!"

If teachers discuss scores, they may find themselves involved in the difficulty of interpreting reliability, validity, and statistical terminology. When parents want to know about children's learning potential, it is safer to talk in language like the following:

For the slow child:

> The tests that John took show that he works a little more
> slowly than some of the other children, but that if we plan

137

work for him that is easier, he will be able to do it well, and can be successful.

Or, in the case of a bright child:

Bill works very successfully in the group. He is doing work that is equal to that of children two years older than he is. He should be a person who can go through college and be successful.

Or, for the child with a specific learning problem:

We have found that Marian needs some help with carrying. I have her with a small group in which we're doing some special drill, and I'm confident that we can cure the difficulty soon.

ROLES OF PERSONNEL IN EFFECTIVE USE OF TESTS

The contributions that may be made by school personnel depend in large measure upon the specialized training and group-work skills of the various individuals. The following suggestions regarding responsibilities are made on the assumption that all persons in the school system are participants in a coordinated effort to develop a sound testing program, and that the specialized skills of each are used in the best fashion possible. The assumption is made that the guidance person has had more training in statistics and measurement than principals, curriculum personnel, or teachers have had. Otherwise, he probably should not hold his position. Principals know their own building problems best; curriculum personnel know materials better than others. Teachers have the responsibility of evaluating and appliy valid suggestions in their daily work. Without the application by teachers, the total program would be pointless. Variations in the suggestions below would depend on available personnel and their backgrounds. Small school districts may depend very successfully upon a highly trained principal to assume special responsibilities.

1. The principal contributes to the testing program by
   a) coordinating test orders and test distribution for his building.

b) planning testing schedules with the teachers.
c) participating in meetings on test interpretation.
d) participating on committees for test selection.
2. The curriculum consultant contributes by
   a) participating on committees for test selection.
   b) serving as a resource to teachers in groups and individually regarding the selection of curriculum materials.
3. The guidance consultant contributes by
   a) serving as chairman of district committees on test selection.
   b) coordinating district test orders and test schedules.
   c) giving instruction through bulletins (and meetings for new teachers and others) on test administration, scoring, and recording of data.
   d) meeting with groups concerning the interpretation and proper use of test results.
   e) preparing class group and district charts of test results for in-service discussions.
   f) meeting with lay groups on test use and interpretation.
4. The teacher contributes by
   a) participating on committees for test selection.
   b) administering tests and scoring and recording test results.
   c) participating in meetings on test interpretation.
   d) applying knowledge gained from study of test results to advantage of children in her group.

summary

The testing program, within the context of the entire guidance program, aids teachers in selecting materials for groups, in identifying children with special needs who need further study, and in making long-range studies of children's growth. Test results may be used to interpret children's needs and modern educational programs to lay groups.

Tests should be selected carefully according to established criteria by qualified persons. The testing program should be planned so that the test results have maximum meaning, and so that the process of testing is not unduly burdensome to teachers. Careful and systematic training for the administration and use of tests is essential. Persons who require further training or review are urged to consult books in measurement such as those listed in the chapter. All professional personnel need to work together and make the best use of their training and experience in order to make the total program truly effective.

7

SCHOOL RECORDS

Use 163

Contents

School records, commonly referred to as "cumulative records," are basic to the guidance program. It is difficult to conceive of an organized, functional program without records, yet Traxler[1] states that *cumulative record* is a term of comparatively recent origin in educational terminology, rarely mentioned before 1925, and commonly used only since 1930. This period parallels roughly the periods of development of school-wide group testing programs and the beginning of the elementary guidance program. The growing recognition of individual differences and the need to base curriculum planning upon children's needs undoubtedly spurred the search for efficient forms on which significant data could be recorded.

Cumulative records vary greatly in size, shape, service and significance. They all have certain characteristics in common however. The term, *cumulative*, refers to a form that permits the accumulation of data concerning a given individual. The record may consist of a single card on which little more than standardized test scores are recorded, or it may be a well-padded folder that contains information comprehensive enough to classify it as a junior case study.

The importance of adequate records in schools is well recognized by present-day educators. Modern educational planning makes such records indispensable. The evolution of satisfactory records has been a multi-pronged effort, involving countless thousands of

[1] Arthur E. Traxler, *Techniques of Guidance* (New York: Harper & Brothers, 1945), p. 215.

141

hours and countless personnel throughout the country. Improvements will always be necessary, as new learnings occur in education. The search for improvements in education has periodically focused attention upon data concerning children, and has led to improvement of record systems. The New York Regents' Inquiry is a good example of the kind of study that fosters inquiry concerning records. Among other things, the investigators had this to say:

> In none of the schools were adequate cumulative pupil record cards for recording the kinds of information essential for future guidance found, nor did the schools have a means of transmitting such information as is available to places to which pupils move.[2]

The major questions of educators concerning records probably resemble the following: Why are records important? What should be contained within them? How can we plan worthwhile records in our local district? How can we be sure that personnel will use them wisely and well? How do district personnel work together best in planning and using records effectively? These questions will be the core of discussion within the present chapter.

IMPORTANCE OF RECORDS

There comes a time in the life of every teacher when she has questions about certain aspects of her profession. One of those areas is that of clerical responsibility, some of which is unavoidable. As she records information from tests and forms on the cumulative record, she speculates on this use of her valuable time. Will the data do the good that they should? Our contention is that they can. Without records, teachers cannot know their pupils and base planning upon their needs. This knowledge of children and its benefits are the primary reasons for any kind of record system.

School records assume proper importance also when one realizes that they provide a means for the scientific study of education. With data available in planned, orderly sequence, educators have many guides that can be utilized in evaluating the effectiveness of their

[2] Leo J. Brueckner, *The Changing Elementary School* (Inor Publishing Company, 1939), p. 142.

programs. Longitudinal studies of individuals and class groups can be used as the basis for periodic curriculum evaluation. Answers to problems of grouping and placement, types of individual and group curriculum needs, special individual requirements, and needs for special resource help often come from record data.

Many answers to questions that teachers ask concerning new groups at the start of the school year come from records. The teachers learn not only what their children are like educationally, intellectually, socially, emotionally, and physically, but learn also what plans have been made for them and what special needs they may have. From the study of this information, teachers may then go on to the specific problem of curriculum planning and to the selection of appropriate experiences and materials.

Through the study of longitudinal data concerning children, teachers learn educational perspective. As they review growth records of children, they develop appreciation for the growth process as an important factor in the educational pattern of the child, and develop understanding of the need for individualized developmental planning for children rather than the all-or-none, here-and-now approach. The study of records tends to develop recognition of the efforts of other teachers, and a realistic picture of one's place in the total educational life of the child.

The cumulative record makes an important contribution to home-school communication. Teachers who conduct individual conferences with parents find that the record is essential in two ways: (1) it provides data vital to intelligent discussion of children and their needs, and (2) it often contains information concerning past conferences, their content, tenor, and results.

Cumulative records are the source of basic materials for intensive case studies. They contain much pertinent information and serve not only to supplement case study data, but also to inform teachers, in many instances, that such studies have been made, and where they may go to get additional information about a child. All services to a wide variety of exceptional children stem from the background information of the cumulative record.

Two highly important groups—teachers and parents—can use the cumulative record in study-group activities. Teachers who use record data on their groups in professional discussions benefit

143

from the experience and backgrounds of their colleagues. Parents who work with educators in the study of anonymous record materials learn firsthand about the modern educator's interest in thorough and adequate planning for their children, and tend to increase their support of education.[3]

Without cumulative records, many research programs that are carried on would be impossible. University and college personnel, working in cooperation with public school officials, frequently consult group records in their study of educational problems. Even in experimental programs, the data on class groups are essential in the structuring of experimental and control groupings.

Finally, the record is a reflection of the school district's educational philosophy. With the assumption that philosophies change, the record also changes. A record for X district, which shows evaluative data developed on an individual basis, reflects the district philosophy. A record that is comprehensive, with provisions for data in all growth phases, also is a reflection of philosophy. This fact makes remote the possibility of uniform records for an area or for a given state, since all educators know that neighboring school districts may be poles apart in their educational beliefs.

CONTENT OF RECORDS

The problem of record content depends in part upon the structure of the record form. Since most schools differ somewhat in evaluation procedures at the elementary and secondary levels, with letter grades less frequently used for elementary children, and since other differences in curriculum structure and student vocational needs appear in the secondary school, many districts use a basic folder for the elementary school, with insert cards for the high school and college. The content listed here will deal only with the elementary school record.

Since the record system is planned ideally to meet the needs of the school district, a listing of items for inclusion does not serve as the goal for all districts. The best use of such a listing occurs when personnel who are working on the formulation of records check the

---

[3] Marian W. Hodge and Esther Grace Nolan, "Cumulative Records in Guidance," *California Journal of Secondary Education*, December, 1947, p. 2.

items in relation to their use in better understanding of children. If an item can be used well by the staff, it should be included.

The following items should be considered in the planning of a record:

1. Home background.
   a) birthdate (verified)
   b) birth place
   c) siblings (age and sex)
   d) other persons in the home
   e) race
   f) other language predominant in the home
   g) marital status of parents
   h) occupation of parents
   i) any significant additional information that might affect the child's school performance.
2. Physical condition and maturity. (These items should be kept on a health card by the nurse. Space should be provided on the teacher's folder for notation of special needs.)
   a) history of childhood illnesses
   b) vision and hearing tests, with follow-up record
   c) inoculation and immunizations
   d) dental inspection
   e) height and weight deviations
   f) disabilities.
3. Social-emotional data.
   a) attitudes toward others
   b) acceptance by others
   c) attitudes toward self
   d) attitudes toward regulations
   e) work habits
   f) special interests
   g) test data.
4. Attendance.
   a) schools attended
   b) attendance record with reasons for marked deviation.
5. Aptitude.
   a) group tests
   b) individual tests.
6. Achievement.
   a) areas of study
   b) achievement test data.
7. Sources of additional data.
   a) referral listings
   b) teacher comments.
8. Transfer data.

145

PLANNING OF RECORDS

The planning of a record system should involve as many adults within the schools as will have any reason to make use of the data. This means not only the guidance person, but also teachers, nurses, special consultants, and administrators. The operating principle should be that of the use of many minds and therefore many ideas. A record system that is planned by a limited number of people is likely to be limited in its scope and in its usefulness to others. If many persons have a part in the design of the record system, they would tend to be helpful also in planning for the best use of their product. The solicitation and use of teachers' reactions to the form and content of the record will mean that the final form will be more acceptable to them than if they had not been consulted.

Not only should all of the possible personnel at the elementary level participate in the development of a record system, but also those persons should be included who will be making future use of the records—namely, personnel from high schools and colleges to whom the elementary children will go for future education. This is important so that the elementary records will contain information useful to future as well as present instructors, and so that the data throughout will be recorded in the most uniform and usable style possible. A further important benefit of vertical planning by elementary and secondary groups is that of in-service growth and understanding by the participants.

The planning of record revision should begin with a survey of reactions to current forms. Suggestions should be solicited through small group meetings and written reactions on needed improvements. The next step might then be the summarization of suggestions, and the establishment of building study groups, with one person in the district designated to coordinate study activities. Functioning simultaneously with the building study groups could be a central group, composed of representatives from elementary and secondary levels, with various interests represented.

After preliminary planning and discussion of needs, a second step might involve the study of literature on the development of records and various records from other school systems. It is particularly necessary that school districts study other records to avoid

146

repetition of work covered by countless others. In other words, schools should attempt by all possible means to learn from others' experiences.

After initial discussion, review of materials, and study, the participants are ready to begin the most difficult part—deciding the essential content. The materials contained in the record should be there for functional use by school personnel, and the purposes should be accepted. Any material that is not of value informationally should be deleted.

Several problems within the content itself will occur, and will make initial trial forms desirable. One problem is the planning of items that consistently establish trends in development in important growth areas throughout the grades. Another is that of optimum space for recording each item. A third is that of instructions for recording data. A fourth is the planning of items in such fashion that they are non-repetitive, easily recorded, and easily understood. A fifth is that of a single form versus separate forms established on the principle of primary use—a basic folder with the teacher, a detailed health form with the nurse, with only exceptional health needs going to the teacher. A final problem is that of housing, in which many considerations appear, among them size, structure, shape, and potential content of the record.

Mention is made of these problems to indicate the complexity of establishing worthwhile records. The learnings contained within the experience are great, but the total program of revision should be projected over a period of several years.

One group of participants in planning a record system should be given special attention. This group is the parents, who can make valuable suggestions concerning background data. They often have ideas concerning data which might be overlooked, and themselves gain in appreciation of the teaching profession through a working association with them.

An outstanding record form has been developed by the Denver Public Schools (see pages 149-156).[4] The form is of the folder type, allowing for flexibility in auxiliary materials and providing space for many of the items listed on page 145. Two features of this record merit study—the graphic chart, which furnishes comparative

[4] Permission to reproduce the record forms has been granted by the Denver Public Schools.

data on achievement and aptitude, and the cumulative direction folder, which is so organized that a teacher may use it as a guide in filling out her own records. The cumulative direction folder is supplemented by a manual in case the teacher desires more complete directions.

A record form of this type can be used easily for in-service discussions by teachers. Graphic data taken from the record and charted for a class group can be readily employed in planning and selection of curriculum materials.

An additional form that has been developed on a somewhat different basis is one recently installed in selected California schools.[5] Local school districts may use the form if they wish, or they may develop their own forms. The California form includes two folders, one for the elementary level which can be inserted into a folder for the junior and senior high school, and a card for junior college records. The elementary form, which again is a flexible folder including much vital information is illustrated.

EFFECTIVE USE OF RECORDS

The first consideration in planning effective use of records is the development of records that allow for individual needs of both children and teachers. The majority of children will go through school in satisfactory style with only standard data used in planning for them. There will be others—exceptional in emotional, physical, or intellectual aspects of their growth—who will require special planning based upon detailed data. A folder-type card will serve both groups best. Teachers also vary in the care and skill employed in record keeping. A folder permits this variation without penalizing the teacher who realizes the value of data as complete and comprehensive as her time and ability permit. With the use of folders, teachers' records may range from minimum essentials to detailed studies of selected individuals.

Uniform directions for the recording of data on records are essential. Such directions must be available to teachers in easy-to-read, concise form, such as those appearing on the Denver direction folder, or within a manual. Written directions require supple-

[5] Permission to reproduce the record forms has been granted by A. Carlisle and Company, 645 Harrison Street, San Francisco.

mentary staff discussions on a regular basis, to assure understanding and thus efficient, correct recording of information. The relatively minor problem of whether a score on a group intelligence test should be recorded as 106, I.Q. 106, CTMM 106, A06 (using symbols), or in still another fashion, can be easily and quickly clarified through a staff meeting on the recording of data. In such meetings, too, responsibilities for the recording of certain types of data can be clarified, and schedules of responsibility can be reviewed. How and when the teacher and nurse could confer about a class group and transfer needed health data to a teacher's folder is one important problem that can be reviewed with the entire staff to improve communication and planning.

Individual responsibilities for the recording of data must be planned so that the teacher of a particular class group is not submerged with clerical duties. The importance of such planning is well stated by Hahn and MacLean:

> 1. *Records should demand a minimum of clerical time.* This is a combined philosophical, practical, and budget matter. Those administrators who have not yet been convinced of the importance and values of counseling to them and to their schools, who look upon it as a "fifth wheel" in education—a nice thing to have if it does not curtail something else—fail to provide adequate funds and personnel at various levels to operate it effectively. They load clerical chores on busy teachers, many of whom have little clerical ability or training and who possess no interest in tedious and time-consuming jobs of recording and filing, which they do badly. In the author's opinion more counseling programs have been inefficient, wasteful, and failures for this than for any other single reason. A teacher may strongly approve of a counseling program, see clearly how it can help students, parents, employees, school administrators, and himself, and yet build up a resentment against it and want to throw it out, if he is compelled to give up duties which he likes and for which he is trained, to spend hours typing and shuffling cards and forms.[6]

Two things can be done by school districts to avoid teacher resentment of records. One is to plan for a gradual enrollment of kindergarten children, spread over a period of several days, so that the parents themselves, in conference with the teacher, can supply

[6] Milton E. Hahn and Malcolm S. MacLean, *General Clinical Counseling* (New York: McGraw-Hill Book Company, 1950), pp. 94-95.

149

150

Pupil's Name

Last | First | Second (in full)

Sex — M F

Birthplace — State or Foreign Country

Pupil's Birthdate — Month Day Year

Authority for Birthdate—Verified by Principal

Birth Certificate _____ Hospital Record _____ Other _____
Bureau Vital Stat. _____ Church Record _____
Signature of Principal (Upon verification of birthdate)

1.

2. Own Father — Race C N M — Occupations (Note changes in type of occupation and dates)

3. Own Mother — C N M

4. Step-Parent — C N M

5. Language Used in Home (When important to school)

6. Culture Pattern (When important to school)

7. HOME SITUATION (Give dates when known)

Deceased { Mother / Father — Parents { Separated / Divorced — Remarried { Mother / Father

8. WHEN BOTH PARENTS ARE NOT IN THE HOME — WITH WHOM DOES PUPIL LIVE?

Relationship | Name | Date

9. ADDITIONAL INFORMATION FROM HOME

10. REGISTRATIONS, TRANSFERS, WITHDRAWALS
(Make entries only when pupil enters and leaves)

ENTERING		LEAVING	
Grade	School Entered	DATE	Destination	DATE

11. SERIOUS PHYSICAL HANDICAPS AND DISABILITIES
(Only those important for teacher to know. Notes should be made by teacher in consultation with nurse. Date each entry.)

	Grade
Vision	
Hearing	
Heart, Organic	
Metabolic (diabetes, thyroid, etc.)	
Skin	
Nutrition	
Orthopedic	
Nervous System (epilepsy, chorea, spastic, etc.)	
Other	

12. ADDITIONAL HELPFUL INFORMATION
Can be secured by consulting with: (Write in grade or date to above source.)

	Elementary	Junior High	Senior High
Principal			
Ass't Principal			
Dean			
Nurse			
Psychologist			
Social Worker			

PUPIL CUMULATIVE RECORD—GRADES K-12

DENVER PUBLIC SCHOOLS
FORM 439-518

PAGE 1

26. COMMENTS TO SHOW SPECIFIC STRENGTHS AND PROBLEMS NOT REVEALED ELSEWHERE
(Grade and teacher's name should follow each entry.)

Educational Plans

Vocational Preference

Work Experience

GRAPHIC CHART OF PUPIL'S AGE AND GRADE AND STA
Use chart to see quickly general levels of achievement, relation between academic aptitude and

13. DIRECTIONS: First determine pupil's September age and write it in proper column in relation to normal age range, Items 15-16. Give pupil's September
Expectancy grade levels in each column give upper limits of intervals. Use symbols given below to indicate type of test. Make letters very plain. Use

14. Normal grade placement		KINDERGARTEN		GRADE 1		GRADE 2		GRADE 3		GRADE 4		GRADE 5	
15. Normal age range for September	4-4 : 4-9	4-10 : 5-9		5-10 : 6-9		6-10 : 7-9		7-10 : 8-9		8-10 : 9-9		9-10 : 10-9	
16. Pupil's age as of September													
17. Pupil's grade													
18. Very superior ability in the factors measured. Approximately highest 7% of same age.				2.0	2.5	3.4	3.7	4.6	5.1	5.9	6.3	7.2	7.6
				1.9	2.4	3.3	3.6	4.4	4.9	5.7	6.1	6.9	7.4
				1.8	2.2	3.1	3.5	4.2	4.6	5.5	5.9	6.6	7.1
				1.7	2.1	3.0	3.3	4.1	4.5	5.4	5.7	6.5	6.9
19. High ability in factors measured when compared with children of same age.				1.6	1.9	2.8	3.1	4.0	4.3	5.1	5.5	6.3	6.6
				1.5	1.8	2.7	3.0	3.8	4.1	4.9	5.4	6.0	6.5
				1.4	1.7	2.5	2.9	3.6	4.0	4.7	5.2	5.7	6.2
20. Range of average achievement. Approximately middle 40% of children of same chronological age.				1.3	1.6	2.4	2.8	3.5	3.8	4.5	5.0	5.6	6.0
				1.2	1.5	2.3	2.6	3.3	3.6	4.4	4.7	5.5	5.7
				1.1	1.4	2.2	2.5	3.2	3.5	4.2	4.5	5.3	5.5
				1.0	1.2	1.9	2.3	3.0	3.3	4.0	4.5	4.9	5.2
21. Scores in this lane indicate that abilities measured are distinctly below average compared with pupils of same age.				1.1	1.8	2.2	2.8	3.1	3.8	4.1	4.7	5.1
				1.0	1.7	2.0	2.7	3.0	3.6	4.0	4.5
					1.5	1.9	2.5	2.9	3.4	3.9	4.4	4.6
					1.4	1.7	2.4	2.6	3.2	3.5	4.0	4.4
22. Abilities scored in this lane, if measured correctly, are very limited. Look for other abilities to capitalize.					1.3	1.5	2.2	2.5	3.0	3.2	3.5	4.0
					1.1	1.4	1.9	2.2	2.7	3.0	3.5	3.8
					1.0	1.1	1.7	2.0	2.5	2.7	3.2	3.5
						1.0	1.5	1.6	2.2	2.5	3.0	3.1

23. SYMBOLS: 106, etc. = IQ, Group Academic Aptitude Test (Binet) 106 = IQ, Individual Binet Test (W-B) 106 = IQ, Full Scale, Wechsler-Bellevue (W-BV) 106 = Verbal IQ, Wechsler-Bellevue (W-BP) 106 = Performance IQ, Wechsler-Bellevue AF = Arithmetic Fundamentals AR = Arithmetic Reasoning EM = English Mechanics G = Geography

24. REPORT CARD GRADES OF ACADEMIC ACHIEVEMENT*

SCHOOL YEAR, e.g. 52 53											SCHOOL YEAR									
GRADE	1	2	3	4	5	6	7	8	9		GRADE	1	2	3	4	5	6	7	8	9
Art											Music, Instrumental									
											Music, Vocal									
English											Penmanship									
											Physical Education									
											Reading									
Guidance											Science									
Home Economics											Social Studies									
Industrial Arts											Spelling									
											Typewriting									
Mathematics																				

*See senior high school for academic record in grades 10-12.

NDARDIZED TEST DATA IN BASIC SKILLS AND KNOWLEDGE   PAGE 3

achievement, and consistency of growth. Do not expect high accuracy of placement and comparison.

grade directly below his age. Item 17. Bring these items up to date each September. Record test data in the column of pupil's grade and semester. only blue or black ink. *See Manual.*

Quotient Scale	%ile Scale	Grade 6 (10-10 : 11-9)		Grade 7 (11-10 : 12-9)		Grade 8 (12-10 : 13-9)		Grade 9 (13-10 : 14-9)		Grade 10 (14-10 : 15-9)		Grade 11 (15-10 : 16-9)		Grade 12 (16-10 : 17-9)	
130-up	99+														
127-129	99	8.5	8.9	9.8	10.2	11.1	11.6	12.5	12.8	13.6	14.0	14.9	15.3	15.7	15.8
123-126	97-98	8.2	8.7	9.5	10.0	10.8	11.2	12.1	12.5	13.3	13.7	14.4	14.9	15.3	15.8
120-122	94-96	7.9	8.3	9.2	9.5	10.3	10.8	11.6	12.0	12.8	13.2	14.0	14.3	14.8	14.9
117-119	83-93	7.7	8.1	8.9	9.3	10.0	10.4	11.3	11.6	12.5	12.8	13.6	14.0	14.3	14.4
114-116	82-87	7.5	7.8	8.6	8.9	9.7	10.1	11.0	11.3	12.1	12.5	13.3	13.6	14.0	14.1
110-113	76-81	7.2	7.5	8.3	8.7	9.5	9.8	10.5	11.0	11.7	12.2	12.8	13.2	13.6	13.7
108-109	71-75	6.8	7.2	7.9	8.3	9.0	9.4	10.1	10.4	11.3	11.6	12.5	12.8	13.0	13.1
105-107	61-70	6.6	7.0	7.7	8.1	8.8	9.2	9.9	10.2	11.1	11.4	12.2	12.5	12.6	12.7
102-104	51-60	6.5	6.7	7.5	7.7	8.5	8.8	9.5	9.9	10.7	11.1	11.7	12.0	12.3	12.4
98-101	41-50	6.2	6.5	7.2	7.5	8.2	8.5	9.2	9.5	10.2	10.5	11.3	11.6	11.7	11.8
95-97	31-40	5.9	6.2	6.8	7.2	7.7	8.1	8.7	9.1	9.8	10.1	10.8	10.8	11.1	11.3
93-94	26-30	5.6	6.0	6.5	6.8	7.5	7.8	8.4	8.7	9.5	9.7	10.2	10.2	10.5	10.7
90-92	20-25	5.3	5.8	6.4	6.6	7.2	7.6	8.2	8.5	9.2	9.5	10.0	10.0	10.1	10.2
86-89	14-19	5.3	5.6	6.1	6.4	6.9	7.3	7.9	8.2	8.8	9.2	9.5	9.5	9.8	9.9
82-85	8-13	4.9	5.2	5.7	6.2	6.5	6.9	7.5	7.7	8.3	8.7	9.0	9.0	9.3	9.4
78-81	5-7	4.5	4.8	5.5	5.6	6.1	6.5	7.0	7.4	7.9	8.2	8.5	8.6	8.7	8.8
74-77	3-4	4.2	4.5	5.0	5.4	5.8	6.1	6.6	6.9	7.5	7.7	8.0	8.1	8.2	8.4
70-73	2	3.9	4.1	4.6	4.9	5.5	5.7	6.3	6.5	7.0	7.3	7.5	7.6	7.7	7.8
0-69	0-1	3.5	3.8	4.3	4.5	5.1	5.4	5.8	6.0	6.5	6.7	7.1	7.2	7.4	7.5

H = History   McAp = Mechanical Aptitude   RV = Reading Vocabulary   Sp = Spelling
Lit. = Literature   RC = Reading Comprehension   Sc = Science   SS = Social Studies

25.   PERSONAL—SOCIAL DEVELOPMENT

DIRECTIONS: Rate as many of the following items as practicable on the basis of observations made. Judgments of as many teachers as possible are of value. Use the symbol *H* for highly desirable functioning; *S* for satisfactory or average functioning; *U* for undesirable or limited functioning.

Grade	K	1	2	3	4	5	6	7	8	9	10	11	12
In relation to his age, this pupil:													
1. Has a healthy attitude toward authority													
2. Cooperates in observing rules and regulations													
3. Shares in meeting group responsibilities													
4. Is well-liked by other pupils													
5. Shows respect and consideration for the rights of others													
6. Shows friendliness toward others													
7. Shows leadership ability*													
8. Adjusts well to own sex													
9. Shows satisfactory adjustment to opposite sex													

*If high but anti-social, please comment.

Grade	K	1	2	3	4	5	6	7	8	9	10	11	12
10. Shows good habits of work													
11. Is usually cheerful and happy													
12. Has a sense of humor													
13. Cares for his health and safety													
14. Is acceptably groomed													
15. Has reasonable self-confidence and self-respect													
16. Displays enthusiasm over a good range of interests													
17. Is learning to think for himself													
18. Is well poised and emotionally stable													
19. Is developing sound values													
20. Shows creative ability*													

*If rated *H*, comment.

PUPIL CUMULATIVE RECORD—GRADES K-12

DENVER PUBLIC SCHOOLS

Page 1

Pupil's Name

Last — First — Second (in full)

1. Name. Type or print. Use birth certificate name if possible.
— Underline second name if used.

2. Own Father

Occupation. Give the type of occupation rather than the place where he works. Example: Profession (specify), merchant, contractor, military service, skilled laborer, unskilled laborer, etc. If mother does not work outside the home, write the word "Home" under occupation. If she does work regularly, give the kind of work she does. Record in pencil after first entry. Do not erase former entries.

3. Name. Give surname first. Name of child's own father and mother should be recorded even though they are deceased or divorced. Record name, race, birthplace, and occupation.

4. Step-Parent

Sex
Check to indicate sex.

Race
Circle one.
Cau-casian
Negro
Mon-golian

Birthplace
City and State or Foreign Country

Pupil's Birthdate
Month — Day — Year

Occupations (Note changes in type of occupation and dates)

Authority for Birthdate—Verified by Principal
Indicate authority for birthdate. Principal will sign upon verification.
Signature of Principal (Upon verification of birthdate)

5. Language Used in Home (When important to school)
5-6. Give information when important in school adjustment.
6. See manual.

7. HOME SITUATION (Give dates when known)
Clarify the family picture. Give the approximate dates when known of important changes.

8. WHEN BOTH PARENTS ARE NOT IN THE HOME WITH WHOM DOES PUPIL LIVE?

Relationship — Name — Date

If either parent, including the step-parent, is out of the home for an indefinite period, the information of Item 8 should be recorded.

9. ADDITIONAL INFORMATION FROM HOME

Classroom teacher, social worker, nurse, and other staff members may get this significant information through their contacts with the child and his parents and should see that it is recorded. See manual for types of valuable comments.

10. REGISTRATIONS, TRANSFERS, WITHDRAWALS
(Make entries only when pupil enters and leaves)

Grade	ENTERING		LEAVING	
	School Entered	DATE	Destination	Grade

When a pupil enters, re-enters, or is received by transfer, record the grade, name of school, and the date.
When a pupil leaves the school either by transfer or withdrawal, record on the line below the last entry the date of leaving, the destination as accurately as possible, and the grade at the time of leaving.
If a school, receiving a pupil from an out-of-Denver school, desires to indicate from where the pupil comes, it is suggested that this item be recorded in parenthesis in the line directly below the record of the pupil's entry.

11. SERIOUS PHYSICAL HANDICAPS AND DISABILITIES
(Only those important for teacher to know. Notes should be made by teacher in consultation with nurse. Date each entry.)

Grade		
Vision		
Hearing		
Heart, Organic		
Metabolic (diabe		
Skin		
Nutrition		
Orthopedic		
Nervous System (epilepsy, chorea, spastic, etc.)		
Other		

The guidance teacher should record significant health and physical information in consultation with the nurse. Include information a teacher can understand and use in working intelligently with the child.
She should also bring up-to-date any existing comments regarding conditions which no longer limit the child's activities.

12. ADDITIONAL HELPFUL INFORMATION
Can be secured by consulting with: (Write in grade or date to show source.)

	Elementary	Junior High	Senior High
Principal			
Ass't Principal			
Dean			
Nurse			
Psychologist			
Social Worker			

The purpose of this section is to acquaint the teacher with sources of information too detailed or too confidential to be recorded on the Record. Give grade or date in the proper space to show school level and source. See manual for examples.

PAGE 4

26. COMMENTS TO SHOW SPECIFIC STRENGTHS AND PROBLEMS NOT REVEALED ELSEWHERE
(Grade and teacher's name should follow each entry.)

Teachers are not under obligation to make comments each year. In many cases the rating of the personal-social development will be sufficient. Comments should be added when a significant contribution can be made to the child's total picture. Give grade, date, and name of person making comments. Comments should be concise and space should be utilized with consideration for the needs of all grades.

Excessive tardiness or absence should be noted with apparent causes and family attitudes toward attendance.

Comments should help to give a picture of the child's abilities and achievements and the material, physical, psychological, and emotional factors not covered elsewhere, which influence his activities and reactions.

Comments may also indicate deviations and may suggest procedures which have been found successful in dealing with them. Special interests and emotional problems should be noted. See comments in manual.

Try to avoid merely describing or listing symptomatic misbehavior. If possible, state probable reasons for child's undesirable behavior patterns.

Avoid emotionally charged words that tend to prejudice or to stereotype the thinking of teachers. (To refer to a child as impudent or lazy or immoral or untrustworthy, tends to make it difficult for most of us to be constructive in dealing with his problems.)

Educational Plans

Junior and Senior High School teachers should make entries here whenever a fairly definite decision has been made by the child and his parents.

Vocational Preference

Work Experience

Record the types of jobs and records of success and dependability on the jobs.

155

SCHOOL RECORDS

GRAPHIC CHART OF PUPIL'S AGE AND GRADE AND STA
Use chart to see quickly general levels of achievement, relation between academic aptitude and :

13. DIRECTIONS: First determine pupil's September age and write it in proper column in relation to normal age range, Items 15-16. Give pupil's September Expectancy grade levels in each column give upper limits of intervals. Use symbols given below to indicate type of test. Make letters very plain. Use

14. Normal grade placement	KINDERGARTEN	GRADE 1	GRADE 2	GRADE 3	GRADE 4	GRADE 5
15. Normal age range for September	4-4 : 4-9 | 4-10 : 5-9	5-10 : 6-9	6-10 : 7-9	7-10 : 8-9	8-10 : 9-9	9-10 : 10-9
16. Pupil's age as of September	5-3	6-3			9-1	10-1
17. Pupil's grade	K K	1 1			3 3	4 4

18. Very superior ability in the factors measured. Approximately highest 7% of same age.

19. High ability in factors measured when compared with children of same age.

20 Range of average achievement. Approximately middle 40% of children of same chronological age.

21. Scores in this lane indicate that abilities measured are distinctly below average compared with pupils of same age.

22. Abilities scored in this lane, if measured correctly, are very limited. Look for other abilities to capitalize.

Sample—Susie; Age 5-3; Kdg.
Determine the pupil's age as of September irrespective of the time of year the pupil enters.
Locate the age range interval (Item 15) which includes the pupil's age. Directly below this, record the pupil's September age as Item 16. In the same column give the pupil's grade as Item 17. Then on each succeeding September simply add one year to the age and enter in the proper column to the right.
In recording the IQ find the proper interval on the quotient scale located near the center of the graphic chart. Follow this line across to the column in which the pupil's present age-grade is recorded. There write the IQ numbers.
Enter test data according to the symbols given in Item 23. Most standardized test results are expressed in grade level. In pupil's age-grade column locate the grade level obtained by the pupil on the test. Enter in this square the symbols for the test given.

Sample—Billy; Age 9-1; Grade 3 IQ 84; RV 3.6; RC 2.8; AR 3.0; AF 3.2; EM 2.9; SP 3.5.
Find the interval in Item 15 that includes his age. Below this write Billy's age 9-1 as Item 16. Write 3 for the grade as Item 17. Since this is under the normal placement of grade 4, it indicates one year retarded.
To record IQ find the quotient scale in the line with the interval which includes 84 (82-85). Record 84 at same level in his age-grade column.
For recording tests use the grade-level figures. RV is in the square with 3.6. RC 2.8 will come between 2.7 and 3.0. Record in the square with the upper limit of 3.0. AR 3.0 will be recorded in the square with upper limit of 3.0. AF 3.2 comes in the square with that upper limit. EM 2.9 will be recorded in the square with the upper limit of 3.0. SP 3.5 will be recorded in the square with the upper limit of 3.6. In Grade 4 these are his scores: In October, IQ 81; in February, RV 4.6; RC 4.1; AR 4.0; AF 4.4; EM 4.0; SP 4.5. Record his IQ in the September age-grade column. The second semester tests are recorded in the column to the right.

Put Billy's picture here. Photographs should be placed outside the range of the pupil's test score, but in his age-grade column.

126

RV 2.0   2.5   3.4
RC 1.9   2.4   3.3
1.8   2.2   3.1
2.1   3.0
1.9   2.8
1.8   2.7
1.7   2.6
1.6   2.4
1.5   2.3
1.4   2.2
1.2   1.9
1.1   1.8
1.0   1.7
1.5
1.4
1.3
1.1
1.0
1.6

3.3   4.0
3.1   3.8
3.0 SP 3.6   4.0   4.6
    RV
2.9   3.4   3.8   4.4 SP 4.6
                        RV
2.6 AF 3.2   3.5   4.0 AF 4.4
    84   RC
2.5 AR 3.0   3.2   3.8 AR 4.0
    RC EM   81   EM
2.2   2.7   3.0   3.5   3.8
2.0   2.5   2.7   3.2   3.5
1.6   2.2   2.5   3.0   3.1

6.3
6.1
5.9
5.7 6.5 6.8
5.6 6.3 6.6
5.4 6.0 6.5
5.2 5.7 6.2
5.0 6.0 6.0
4.7 5.5 5.7
4.5 5.3 5.5
4.3 4.9 5.3

23 SYMBOLS: *106, etc. = IQ, Group Academic Aptitude Test* · (W-B) 106 = IQ, Full Scale, Wechsler-Bellevue · AF = Arithmetic Fundamentals · EM = English Mechanics
(Binet) 106 = IQ, Individual Binet Test · (W-BV) 106 = Verbal IQ, Wechsler-Bellevue · AR = Arithmetic Reasoning · G = Geography
(W-BP) 106 = Performance IQ, Wechsler-Bellevue

24. REPORT CARD GRADES OF ACADEMIC ACHIEVEMENT*

SCHOOL YEAR, e.g. 52/53										SCHOOL YEAR									
GRADE	1	2	3	4	5	6	7	8	9	GRADE	1	2	3	4	5	6	7	8	9
Art										Music, Instrumental									
English										Music, Vocal									
										Penmanship									
Guidance										Physical Education									
Home Economics										Reading									
Industrial Arts										Science									
Mathematics										Social Studies									
										Spelling									
										Typewriting									

The final grades for the year should be placed on the Cumulative Record.
If a child is retained in a grade, change the grade numbers for the following columns. Use one column for each year.
If a child withdraws or transfers from the school during the school year, it will help greatly to record his latest grades in pencil before sending in his record.
Whether or not grades are written in the teacher's register at the end of the year is a question for each building to decide. There is no city-wide policy requiring such a double entry.

*See senior high school for academic record in grades 10-12.

156

STANDARDIZED TEST DATA IN BASIC SKILLS AND KNOWLEDGE — PAGE 3

...chievement, and consistency of growth. Do not expect high accuracy of placement and comparison.

...grade directly below his age, Item 17. Bring these items up to date each September. Record test data in the column of pupil's grade and semester. ...nly blue or black ink. *See Manual.*

(Right margin, vertical:) CUMULATIVE DIRECTION FOLDER — See Manual for more complete suggestions. / Last Name / First / Second in Full / Nickname / Grade / Room or Group / Location of Record

Quotient Scale	%ile Scale	Grade 6 (10-10:11-9) 10-11 — 6	6	Grade 7 (11-10:12-9) 11-11 — 7	7	Grade 8 (12-10:13-9) 12-11 — 8	8	Grade 9 (13-10:14-9)		Grade 10 (14-10:15-9)		Grade 11 (15-10:16-9)		Grade 12 (16-10:17-9)	
130-up	99+														
127-129	99	8.5	8.9			11.1				13.6	14.0	14.9	15.3	15.7	15.8
123-126	97-98	8.2	8.7			10.8				13.3	13.7	14.4	14.9	15.3	15.3
120-122	94-96	7.9	8.3			10.3				12.8	13.2	14.0	14.3	14.8	14.9
117-119	88-93	7.7	8.1	8.8	9.3	10.0				12.6	12.8	13.6	14.0	14.3	14.4
114-116	82-87	7.5	7.8	8.6	8.9	9.7				12.1	12.5	13.3	13.6	14.0	14.1
110-113	76-81	7.2	7.5	8.3	8.7	9.5				11.7	12.2	12.8	13.3	13.6	13.7
108-109	71-75	6.8 AF	7.2	109 7.9 (W-BP)		8.3 AF	9.0			11.3	11.6	12.5	12.8	13.0	13.1
105-107	61-70	6.6 AR	7.0	7.7		8.1 AR	8.8			11.1	11.4	12.2	12.5	12.6	12.7
102-104	51-60	6.5	6.7	104 7.5 (W-B)		7.7 SP	8.5			10.7	11.1	11.7	12.0	12.3	12.4
98-101	41-50	6.2	6.5	98 7.5 (W-BV)		7.5 RC	8.2			10.2	10.5	11.3	11.6	11.7	11.8
95-97	31-40	5.9 95	6.2	6.8		7.2 RV EM	7.7			9.8	10.1	10.8	10.8	11.1	11.3
93-94	26-30	5.6 RV	6.0	6.5	6.8	7.5				9.5	9.7	10.2	10.2	10.5	10.7
90-92	20-25	5.5 SP	5.8	6.4	6.6	7.2	7.6	8.2	8.5	9.2	9.5	10.0	10.0	10.1	10.2
86-89	14-19	5.3 RC	5.6	6.1	6.4	6.9	7.3	7.9	8.2	8.8	9.2	9.5	9.5	9.8	9.9
82-85	8-13	4.9 EM	5.2	5.7	6.2	6.5	6.9	7.5	7.7	8.3	8.7	9.0	9.0	9.3	9.4
78-81	5-7	4.5	4.8	5.5	5.6	6.1	6.5	7.0	7.4	7.9	8.2	8.5	8.6	8.7	8.8
74-77	3-4	4.2	4.5	5.0	5.4	5.8	6.1	6.6	6.9	7.5	7.7	8.0	8.1	8.2	8.4
70-73	2	3.9	4.1	4.6	4.9	5.5	5.7	6.2	6.5	7.0	7.3	7.5	7.6	7.7	7.8
0-69	0-1	3.5	3.8	4.2	4.4	5.1	5.4	5.8	6.0	6.5	6.7	7.1	7.2	7.4	7.5

(Text box in Grade 7–8 area:) Pictures are optional. John's seventh grade picture may go here. Use rubber cement, glue, or Scotch tape. Do not use staples.

(Sample text box:)
Sample — John; Age 10-11; Grade 6. John entered sixth grade in February, but the age and grade are always recorded as of September. Test grades are recorded in the column for the second semester. The following tests have been recorded to illustrate method of recording. More detailed directions may be found on the left half of the chart. Further instructions are to be found in the Test Handbook.
Grade 6 (February) Group IQ 95; RV 5.9; RC 5.5; AR 6.8; AF 7.2; EM 5.1; SP 5.8.
Grade 7 (October) (W-B) 104; (W-BP) 109; (W-BV) 98.
Grade 8 (September) RV 7.6; RC 8.1; AR 8.8; AF 8.9; EM 7.6; SP 8.4.

H = History   McAp = Mechanical Aptitude   RV = Reading Vocabulary   Sp = Spelling
Lit. = Literature   RC = Reading Comprehension   Sc = Science   SS = Social Studies

25. PERSONAL—SOCIAL DEVELOPMENT

DIRECTIONS: Rate as many of the following items as practicable on the basis of observations made. Judgments of as many teachers as possible are of value. Use the symbol H for highly desirable functioning; S for satisfactory or average functioning; U for undesirable or limited functioning.

	GRADE	K	1	2	3	4	5	6	7	8	9	10	11	12
In relation to his age, this pupil														
Has a healthy attitude toward authority														
Cooperates in observing rules and regulations														
Shares in meeting group responsibilities														
Is well-liked by other pupils														
Shows respect and consideration for the rights of others														
Shows friendliness toward others														
Shows leadership ability*														
Adjusts well to own sex														
Shows satisfactory adjustment to opposite sex														
If high but anti-social, please comment														

Careful evaluation of characteristics in Item 25 should replace writing voluminous comments. A teacher shou'd not rate a pupil on any characteristic when evidence is insufficient to justify a conclusion. Evaluations should be made in relation to pupils of the same chronological age and not in relation to ideal behavior.

Anecdotal notes and other records should help to recall the history of the child and specific responses on which to base judgment rather than relying on general impressions and immediate situations. Other teachers should share the evaluation of these characteristics with the guidance teacher. Many youngsters show different characteristics in different situations and in different subjects. Comments may help clarify.

	GRADE	K	1	2	3	4	5	6	7	8	9	10	11	12
10. Shows good habits of work														
11. Is usually cheerful and happy														
12. Has a sense of humor														
13. Cares for his health and safety														
14. Is acceptably groomed														
15. Has reasonable self-confidence and self-respect														
16. Displays enthusiasm over a good range of interests														
17. Is learning to think for himself														
18. Is well poised and emotionally stable														
19. Is developing sound values														
20. Shows creative ability*														

*If rated H, comment.

Specific abilities which are outstanding or deficient should be described on page 4 when they influence markedly the child's development. The evaluation made near the end of the year should be recorded here.

157

1. IDENTIFICATION DATA

PHOTOGRAPHS

CALIFORNIA CUMULATIVE RECORD
ELEMENTARY FORM

Confidential Information for use by Professional Personnel

FILE No. (Pencil)

LAST NAME   FIRST NAME   MIDDLE NAME   CHECK SEX M F

NICKNAME: (Pencil)

SCHOOL DISTRICT

BIRTH DATE BIRTH DATE VERIFICATION   PLACE OF BIRTH
CITY (OR COUNTY)   STATE (OR NATION)

By

DATES PHOTOGRAPHED (Pencil)

HOME
NAME   ADDRESS   TELEPHONE (OR)   NAME (Pencil)   (OR)   TELEPHONE (Pencil)   NAME   ADDRESS   TELEPHONE

IN CASE OF EMERGENCY NOTIFY
ADDRESS   TELEPHONE

COMMENTS

COMMENTS

2. GROUP SCHOLASTIC CAPACITY TESTS (LABEL OTHER SUB SCORES USED, e.g., PERFORMANCE, PERCEPTION, ETC. DOUBLE SPACES PROVIDED.)

DATE TEST GIVEN	GRADE	NAME OF TEST	FORM	LEVEL	C.A.	M.A.	Total	Verbal	Non-Verb	8	9	10	11	12	13	COMMENTS	EXAMINER

3. INDIVIDUAL TESTS

DATE TEST GIVEN	GRADE	NAME OF TEST	C.A.	RESULTS AND REMARKS	EXAMINER

4. GROUP ACHIEVEMENT TESTS (Including Reading Readiness) (LABEL VARIOUS SUB SCORES, e.g., VOCABULARY)

DATE TEST GIVEN	GRADE	NAME OF TEST	FORM	LEVEL	READING	ARITHMETIC	LANGUAGE	13	14	15	COMMENTS	EXAMINER

5. PERSONALITY AND INTEREST INVENTORIES, APTITUDE TESTS, AND OTHER TESTS (LABEL VARIOUS SUB SCORES, e.g., EMOTIONAL, SOCIAL)

DATE TEST GIVEN	GRADE	NAME OF TEST	FORM	LEVEL	5	6	7	8	9	10	11	12	13	14	15	COMMENTS	EXAMINER

158

6. INFORMATION CONCERNING INDIVIDUAL ADJUSTMENT

YEAR AND GRADE	INTERESTS, ACTIVITIES, LEADERSHIP	FAMILY AND HOME RELATIONSHIPS OUT OF SCHOOL RESPONSIBILITIES	ATTITUDES AND FEELINGS ABOUT: SELF, PEERS, SCHOOL	REFERRALS TO SCHOOL SERVICES AND/OR COMMUNITY AGENCIES
YEAR 19 -19 KINDERGARTEN				
YEAR 19 -19 GRADE				
YEAR 19 -19 GRADE				
YEAR 19 -19 GRADE				
YEAR 19 -19 GRADE				
YEAR 19 -19 GRADE				
YEAR 19 -19 GRADE				
YEAR 19 -19 GRADE				
YEAR 19 -19 GRADE				

FORM L.M.—A. Carlisle & Co. S.F. 1955

7. GROWTH AND DEVELOPMENT THROUGH SCHOOL EXPERIENCES

INDICATE MAJOR CURRICULUM UNIT, DESCRIPTION OF EXPERIENCE, AND DURATION. INITIAL EACH ENTRY. THIS SPACE MAY ALSO BE USED FOR INDICATING DEGREE OF SUCCESS IN SCHOOL EXPERIENCES AND READERS USED.

YEAR 19 -19 KINDERGARTEN	YEAR 19 -19 GRADE	YEAR 19 -19 GRADE	YEAR 19 -19 GRADE	YEAR 19 -19 GRADE

YEAR 19 -19 GRADE	YEAR 19 -19 GRADE	YEAR 19 -19 GRADE	YEAR 19 -19 GRADE

Requirements of U. S. Constitution, American History, State and Local Government satisfactorily completed.

Date Certified _____ INITIAL _____

8. SCHOOL HISTORY

DATE ENTERED	HOME ADDRESS & TELEPHONE	CITY OR COUNTY	SCHOOL & SCHOOL DISTRICT	GRADE	TEACHER	ATTENDANCE	TRANSFERRED TO	DATE LEFT

COMPLETED GRADE 6 OR 8 OR ( ) ON — CIRCLE — Month Day Year

9. PARENTS' EDUCATIONAL AND/OR VOCATIONAL PLANS FOR PUPIL: (Pencil)

	HOME ADDRESS (Pencil)	SPECIFIC OCCUPATION (Pencil)	BUSINESS ADDRESS AND TELEPHONE (Pencil)	CIRCLE (Pencil)	CIRCLE
10. FATHER'S NAME				Pupil Living With Yes No	Living? Yes No
11. MOTHER'S NAME				Pupil Living With Yes No	Living? Yes No
12. OR GUARDIAN'S NAME				Pupil Living With Yes No	Living? Yes No

13. CHILDREN OF FAMILY

NAMES	Year of Birth	RELATIONSHIP TO PUPIL	Living at Home (Check)

14. ADULTS OTHER THAN PARENTS LIVING CONTINUOUSLY IN PUPIL'S HOME (Pencil)

NAME	RELATIONSHIP TO PUPIL

15. SIGNIFICANT HEALTH FACTORS

DATE	RECOMMENDATIONS OF HEALTH ADVISER	ADVISER'S NAME

DATE	TEACHER'S COMMENTS ON PUPIL'S HEALTH CONDITIONS	TEACHER

any basic family data that appear on the child's folder. Such an arrangement would presuppose in-service meetings, in which the teachers concerned would orient themselves to means for acquainting the parents with the records, their use, and the confidential, professional nature of the information. Another is to plan a schedule for recording specific information, so that the teachers can see readily the cumulative, cooperative approach that is taken by the entire staff to building information regarding children. The plan for recording data might resemble the following:

1. *Basic Data:* kindergarten teacher and parent (September); new entries, principal or counselor and parent.
2. *Health Card:* nurse and physician.
3. *Health Needs:* nurse with kindergarten and second grade teachers (November).
4. *Health Needs:* nurse with fourth and sixth grade teachers (December).
5. *Health Needs:* nurse with others (January).
6. *Individual Tests:* counselor with teachers (as needed).
7. *Group Tests:* teacher (upon completion).
8. *Additional Information:* teacher.

The teacher remains the primary source of information under such an arrangement, but the actual time consumed at any one recording period is not excessive.

If records are to be used efficiently and with a minimum of confusion, two additional points should be considered. When records are revised or new ones are adopted, old records should be abandoned within the district. Otherwise, the teacher is confronted with several forms, several sets of directions, and complete irritation. Record data may be transferred to new forms by trained clerks, or old forms may be inserted into new folders, to be eliminated gradually. All records should be within easy access of the person who makes the greatest use of them. This would mean locating the basic records in the teacher's classroom rather than in the principal's office, the health card in the nurse's office, and highly confidential data with the counselor. Sources for additional information should be noted on the teacher's folder, so that she may know of them.

Since records are the framework of the guidance program, they should form the background for in-service discussions. Teachers may use them in presenting and reacting to group variations in ability and achievement, studying selected exceptional children, evaluating techniques of recording subjective information, studying economic and social structures of their groups, studying family compositions, and in many other ways. Frequent use of records in such fashion will tend to improve planning within the classroom, and will enhance the importance of the records themselves.

ROLES OF PERSONNEL IN EFFECTIVE DEVELOPMENT AND USE OF RECORDS

Separation of the roles of personnel in the development of an effective record system is difficult because of the great variety of resources within given schools. However, some indication of how school people may work together may be given through mention of contributions that each person makes to the total effort.

1. The *teacher* contributes to effective records through
   a) serving on planning committees to develop records.
   b) keeping data up-to-date and complete.
   c) participating in in-service discussions based upon record information.
   d) contacting others for special information.
2. The *principal* contributes to effective records through
   a) working with planning committees.
   b) appointing committee members.
   c) scheduling meetings for planning and use of record data.
   d) scheduling time and responsibility for recording data.
   e) serving on district committee.
   f) recording, or arranging for recording, of data on new entries.
   g) providing trained clerical help for recording.
   h) checking the recording of data.
3. The *guidance person* contributes to effective records through
   a) working with planning committees.
   b) coordinating work of committees.
   c) supplying resource materials.
   d) serving as chairman of coordinating committee.
   e) assuming responsibility for distribution of trial forms.
   f) serving as resource to principals in planning and conducting in-service meetings.

The development of successful records is a team affair. All persons in the school system, in addition to those listed above, have contributions to make, and would have points similar to the above related to them. The success of the record system of a district depends in large measure upon the *personal* investment of district personnel in it.

Yes responses to the ten questions below would serve to indicate a successful record program within a district:

	Yes	No
1. Do the records permit flexible recording of data?	—	—
2. Are the basic records kept in the classroom in locked files?	—	—
3. Did many district personnel assist in developing the records?	—	—
4. Does the record reflect district philosophy?	—	—
5. Are regular meetings held concerning the recording of data?	—	—
6. Do principals confer with individual teachers concerning their records?	—	—
7. Do resource persons (principal, counselor, nurse, etc.) use the teacher's records in discussions with her?	—	—
8. Do teachers use records as bases for regular in-service meetings?	—	—
9. Are data recorded systematically?	—	—
10. Are the records evaluated periodically?	—	—

summary

School records are essential for educational research, curriculum development, and studies of children. They contribute information that enables teachers to study children with proper perspective and to work with parents intelligently. The philosophy of a school district is based upon the records employed within it.

The content of records should be comprehensive, planned by individuals at as many varying levels of the educational pattern as possible. Personnel from secondary and college groups should be invited to work with elementary school committees in the study of resource materials, of forms from other districts, and in the initiation of trial forms. Record content should be planned carefully to insure comprehensiveness and efficiency in use.

The effective use of records involves numerous factors, among them form, location, training for recording and use of data, in-service use of records, and the utilization of many district personnel in their planning and maintenance.

8

THE NEED FOR
GUIDANCE PERSONNEL

Guidance personnel at the secondary level have been an accepted
part of the educational scene since the early part of the century.
The vocational guidance movement and the departmental organization of secondary schools made the addition of specialized guidance
workers logical and necessary. With many teachers having limited
contact with their students, the guidance worker became the staff
person within the school who could work with students on a flexible
time schedule geared at least in part to their needs. The many and
varied specializations of the high school staff members, too, meant
that their preparations for dealing with guidance problems and
services differed greatly.

It has been only recently that guidance workers in any number
have been found in elementary schools. The historical guidance
worker in the elementary school has been the teacher, who relied
upon the judgment and action of the principal when her own efforts
failed. In the past, when little was known of growth differences, and
the curriculum was poured into all children in regular, uniform
doses, teachers had little need for guidance services as we know
them today. Our increasing knowledge of children with their tremendous variations in all growth factors, the ever-growing realization of the intricacy and individuality of personality development,
the modern elementary school program with its emphasis upon child
study, expanding resources in all branches of special education—

all have contributed to the need for specialized, skilled personnel at the elementary level.

The realization of need and the provision for meeting the need have not been parallel factors. Part of this is due to the comparative recency of the need itself, and part to the traditional organization of the elementary school. In schools at this level, emphasis has been placed upon an integrated program in charge of the classroom teacher, and fear may exist in some quarters that specialization of personnel may lead to specialization within the program itself, with guidance activities divorced from the classroom situation. Within the next several chapters, the contributions of guidance workers will be discussed from the standpoint of reinforcement and support of other adults interested in children, rather than compartmentalization.

FROM THE STANDPOINT OF PARENTS

Why do parents need guidance personnel? Modern society furnishes several answers. Children no longer live in close, cohesive family units, with their educational and vocational goals prescribed for them. Society is becoming increasingly urban, industrial, and anonymous. Neighborhoods lack the opportunities for close contact and acquaintance; they no longer offer the wide, open spaces of the past. The increase in working mothers has led to less intimacy of contact and supervision within the home.

Parents, along with school people, have become interested in psychology. Magazines by the hundreds have sold issues containing articles on what to do and what not to do. Series of features on love, jealousy, and delinquency have given parents many views concerning the mechanisms of behavior. The importance of the first years of life has been stressed through articles and books to parents as it has been to teachers. The flood of information about child rearing has increased parental concern to "do the right thing," and the changes in recipes for bringing up the young that have accompanied new learnings in psychology have developed uncertainties in many parents about what the "right thing" actually is.

The guidance person, working with parents in study groups, can do much to help them in their search for wholesome approaches to the business of proper upbringing for their children. The very knowledge that they have a trained resource person within the district to work with them and with school personnel toward the best possible adjustment of all children is satisfying to parents.

There may be times when parents wish to confer with someone who is not in direct contact with their children. They may be hesitant to discuss aspects of family life with the teacher or principal within the school, because of the groundless, but nevertheless real, fear that their child's future relationships within the school may suffer. Having a person with whom they can discuss the child away from the school environment, with the knowledge that the person has no stake in the school program other than the adjustment of the child, is an additional source of satisfaction.

Occasionally, parents are themselves in need of help. They may feel less reserve in talking with a person whose orientation is primarily guidance, rather than teaching or administration. They tend, too, to work through referrals willingly with a person whose business it is to maintain close contact with the best referral agencies available.

FROM THE STANDPOINT OF THE ADMINISTRATOR [1]

The school administrator is a busy person. He is expected to supervise the educational program of his school, provide leadership in interpreting the program to the public, organize schedules for buses, yard duty, lunchroom and special activities, schedule and plan meetings, work with PTA groups, serve on committees, interview teachers, supervise custodial activities, and plan budgets. These represent only a few of his responsibilities. The administrator is the chief officer in the school, but this does not mean that he does all of the work, or should be responsible for all decisions and planning. To ask him to be a soothsayer in all fields is asking the impossible. He would then be placed in the position of having to carry on in-service and supervisory activities in all areas of curriculum and guidance, as well as to perform the administrative functions of the school. Versatility that would enable an individual to carry on workshops in the recording of children's creative songs, the teaching of form and perspective, the latest children's resources on Latin America, books for retarded readers, remedial techniques, needs of various types of exceptional children, kindergarten rhythms, and

[1] The administrator in this discussion is the principal.

168

emotional problems, is exceedingly rare. In most cases, the administrator relies upon a resource person who has specialized in a given field as he has in his, or works with the teachers on the basis of whatever skills he has been able to develop. In any field, the wise person realizes his skills and limitations, and uses any resource that can be of aid to him and his teachers.

In working with individual children, the administrator has much to offer. His attitude and the attitude that he fosters within his school affect the school and classroom relationships tremendously. Many times he is able to make suggestions to teachers regarding the needs of children whom he has come to know well. At other times, he is able to rely upon the guidance person to work with him to interpret the needs of children with more involved problems than the ordinary. The work in case conferences provides opportunity for in-service study on the part of all, including the administrator and guidance worker.

The contact of the administrator with children in a true guidance capacity is difficult, since situations arise in which he is called upon to perform on a disciplinary plane. This fact, plus the lack of time in his schedule, often makes it difficult for him to attain a permissive, accepting relationship with a child.

The availability of a guidance specialist is a boon to the conscientious administrator who sees the need for in-service work for his teachers. He can plan with the resource person for meetings in which he serves as an active resource without the responsibility for the entire content and conduct of the meeting itself. Similarly, he can use the services of the guidance specialist to meet the needs of parent study groups without involved preparation on his part.

FROM THE STANDPOINT OF THE TEACHER

The question from the standpoint of the teacher is not whether she should do the guidance work within the school, since all teachers inevitably guide, but to what extent she should have reinforcement. The training background of the elementary teacher usually includes courses in child growth and learning. She may or may not be required to take courses in measurement, and probably is not required to takes courses in psychology beyond the general survey course. The institution that requires, or even provides, a course in guidance at the elementary level is still rare. Her training does not supply her with all of the answers, and it is helpful to her to have someone who can help her to find them.

The modern teacher frequently has had enough training so that she is sensitive to special needs, but being sensitive is not enough. It can be extremely frustrating unless the teacher knows that someone is available to apply special skills in assisting her to work through a problem.

Teachers participate in guidance activities when they understand how to carry them on. It is not enough to suggest to a teacher that a social-distance scale might be a good idea—or has she ever tried sociodrama to work out X problem? Teachers feel more comfortable if they can plan activities in any area that is new to them with someone who can work with them as a resource, and who can give them opportunities for preliminary tryout of a skill in a workshop session. When they have worked with a guidance technique, have found it of value, and understand how to use it properly, then they are ready to use it independently. The total field of home-school communication, with its many ramifications, is an example of one in which the teacher often seeks help.

PERSONNEL ARRANGEMENTS

The identification at the elementary level of guidance workers and their functions has been difficult, in part because of the multitude of associated duties and titles under which they operate. This confusion is not restricted to schools. In the community, we find many persons doing guidance work—the minister, the attorney, the pediatrician, the youth group director, the social worker, the president of the ladies' church group, the interested neighbor—and countless others. In the final analysis, any person who at some time attempts to help another does guidance work, which accounts for all of humanity.

This broad interpretation of guidance has affected somewhat the classification of guidance personnel within the school. In a study of guidance workers, even after the superintendents, nurses, and curriculum directors who performed only limited functions as guidance workers had been eliminated, it was found that 23 titles were used, including research assistant, vice-principal, assistant superintendent, supervisor, and remedial reading teacher.[2] We may find, within the elementary school system, that superintendents have delegated responsibility for guidance to teachers, counselors, administrators, psychologists, supervisors of attendance and child welfare, curriculum coordinators, nurses, doctors, visiting teachers, or social workers, to name but a few.

The title of the functionary is not tremendously important. What is important is that the individual concerned possess the necessary skills and assigned time to make his job as a guidance worker effective. His primary function, in other words, should be that of a guidance worker if he is called one. If he shares work responsibility in another area, such as curriculum, then it is important that his responsibilities be clearly defined, so that his time can be divided equitably in both fields. If a district is small, such joint work assignment may be necessary. It is difficult from the standpoint of training, since a person may possess more background in one field than another and may tend therefore to concentrate his efforts in the area of his own specialization. If a teacher is called upon to perform guidance duties, it is mandatory that her total working schedule be carefully scrutinized, to prevent excessive demands upon her time. If she teaches a half session, for example, her work should be scheduled within a limited portion of the other half day, so that she will have time for written summaries and preparations of various sorts. It goes without saying that if she does the full work of a teacher, plus one-fourth or one-half of a counselor's assignment, she should be compensated fairly for both.

In small districts, guidance responsibility is often shared with other duties. In order to make the administrator or supervisor effective in guidance work, it is necessary not only to plan time for the activities, but also to clarify with the staff the guidance contributions that he can be called upon to make. Unless this is done regularly, there is the danger that teachers will work with him only in terms of his job title.

If a district is too small to afford a guidance consultant—and many of them are—guidance responsibilities should be coordinated by someone on an assignment basis. This may be one of the individuals listed above, alone, or one of them working with others who have special interests and training in guidance on a committee

[2] Ruth Martinson, *The Elementary School Counselor in California*, p. 11.

basis. The structure of the guidance program depends upon many things, chief among them the interest of the chief administrator and his staff, and finance. It is the hope of the writers that guidance would be a district necessity rather than a luxury, and that staff planning would be directed toward the systematic organization of personnel efforts so that good guidance can become a reality, even in the smallest schools. Somehow, through individual or shared responsibility, guidance should be a planned part of the program.

summary

Guidance workers are increasing in the elementary school, because of their contribution to the modern, child-centered program. They provide assistance to parents, administrators, and teachers in the understanding of growth variations and children's needs. Their role is that of support and resource, adding their special skills to those of others in the task of planning properly for children.

Guidance responsibility has been delegated to many persons at the elementary level. This variation is acceptable and desirable if those assigned guidance duties are assigned time to perform them, and if they possess the necessary qualifications. Otherwise, the guidance program becomes a "lip-service" appendage, functioning with no real satisfactions to teachers or to the public.

QUALIFICATIONS AND
DUTIES OF PERSONNEL

A discussion of the qualifications and duties of guidance personnel becomes a difficult problem when one considers the vastly heterogeneous administrative arrangement under which they may operate, and when one reviews the assorted assignments through which they perform their guidance functions (see Chapter 8). The more individuals with work assignments other than guidance are grouped together, especially in a consideration of qualifications, the greater the problem. For example, when one refers to the guidance functions of social workers, pediatricians, curriculum coordinators, administrators, guidance workers, and teachers, one is forced to differentiate functions in terms of training. It is perhaps easier to discuss personal qualifications for persons with varied assignments than to discuss educational qualifications and duties.

PERSONAL QUALIFICATIONS

When we search for individuals who possess the qualities that we deem necessary for the guidance worker, we feel somewhat like one psychologist who read a list of qualifications and observed:

> All we want to be is George Washington, Abraham Lincoln, and Albert Einstein made into one—only we wish Einstein had been a kindergarten teacher.[1]

[1] Norma E. Cutts, ed., *School Psychologists at Mid-Century*, p. 114.

The concept of a continuum may comfort us. Leadership, humble wisdom, and high intelligence are important. We seek these qualities, and those discussed below, not in relation to equaling the attributes of great leaders, but in terms of their existence to such an extent that the person who is considering or is being considered for guidance work may serve others effectively.

The ten areas below seem particularly important for guidance workers:

1. *Intelligence and good judgment.* Because the guidance worker serves as a resource to many individuals and groups in varied situations, he should possess high ability, ingenuity, and flexibility. Because he often works on a confidential basis, he needs to exercise good judgment in his service to others.

2. *Ability to work effectively with others as a team member.* The ability to work with others extends to both individuals and groups. The successful guidance worker is able to establish rapport with children and adults. He has the confidence and respect of the administrative, supervisory, teaching and non-instructional staff. He is able to gain the confidence and co-operation of parents. He is sensitive to the reactions and needs of others.

3. *Desire to serve others.* The guidance worker needs faith in the ability of others and an appreciation of his role in relation to them. His real function is to help others to help themselves, to improve their competencies. The good guidance worker works to develop guidance skills in others. He is willing to work when he is needed, without a set alarm clock.

4. *Good personal adjustment.* A person who enters the field of psychology because of personal problems is a poor risk as an effective guidance resource. The varied and exacting demands of the occupation make mandatory sound mental health and emotional maturity.

5. *Appreciation of one's role in relation to the total program.* The successful guidance worker has a broad point of view centered upon the whole educational program. He understands the relationship of guidance to the total educational effort. He does not perform as an individual with mystic, profound knowledge that sets him apart from the "educators." His work is also that of education.

6. *Leadership and organizational ability.* The ability to work with groups effectively is an important quality of success. The guidance person needs to lead discussions, to coordinate and follow through programs and projects. He needs skill in interpreting aspects of his role to the school and community.

7. *Good appearance and health.* The demands of the profession, both social and physical, make this important.

8. *Willingness to improve.* The area of school guidance is relatively new. Personnel are constantly evaluating and revising their working skills and techniques. Self-evaluation is a continuous aspect of the guidance worker's performance.

9. *Breadth of interests.* Because guidance activities may go on during both day and evening, the guidance person needs to plan a definite recreational schedule. Gardening, painting, fishing, or many other activities, may serve this need. Many counselors recommend summer occupations that differ greatly from their guidance responsibilities, such as "following the crops," both for the diversity and for the value of getting to know persons in other social groups.

10. *Humor.* This is last but not least. Ability to laugh at oneself and with others is of primary importance.

EDUCATIONAL QUALIFICATIONS

Educational qualifications for guidance work are related to the individual functions of the guidance person. In large city systems in which guidance services are well established, one may find that a director or supervisor of guidance coordinates the activities of many persons of varied skills and training. Such a system might have a counselor for every building or every two buildings, depending upon the building enrollment. Resource personnel to the teachers and counselors might include psychometrists, psychologists, and social workers, in addition to resource personnel in health and other areas. In other systems the psychologist or psychometrist may be the only resource for a number of schools. County or state consultants who work with local guidance personnel perform different functions and need somewhat different skills. It becomes necessary, therefore, to start with background training that might be common to all school guidance workers, and to diversify the training with increasing specialization.

One area of training that contributes to success in school guidance work is that of teaching. Teachers have confidence in others who have had experience in education when recommendations are made concerning educational methods and practices. Indeed, they are quick to identify those who are unable to go beyond the identification of needs or who make recommendations contrary to accepted good practice. They feel that someone who has had their experience is much more likely to be practical, and the guidance worker with teaching background has made a long, automatic step toward acceptance as a peer.

Numerous state and national conferences have wrestled with the problem of teaching experience or certification for guidance workers. One such conference made this observation:

> The Conference had no doubt that the school psychologist needs an intimate and thorough understanding of the processes of education. The disagreement over whether or not he had to have classroom teaching experience was largely about the most efficient method of acquiring the knowledge necessary and only partly about how much knowledge was needed. In fact, there was general agreement that sometime, somewhere, the school psychologist should acquire: (a) basic knowledge of education, including its history and philosophy, curriculum construction, methods and materials, remedial methods, test construction, exceptional children; (b) skill in educational diagnosis along with his other assessment skills; (c) practical knowledge of the classroom and the school, the roles and responsibilities of the teachers, principals, supervisors, and other specialized services, the necessary rules and courtesies for work in the schools, including a respect for what other school workers do, the practical limitations of the school situation, the school hierarchy, and the relations of the school to the various forces in the community.[2]

Added to the above is the practical consideration that in repeated surveys school administrators have indicated that they prefer to hire guidance workers who have had teaching experience. It would seem that the most practical way to insure adequate training and acceptability for placement might be likened to swimming: one might discuss theories and methods of swimming endlessly, but he needs also to get his feet wet!

The need for teaching experience as a preliminary step to guidance work is indicated in the certification requirements of some states. The Division of School Psychologists of the American Psychological Association takes the position that trainees will include enough educational background in their training to qualify for teaching and may welcome the income from teaching during their graduate training period. The Division now makes this additional significant comment.

[2] Norma E. Cutts, *op. cit.*, p. 129.

The people who have the contempt for teaching which makes such a requirement seem preposterous should neither be entering upon, nor training people to enter upon, a profession whose daily work and ultimate satisfaction will depend upon their close, sympathetic, understanding and respectful relationship with teachers.[3]

Because of the varying titles and functions of school guidance workers, several states have developed credentials that reflect differing levels of specialization. One example is the Pupil Personnel Services Credential in California, effective in September, 1956. Within this credential pattern, all trainees take courses in the general area and then may qualify in one or several areas, depending upon additional training. The credential requires from one to two years of graduate training and school experience.

GENERAL PUPIL PERSONNEL SERVICES CREDENTIAL[4]

Requirements:

A. Bachelor's degree.

B. Two years of successful teaching experience, or one year of successful teaching experience and one year of supervised field experience in pupil personnel activities with school-age pupils, or two years of supervised field experience in school social work, school psychometry, or school psychology of which at least one year shall have been in a public school.

C. One year of 30 semester hours of postgraduate work of upper division or graduate level.

1. The general area shall include each of the following:
   (a) Counseling procedures and techniques, including interviewing.
   . (b) Mental hygiene.
   (c) Case study and case conference techniques.
   (d) Psychology and education of exceptional children.
   (e) The dynamics of family, pupil-teacher, teacher-parent, and pupil-pupil relationships.
   (f) The methods and materials of family counseling including experience in working with parent groups, home visits, parent conferences, and problems of home and school.
   (g) The use of community resources including agencies and

---

[3] Division of School Psychologists, American Psychological Association, *Newsletter*, January 3, 1955, p. 11.

[4] Adapted from California State Department of Education, California Administrative Code, Title 5, Education, Chapter 1, Subchapter 2, Article 34.

177

organizations that provide services to individuals and/or groups.
(h) Laws relating to children and child welfare.
(i) Organization, administration, and evaluation of pupil personnel service programs.
2. The specialized area shall include at least one of the following:
(a) Pupil counseling, including:
(1) Educational, vocational, and personal guidance.
(2) Advanced training in procedures of counseling including supervised field experience.
(b) Child welfare and attendance work, including:
(1) Appropriate case work, with supervised field experience in a recognized agency or clinic dealing with family or children's problems.
(2) The application of local, federal, and state laws relating to the education, employment, and welfare of school-age youth.
(c) School social work, including:
(1) Appropriate case work, with supervised field experience in a recognized agency or clinic dealing with family or children's problems.
(2) The application of local, federal, and state laws relating to the education, employment, and welfare of school-age youth.
(d) School psychometry, including:
(1) Advanced training and experience in individual and group testing, including testing of exceptional children.
(2) Advanced training in educational psychology, including measurement and statistics, and the psychology of learning.
(e) School psychology:
(1) An additional year of graduate work including:
(A) Individual diagnostic procedures.
(B) Advanced case study techniques.
(c) Remedial instruction techniques.
(D) Individual and group therapy, including supervised laboratory and field experience with school-age pupils.

A training program that would serve to train promising students early has been worked out by the University of Hawaii and public school representatives. The program is based upon regular teacher training with counseling as a secondary field of concentration. The individual in training would be required to teach for at least two years prior to appointment as a counselor. The outline appears below in brief:[5]

1st year	Anthropology
	Educational orientation
	Sociology (orientation)
2nd year	Psychology (introduction)
	Psychology (developmental)
3rd year	Sociology (community forces)
	Psychology (elementary measurement and statistics)
	Psychology (mental hygiene)
4th year	Psychology (counseling)
	Psychology (clinical)
5th year	Social work (field of)
	Psychology (advanced)
	Education (evaluation)
	Education (counseling laboratory)
	Social work (dynamics of human behavior)

At this point the candidate is certified as a teacher with a minor in counseling.

6th year	On the job as full-time teacher but should take six credits summer school or at other times as follows.
7th year	Required education (materials and resources of guidance)
	Select one Psychology (group techniques in guidance)
	Social work (child welfare)
	Occupational information

At this point the candidate is eligible to receive a provisional certificate as a counselor and for appointment.

| 8th year or later | The final state of the training does not take place until the prospective counselor has an actual appointment. During the first year of counseling a plan of supervision including seminar discussions to be worked out. |

At the end of this year the candidate receives full certification as a counselor.

[5] Proposed Guidance-Counselor Training Program (as suggested by a committee composed of University of Hawaii and D.P.I. staff members). Mimeographed.

179

Training programs for school psychologists are necessarily more comprehensive and specialized than those of counselors. The psychologist is most often the terminal resource person in districts with personnel of differing levels of training. The programs outlined by the Connecticut Association of School Psychological Personnel and by the Division of School Psychologists of the American Psychological Association indicate the breadth of training necessary for this person.

THE CONNECTICUT STATEMENT OF REQUIREMENTS [6]

General Psychology. This includes basic psychological theories and principles of behavior, such as intelligence, feelings and emotions, motivation and learning, racial and cultural differences, perception and thinking.

Human Behavior and Development. Courses in this area treat the behavior and psychological development of humans from birth to maturity, the influence of heredity and environment, the psychology of deviates, mental health, etc. Emphasis is given to childhood and adolescence.

Diagnostic Skills. This includes training in clinical methods and techniques for appraising individual functioning and behavior, as well as in group testing techniques applicable to the school situation.

Educational Principles and Methods. This seeks to increase the psychologist's understanding of the pupil in the school situation, and his ability to improve the school situation for the pupil.

Counseling Skills. This includes training in principles and procedures in counseling, necessary in the readjustment of individual pupils.

Research Skills. Courses in this area include scientific methods of psychological and educational research. Statistical techniques are, of course, part of this area.

Orientation to Problems and Resources of Family and Community. This fosters an awareness of the forces that are at work and the resources that are available in the family and in the community.

Practicum. This refers to supervised practice in the diagnosis and correction of learning and behavior difficulties, with participation in case studies. It is a type of internship taken in a school or other clinic dealing with school age children.

[6] Norma E. Cutts, ed., *School Psychologists at Mid-Century*, pp. 124-125.

180

CERTIFICATION STANDARDS—July, 1952 [7]
DIVISION OF SCHOOL PSYCHOLOGISTS
AMERICAN PSYCHOLOGICAL ASSOCIATION

Recommended educational background:

The psychological background:

Should assure knowledge of psychological theory, experimental psychology, child and adolescent psychology, psychology of exceptional children, psychology of learning, clinical and abnormal psychology, mental hygiene, personality dynamics, and statistical techniques.

Should assure efficiencies in individual clinical diagnoses, case study procedures, case conference techniques, and an acquaintance with individual and group therapies. Field work in school psychology.

The educational background:

Should assure knowledge of educational philosophies, methods and techniques, including remedial techniques, administrative insights, as well as a practical knowledge of classroom procedures.

Should assure efficiencies in educational psychology, in the critical analysis and use of group measurement techniques as teacher and administrator guides to understanding child growth and curriculum adjustment needs.

The socio-anthropological background:

Should assure a knowledge of the socio-economic factors which influence child behaviors and learnings and insight into the satisfactory adjustment patterns of other cultures.

Desirable additional backgrounds:

An understanding of the dynamic inter-relationships between home-child-teacher-administrator, together with the ability to manipulate these.

Acquaintance with group dynamics, with ability to assume leadership in the development of sound learning, adjustment and mental health concepts within the school and community.

A knowledge of the possible contributions of community resources toward the solution of individual problems, and the development of wholesome school-community relationships.

A creative inquisitiveness that promotes research in the many

---

[7] Division of School Psychologists, American Psychological Association, *Certification Standards*, July, 1952 (mimeographed), 2 pp.

uncharted areas of human learning and human relationships in education.

Approved: Business meeting
Division of School Psychologists
September, 1952

It is evident that the training of guidance workers at any level of competence is never totally accomplished, and that a person who keeps abreast of new findings related to his profession will not regard any block of academic training as the final goal. The training of guidance workers assumes a flexibility and on-goingness if the worker keeps up with new trends and developments in his field. In-service training becomes, therefore, an important part of his education.

The foregoing lists of training programs illustrate the various levels of training at which guidance personnel perform. It is important that these personnel learn their capabilities and limitations during the educational training period, and that they operate professionally with an understanding of their limitations. It has been said that realization of one's limitations comes only with complete training, and it has been established that referrals are more frequently made by those with doctoral-level training than those with less background.[8] A realistic understanding of one's own strengths and limitations would aid the guidance person in assessing his own training needs and in giving proper service.

DUTIES OF GUIDANCE PERSONNEL

The presence of a designated guidance resource within the school or school system means that school personnel have the advantage of constant assistance. The reason for the existence of a guidance resource—the social and emotional well-being of the child—means that this person may give assistance to teachers in systematic fashion in their efforts to work with children effectively. The modern teacher, trained to be sensitive to the needs of children, and aware of their complex variations, often feels the need for a person with special

[8] Division of School Psychologists, American Psychological Association, *Newsletter*, December, 1950, p. 4.

training with whom she can work. Increased understanding of individual differences has brought about an increased need for a specialist who can work with all school personnel and parents throughout a child's school career.

The guidance person, then, is seen as a resource who works to increase the guidance activities within a school, and to make easier for teachers and others the complex business of understanding children, individually and in groups. The existence of a good guidance resource means that all persons who contact the child increase their guidance knowledge and activities in that child's behalf. In short, all within the school system, and the parents, improve their skills in child guidance. The guidance specialist works as a contributing member of a comprehensive team, adding his skills and training to those of others to help teachers, parents, and children. He works constantly with and through others.

THE STUDY OF CHILDREN

Good teachers are aware of the need for child study. They feel the need for information concerning their children so that they may teach intelligently. The guidance specialist can contribute to the development of effective child study in several ways:

1. *The guidance specialist assists teachers in the gathering and use of information.*

How much to record and what to record is a problem for busy teachers. Through the help of the specialist, teachers and others in the school may be helped to systematize the gathering of essential data on all children. The specialist may provide leadership in the development of child study materials. Through study groups, teachers may increase their skills in the accurate recording of information.

Teachers often feel the need for help in interpreting information. A teacher may observe that Johnny sits alone in the swing day after day at recess time, but may need to talk with someone about what she may do to help Johnny. She may sense the group rejection of an aggressive child, yet feel somewhat helpless about how to

183

assist the child to gain acceptance. She may be baffled by the child who pays little apparent attention and knows all the answers. She may be annoyed by the inexplicable giggling of a few of her sixth-graders.

The guidance person may help the teacher through specific suggestions regarding the needs of individual children. He may interpret growth patterns and characteristics so that the teacher may understand some of the normal individual variations within her group. He may supplement the efforts of the teacher through more detailed special study, and through interpretation of his findings.

2. *The guidance specialist gives direct help to teachers.*

There may be times when a teacher needs specialized help directly. She may have a child within her group whose behavior is incomprehensible to her. In instances in which the teacher feels inadequate to work with a child or his parents, the guidance person may assume responsibility, and either work with the situation himself, or seek further assistance, to improve the adjustment of the child.

At all times the guidance specialist maintains close communication with other staff members and parents. It is through these contacts regarding individual children that much guidance training is done. Learnings concerning the needs of one child have much transfer value in the understanding of others.

3. *The guidance specialist helps with the identification of children with special needs.*

An important contribution can be made by the trained guidance person to the well-being of exceptional children. Special studies to identify them and the coordination of planning for their educational needs are a major responsibility in guidance. Careful work in this area can make the difference between little educational opportunity or valuable training for more than 10 per cent of the American public school population. Teachers welcome specific suggestions to aid them in planning for these children, whether they are in regular classrooms or in special groups. Whether the child is gifted, retarded, aurally or visually handicapped, emotionally disturbed, or crippled, he needs someone to assist in the interpretation of his needs to teachers and others.

184

4. *The guidance specialist coordinates individual child study.*

The specialist is able to coordinate the efforts and contributions of many persons assisting individual children. He may contact several special school personnel in making plans for a child's adjustment. Because of his special assignment, he is in a better position than any other person in the system to follow the child's progress over a period of time, and to interpret the child's needs in successive situations.

GROUP WORK IN SCHOOL

One of the major objectives of the guidance resource is helping others to understand children. Assistance to teachers in understanding the dynamics of interpersonal relationships in the classroom and their effects on the educational program is a primary goal in his work. He sets his sights toward a positive program rather than a remedial program. To achieve this, he works in several areas:

1. *The guidance specialist helps with the understanding of groups.*

One of the greatest contributions of a guidance person is that of helping school personnel appreciate and be comfortable with children. To this end, he works with groups of teachers and provides outside resource persons and films in the study and interpretation of growth, development, and behavior. He coordinates child study programs, and conducts workshops on guidance techniques.

2. *The guidance specialist assists school personnel in the understanding of children in special groups.*

When a school system provides special groupings for all or part of a day, the guidance person needs to work with all school personnel to develop proper relationships and attitudes. The special needs of the children that make grouping advisable require constant interpretation; their special educational needs require understanding by all who may contact them. Teachers need help so that they may interpret special programs properly to their children in regular classrooms.

185

3. *The guidance specialist assists teachers and others with special problems related to classroom groups.*

The guidance resource helps teachers with the consideration of such problems as grouping and promotion. He works with teacher groups so that they may use the best group tests and so that they may administer them well and use the results effectively. He develops and carries out in-service programs to promote modern home-school reporting procedures. He contributes his ideas as a staff member in the planning of sound curriculum practices based upon group needs.

WORK WITH PARENTS AND COMMUNITY

The educational welfare of children is affected by many forces both in and out of school. Parents and others in the community contribute greatly to the adjustment of the child. The guidance person in the school works with the community to promote desirable conditions for the child in these ways:

1. *The guidance specialist assists parents to understand children.*

He does this through individual conferences and planned study groups. He may involve other school personnel in the study groups and frequently does so to extend learnings, interest, and participation. He works with others to interpret the total school program and the needs of the child population to parents, school board members, and civic groups. Because of the importance of the early years, he enlists the cooperation of kindergarten and primary teachers for extensive child study programs for parents at that level. The programs are carried out on a planned basis throughout the school, since all parents want interpretation of child behavior, regardless of age or grade.

2. *The guidance specialist coordinates school-community guidance efforts.*

The guidance person keeps informed of community resources and the types of services given. He develops referral forms for school use, makes arrangements for the use of community resources

186

in mental health, and serves as a liaison person between the school and community. One of his important responsibilities is that of interpreting the contributions of specialists outside of the school to the school personnel concerned.

RESEARCH

The guidance worker may do research individually or sponsor cooperative research studies. The specialist may individually prepare statistical reports of test results, comparing groups over a period of years. He may do some experimenting with several group tests, and compare results. He may involve others in experimental studies of such areas as grouped versus self-selective reading in classroom groups. He may be asked by parent or administrative groups to prepare summaries of published research on selected topics.

The schools contain many opportunities for on-going active research. The work is probably done best and with greatest effect if it is a team enterprise. The guidance person can contribute much through his knowledge of research design and procedures, and through his training in statistical techniques.

THE IMPORTANCE OF TEAMWORK

The work of the guidance specialist, as outlined above, is broad in scope. It can be of value only with the full cooperation of other school personnel. Teachers and administrators contribute directly to the effectiveness of the guidance worker.

1. *The teacher helps the guidance specialist in his work.*

The teacher is very frequently the person who identifies children who need special study. She does much to observe and record the day-to-day progress of children who are being studied. She gathers information, keeps records, studies children as group members, and if special help is needed, she is often able to give the specialist a comprehensive picture of a child who needs help.

If a special resource is called in, the teacher does much to help him by preparing the child for a pleasant contact. If several contacts

187

are made, she does a great deal in providing support and under-standing for a child who is making adjustments.

The teacher utilizes the contributions of counselors, parents, and others to establish positive relationships within the classroom. She participates in in-service discussions of guidance in order to under-stand the total program. She maintains constant awareness of individual needs, and works constantly to maintain a challenging, interesting, invigorating, and constructive atmosphere in her class-room.

She makes full use of the skills of the guidance person to improve her classroom guidance, and works with him in a group partnership to expand the objectives of the guidance program.

2. *The administrative and supervisory personnel help the specialist in his work.*

Administrators promote the guidance program through employ-ing highly qualified personnel and supporting them in their work. They keep informed concerning guidance activities and assist the guidance specialist to interpret his services to school personnel. Administrative personnel stress the *service* function of the guidance worker, and plan sound working procedures with him. They make him a member of the school team by including him in planning groups, by placing his name on building staff lists, and by inviting him to individual building meetings. They keep in mind the fact that interchange of support and ideas strengthens the professional performance of all staff members.

summary

Personal qualifications for guidance personnel are some-what easier to list than educational qualifications, because of the diversity of training and function of guidance workers within the public schools. Several groups have attempted to establish training programs involving several levels of training and accreditation to care for differing needs within school systems. Criteria for training areas have been outlined by such groups as the American Psy-chological Association, Division of School Psychologists.

The functions of guidance personnel extend into four areas—child study, work with school personnel, work with parents and community groups, and research. The cooperative efforts of all school persons contribute to the effectiveness of the resource person in guidance.

10

RELATIONSHIPS
OF SCHOOL
PERSONNEL IN GUIDANCE

The assumption will be made in the current chapter that the school district has some person designated as a guidance coordinator or resource. Since the guidance program is his primary responsibility, and since many other persons make direct contributions to it, the further assumption will be made that the guidance person has a great responsibility to promote, insofar as possible, optimum human relationships within the program. His chief aim is the coordination of his skills and knowledge with those of other personnel for the benefit of the children, parents, and school personnel.

THE SCHOOL ADMINISTRATOR

The administrator, whether of the district or the school, can "make or break" the guidance person. The chief administrator can govern his working conditions by edict, and can make them intolerable or pleasant. He can promote or negate guidance attitudes on the part of the entire school staff and the community by his own expressions of attitude. He can actually govern in part the home life of the guidance worker through job demands. He can have a part in determining the status of the guidance worker with other specialists on the staff, and can affect directly his recreational

190

tastes, his clothing and even the food he eats by the salary he pays. He may decide whether the guidance specialist shall have adequate office space or none at all. It becomes important, then, that the guidance specialist plan his over-all district activities closely with the chief administrator.

Within individual schools the administrator sets the pace in determining guidance activities. He can plan ineffectual and impossible activities for the guidance person, or plan with him so that his work can be highly effective. The building administrator does much to establish proper attitudes and understandings toward guidance. Because he is responsible for the educational program within his own building, the guidance specialist properly works with him as chairman of the building guidance group. As the spokesman for his school, he has tremendous influence in facilitating guidance activities.

THE PHYSICIAN AND/OR NURSE

Without the aid of the physician or nurse, a complete study of an individual child would not be possible. Through a mutual exchange of information, physicians, nurses, and guidance specialists are able to assess individuals in physical, social, emotional, and intellectual areas, and are able to learn much from one another in the process. The medical staff members should be included in case conferences whenever possible.

THE CURRICULUM CONSULTANT

The curriculum consultant is primarily responsible for the district curriculum program. She should always be directly involved in curriculum planning for individuals and for special and regular groups concerning whom the guidance specialist has made studies. She may work also as a partner in the development of publications regarding children. As a contributor or leader in parent study groups, she has much valuable information to give.

THE TEACHER

The teacher needs someone as a resource in guidance—to give her support and assistance regarding curriculum planning, health

191

needs, library facilities, and other areas. The help that is given her should assist her to grow in classroom guidance skills and attitudes. It is important that her direct influence in the guidance program be recognized. When she needs help with involved problems, the help should be given, and plans should be completed with her. It is important that the guidance specialist maintain frequent contact with her, and give her frequent support and encouragement in the work that she is doing. She, as others, is a co-worker in guidance.

THE TOTAL STAFF

The entire staff can do a good job of guidance if the attitude that permeates their relationships is one of reinforcement and support. All need to respect the unique skills and specializations of the others, and use them wisely. The contributions of all should be centered upon the child, and not upon themselves and their specialties. The establishment of a district-wide guidance committee, with the guidance specialist as coordinator, and of building guidance committees, with the principal as chairman and the guidance specialist and others as participants, can do much to spread interest and promote understanding.

At the beginning of the chapter it was stated that the guidance specialist has tremendous responsibility to other staff members in the promotion of positive attitudes toward his work. The nine rules below, addressed to guidance workers, may help them to maintain perspective:

1. Keep others informed of your work—interpret it well.
2. Help others to develop a comprehensive concept of guidance.
3. Assume always that all school personnel share your interest in children.
4. Make others aware of their potential and real contributions to guidance. Ask them for help.
5. Respect your co-workers. Show your respect.
6. Avoid non-essential professional terminology.
7. Realize that the behavior of adults is caused, too.
8. Plan flexibly, and include others in guidance activities.
9. Remember that your success depends upon your colleagues just as much as upon yourself.

summary

Major responsibility for success and understanding in the guidance program rests with the guidance specialist. He works with others in cooperative planning, and utilizes their skills along with his own to develop a sound educational program for all children. The efforts of all personnel should be centered upon the welfare of the children.

11

GUIDANCE OF
EXCEPTIONAL CHILDREN

Any organized program of guidance in the public schools must necessarily extend to all children—including those with special educational needs. Within this group we find from 10 to 12 per cent of all school children, or from three to four million individuals. Exceptional children are commonly defined as those who deviate from the normal to such an extent that they require some special educational provisions and planning in order to benefit fully from their educational experiences. According to statistics for the year, 1947-48, gathered by the United States Office of Education, approximately 425,000 exceptional children were enrolled in special schools and classes, in residential schools, or were being given home or hospital instruction by local school districts.[1] Although many others are undoubtedly being given much assistance in regular class groups, it is obvious that much remains to be done. About three-fourths of the state legislatures have appropriated funds for special classes.[2]

With advances in learning about exceptional children, we find an extension of special provisions. It is not unusual in larger school districts to find well-organized programs of special education not

[1] National Society for the Study of Education, *Education of Exceptional Children, Forty-Ninth Yearbook,* Part II (Chicago, Illinois: University of Chicago Press, 1950), p. 12.
[2] *Ibid.,* p. 13.

only for the mentally retarded but also for the academically re-tarded, the visually and aurally handicapped, the speech handi-capped, the orthopedically handicapped, the mentally deficient, the socially maladjusted, and the gifted. Multiple arrangements, in-cluding special schools and classes, flexible special and regular groupings, and home and hospital teaching through special teachers and audio-visual materials, are some of the ways in which school districts function to meet the needs of this total group.

NEEDS OF EXCEPTIONAL CHILDREN

Whether a child is mentally retarded or gifted, whether he has one of a variety of physical defects, whether he has social adjust-ment problems or academic problems, his special needs require special planning. The aim of special planning is the best adjustment of the child. The exceptional child has the same needs as other children—the need for belonging, the need for success, the need for affection, the need for social approval, the need for inde-pendence—to name but a few of those commonly listed. To help him meet those needs is a challenge for all school personnel. The building of proper attitudes toward oneself and one's role in society necessitates careful guidance for all children. It becomes a problem that demands closer coordination and greater skills for exceptional children.

One of the great needs for the exceptional child is an acceptance of his difference rather than a denial of it. In order that he may achieve this successfully, he must be placed in an environment in which he works with other children in terms of likenesses rather than differences. In some instances, this may be achieved in a regular classroom by a highly competent teacher, when differences are not pronounced. As differences become magnified, however, the prob-lem increases.

We recognize the problems of adjustment for children with pronounced physical handicaps or severe mental retardation. We are less likely to be aware of the problems of children like these:

An eighth-grade boy of normal intelligence with an extreme reading problem, when asked to name his three wishes, stated them as follows:

195

1. A horse, and to learn to read.
2. Peace in the world, and to read.
3. To learn to read.

A gifted child, who at second-grade level read adult materials with ease, took her turn in the top reading group "because she was supposed to, and she could read other things at home." She learned, during her school career, to make certain adjustments, such as teaching herself the accordion (highly rated with her peers), deliberately missing problems so that the other students wouldn't call her a "brain" all of the time, taking courses geared toward activities such as journalism, along with advanced science and mathematics, and taking six subjects instead of the customary four in high school. The child succeeded as a student leader, but succeeded primarily through somewhat deliberate planning on her own part, rather than on the part of the school.

Examples like the latter serve to illustrate powerfully the intense need of any child for belonging and social approval. Such needs are more easily met when the child has opportunity for association with other children who are peers in actuality. A child who is highly intelligent, for example, is less the exception when in a situation with a few others of similar ability. This does not mean necessarily that segregated groups should be established. Such groups are not feasible in other than the largest metropolitan school districts. It is possible, however, for schools to approach such needs with more flexibility than has been the practice, through small groupings of children of like abilities with teachers who are especially trained to work with them, through special-interest groups in which bright children are included, and through meaningful enrichment. Meaningful enrichment requires thoughtful planning, to avoid penalizing the child of high ability with added assignments of 30 problems instead of 20, or 50 spelling words instead of 25. Enrichment should relate to the special interests and talents of the individual child.

The need for children to learn to live with all kinds of people is often cited as an argument against special provisions, and the argument has some merit. There is great value in association with many types. There is also a great need for functioning in an environment that provides opportunity for stimulation, and that

196

provides a curriculum that will enable a child to learn satisfactorily, whether he be blind, cerebral palsied, or intellectually gifted.

PROBLEMS IN IDENTIFICATION OF NEEDS

The identification of the needs of exceptional children is not the province of a single individual. It is rather a problem that involves many individuals, both in and out of school. To plan adequately for a child with special needs, it becomes necessary to bring together school personnel, parents, and often medical personnel, who work together to state the needs of the child in comprehensive terms and to plan for his proper education.

In addition to the accumulation of extensive cumulative record data, school personnel most commonly are responsible for various types of testing. In the use of achievement tests and tests of intelligence and personality, both teachers and guidance workers perform important functions. Teachers often may refer children for further study through their use and study of group test results. The guidance worker uses a wide variety of individual measures to assess the actual and potential capabilities of the child.

The testing program for exceptional children should be under the direction of a highly trained person. Individual measurement requires that the examiner be able to use appropriate test materials, and often to adapt both materials and the testing situation in order to measure accurately. He needs skill in evaluating such subjective factors as attitudes of the child toward the test, his motivation, problems of fatigue, rapport, effects of environmental limitations upon test performance, and possible effects of poor health or anxiety or coordination upon the test results. He may need to use several individual tests with a given child, and may need to interpret his findings in terms of actual performance and his estimates of the true potential of the person tested. He will avoid the use of classifications in terms of scores. He will instead interpret the results on the basis of what the child can do and what can be done for him.

The following excellent summary by Newland points out vividly the need for a person with extensive clinical training in the evaluation of one kind of exceptional child:

197

. . . The major difficulties exist with respect to the examination of those of moderate and severe neuromuscular involvement. In such cases, communication is a problem, both regarding the use of verbal responses by the subjects and, in some cases, regarding the sensory impairment of such cerebral palsied children. In some instances, where these handicapped children are physically unable to speak, they also are unable to point. In such cases the examiner may have to rely upon the child's eye movements, and, if nystagmus renders this avenue of communication doubtful, even upon the facial expression of the child. In addition to the problem of communication, there are those of the meaninglessness of rigid time limits, the highly varying and often grossly distorted cultural backgrounds, the possibility of the confusion of figure and ground in at least the visual field, the wide age range, the possible relatively higher fatigability as compared with the non-handicapped, the possible interference of more and greater emotional factors such as excessive dependency upon the parents, and conditioning against clinical settings. Add to all these problems the fact that the term "cerebral palsy" has come to include a variety of conditions that might materially complicate the psychological picture, and it will be seen how difficult the intellectual evaluation of these handicapped children actually is. The fact that this handicapped group is numerically smaller, for instance, than the blind group, even after correcting for Phelps' underestimation of prevalence, and regarding as blind those with a Snellen rating of 20/200 or worse in the better eye after maximal correction, also adds to the difficulty of soundly standardizing a test or test battery on this population.[3]

The need for diagnostic skills is not limited to physical handicaps. Any measurement of a being as complex as a child requires the services of many specialists if it is to be complete. The procedures of Helen Robinson, described in her book, *Why Pupils Fail in Reading* (University of Chicago Press, 1946), further illustrate the importance of diagnostic ability:

Robinson studied causal factors in a group of thirty severely retarded readers. To aid in her study, she secured the services of the following specialists: a social worker, a psychiatrist, a pediatrist, a neurologist, three ophthalmologists, a speech specialist, an otolaryngologist, an endocrinologist, a reading specialist. Dr. Robinson acted as psychologist and reading

[3] William Cruickshank, ed., *Psychology of Exceptional Children and Youth* (Englewood Cliffs, N.J.: Prentice-Hall, Inc., 1955), p. 88.

technician. The thirty retarded readers were examined by each of these specialists. After the individual examinations, the specialists met and attempted to evaluate the anomalies that had been identified. They also attempted to identify the possible causes of reading retardation operating in each case. Then, twenty-two of the thirty cases were given intensive remedial work to secure further evidence about each of the possible causes.

Causes especially considered were visual problems, emotional problems, school methods, neurological difficulties, speech and functional auditory problems, endocrine difficulties, insufficient auditory acuity, general physical problems, dominance and intelligence. Robinson says: "This study is not unlike many others in that it has revealed more problems in need of further study than it has solved. . . . The diagnostic examination of severely retarded readers should not end with an attempt to identify a wide number of possible causes. Evaluation of each factor in the light of all information available concerning the child should follow. An anomaly found with one child may be insignificant when all other findings are considered, whereas in another instance with a different constellation of causes, the same anomaly may take on much greater significance . . . At present identifying causes of poor reading is a difficult task. This study indicates that the pooled opinions of several experts in varied fields is more reliable than the opinion of a reading examiner alone. It is not always possible for the examiner to obtain the services of competent specialists in allied fields. *This practical limitation emphasizes the need for a thorough search for symptoms of various causal factors in order that the advice of appropriate specialists may be sought only as particular groups of symptoms are exhibited.*" [4]

The two illustrations above serve to underscore the importance of guidance workers with specialized training. This is not to say that teachers and others do not have much to contribute in an understanding of the needs and capabilities of exceptional children, but rather to emphasize the need for specially trained personnel as well. We all know that many schools do much for children with special needs, sometimes with limited special help, and sometimes with none at all. It seems important, nevertheless, to point out the real complexities of evaluation, and to indicate what might be

[4] Jerry W. Carter, Jr., and J. W. Bowles, Jr., *A Manual on Qualitative Aspects of Psychological Examining*, Clinical Psychology Monographs, No. 2 (Burlington, Vermont: Journal of Clinical Psychology, April, 1948), p. 30. Italics ours.

done by schools with means for the development of auxiliary facilities.

HELPING THE EXCEPTIONAL CHILD
IN THE CLASSROOM

Special resources are of great assistance in the education and care of exceptional children. Most teachers at the present time, however, find that their school districts do not make special provisions, and that they are responsible themselves for any extra planning that may be done. Teachers may be discouraged at the prospect of providing for children who deviate from the "average" along with all of the others, yet much of the discouragement is groundless. Good teachers can and do much to help the exceptional child as well as any other. These are some specific ways in which help may be given:

1. *The good teacher shows through her own attitudes that every child in her group has value.*

This includes the child who may know more about certain areas than she does. It also includes the child who has limited academic potential, but who swings a powerful bat, or the child who cannot run, but who arranges flowers well, or the child who can't sing a tune well, but can do rhythms or express appreciation of recorded music. She seeks contributions that all can make, and prizes the uniqueness of the individual.

2. *The good teacher utilizes a varied program to meet the needs of her pupils.*

Differentiation of activities is necessary in any classroom if the teacher is to meet individual needs. It is especially necessary for the exceptional child. The activity approach holds many possibilities for variation. For example, the class group that is working on the publication of a paper in connection with their study of communication may include a child of high potential who will do research and write a feature story on a subject such as the contributions of insects to human welfare. Within the same group may be a retarded child who does his part through tracing the outline of an enlarged picture of an insect for use with the article.

200

When a mural is planned by the group, the more capable children may do research and help with the over-all planning. A child of limited potential may be responsible for some of the simple figures. A physically handicapped child may not have the control needed for figure drawing, but may help with the background, and thereby make a much-needed contribution.

A seemingly simple area such as the care of a pet in the primary grades is but one additional example of how the resourceful teacher may utilize individual differences in positive fashion. One question that naturally arises concerning a new pet is "What does he eat?"

In seeking answers, children may find pictures, read information on feeding and report to the group, read stories to others, interview adults who have similar pets, or arrange for older children to talk with the class, depending upon their own abilities and interests. They may all take responsibilities for care and feedings.

Another natural problem area is that of housing. Through approaches like those above, the children may work together further for the comfort of their pet. One group of children may plan and measure. Another group may saw—another may assemble. A child who cannot handle a hammer may be involved in a group planning the best location for the new home, and so on. The fun of watching a pet grow, charting his name, his development, his behavior, and his habits, is one means through which the teacher may center the attention of the group upon the activity and thus allow for the cooperation and responsibility of all.

3. *The teacher helps the child succeed through giving individual help when necessary.*

Sometimes this help may be simply a matter of holding a board so that a child can saw it, or giving some help with word analysis. At other times it becomes a problem of physical arrangement: placing a child with hearing difficulties near the front and center of the group, speaking clearly, reinforcing spoken words with necessary directions on the chalkboard, and checking individually to be sure that he understood. The child with visual handicaps may need rest from exacting visual demands, or again, may require preferred seating to reduce strain. The central problem is one of assisting the child so that he can be a regular group member. This is accomplished, not through concentration upon the handicap, but

201

through reduction of situations in which the handicap becomes a crucial problem.

4. The teacher helps the exceptional child to work with others successfully.

At times this is achieved through giving the child a way in which he can make a valuable contribution to the group. The retarded child may do a particularly fine job of housekeeping, or may be one of several who does good work in the classroom garden. The child who is exceptional in a racial or religious sense, through his family and himself, may contribute much to the group appreciation of his culture. Sometimes the teacher may help the child through individual counseling, in which she helps him to think of ways in which he may get along better with the others.

5. The teacher helps parents and others to see values in exceptional children.

The parents who need help in appreciating the positive values of their children are those of handicapped rather than of gifted or talented children. Teachers can do much to point out to them the progress and learnings of the children, to interpret their need for independence and their growth toward it, and to indicate the many ways in which the children contribute to the group. They can indicate also the appreciation of others that their child promotes in the group through his presence.

Teachers and children need much help in understanding the exceptional child. The teacher who plans for a free interchange of activities and many associations between exceptional and other children can help all children to appreciate one another. Exceptional children can go to other classes and contribute to their knowledge and appreciation of what handicapped children can do. For example, a visually handicapped child who performs very well in the school orchestra helps other children and teachers to consider his attributes rather than his limitations.

CONTRIBUTIONS OF THE GUIDANCE WORKER

The contributions of guidance workers encompass much more than diagnosis and testing, discussed on pages 197-199. The diagnos-

202

tic aspects are of extreme importance, but the guidance person finds that his work has just begun with the identification of the exceptional child. It continues through the following areas:

1. *Interpretation of needs.*

The counselor often needs to work with others who contact the child in the school to emphasize his likenesses to others. The tendency of the person who has not worked with exceptional children is to concentrate upon the differentiating factor. If the counselor can help others to see exceptional children as *children* and if he can help them to behave properly toward them, he will be of great assistance. To help other teachers and thereby other children, he may hold group discussions on such topics as "How to Help ———— Child Meet His Basic Needs." In a discussion of the need for independence, for example, the counselor may indicate how the almost automatic desire of the adult to help the blind child up and down steps may retard his growth toward independence.

The interpretation of needs may extend to social and emotional areas, too. Teachers have great difficulty in appreciating the need of some children for time to achieve growth in social development, especially when they have direct contact with them each day. The counselor who maintains contact can do much to help the teacher by commenting on the growth he observes in a child who at first was completely withdrawn from the group, then watched others, then indulged in limited parallel play, then played with another boy and fought with him. Without interpretation and encouragement, the teacher may regard the battle as regression rather than progress! A person who observes and interprets periodically can do much to support the teacher in his day-to-day efforts.

Needs in academic areas require constant interpretation as well. The teacher needs more than the observation that X child is mentally retarded or a slow learner. He needs also specific suggestions on types of things that the child can be expected to do, what kinds of curriculum experiences are best for him, and information concerning his attitudes and learning problems. In academic areas the counselor works in close cooperation with curriculum workers.

2. *Helping the child.*

Often the child needs a great deal of help in learning to accept himself and to live with others. The counselor may work with him individually or in small groups. Special therapy may be provided or arranged for in cases where the emotional problems are great. Emotional problems that affect learning are not confined to the handicapped. With the recent increase of interest in the needs of the gifted has come the realization that gifted children may have problems of adjustment that handicap them seriously in academic achievement.

3. *The need for constant study.*

Flexible planning is the keynote of modern thinking about the education of exceptional children. Special provisions may be made in a variety of ways: special classes, special teaching away from the regular group for an hour or two each day, or special help in the regular classroom through outside assistance. In any event, the progress of the child must be evaluated from time to time to be sure that his needs are being met to best advantage. The basis for any special placement is additional help that will enable the child, if at all possible, to adjust eventually to placement in regular groups.

4. *The use of special resources.*

One of the primary responsibilities of the guidance worker is to serve as a resource in the referral of children to community agencies for additional help. Guidance personnel often collaborate to compile listings of special agencies and civic groups that may give direct financial aid or diagnosis and treatment for exceptional children. The Manual of the Department of Guidance, Child Welfare, and Attendance of the Richmond, California Public Schools contains such a listing for the use of department personnel. In each instance, the name of the agency, the name of the supervising officer, and the telephone number is given. A partial list of agency names is given below, not because it can be adapted directly by anyone outside of the San Francisco area, but because it illustrates the types of agencies that may render real service to the public schools:

Department of Mental Hygiene, Sonoma State Home, Langley-Porter Clinic, Department of Public Health, Youth Authority, County Hospital, County Health Department, County Juvenile Probation Office, County Social Service Department, American Red Cross, Boy Scouts, Campfire Girls, Catholic Social Service, Child Care Centers, Girl Scouts, City Health Center, City Recreation Department, Y.M.C.A., Y.W.C.A., Jewish Family Service.[5]

Other organizations—many of them found in communities of small or moderate size—that are interested in helping children with special needs, are the Kiwanis, Lions, Shriners, Rotary, church groups, and P.T.A.

5. Special classes.

Despite all of the best efforts of school personnel to maintain adequate records, study the needs of children, adjust procedures to individual abilities, and provide special services, some children require school facilities beyond those of the regular classroom, and teachers with highly specialized skills and knowledge. Although some provisions are made, much work remains to be done. For example, Baker[6] estimates that only one out of seven children who are potential candidates for sight-saving classes is actually enrolled in such a class. The ratio of one sight-saving child to every 500 means that every city of 20,000 general population should have one sight-saving class of eight members. The number of blind children is approximately one-fourth that of those requiring sight-saving classes, which would require a class of eight members in every city of 80,000 general population. Only about 6,000 of an estimated 15,000 blind children are currently in classes for the blind.[7] The need in the case of hard-of-hearing children is similar to that in sight-saving, while the problem in relation to the deaf is that of locating the children, according to Baker. The gap between provisions needed and provisions actually being made is similar in other categories of exception.

The statistics above indicate in part the work yet to be done if

[5] *Manual, Department of Guidance, Child Welfare and Attendance* (Richmond, Calif.: Richmond Public Schools, March, 1955).

[6] Harry J. Baker, *Introduction to Exceptional Children* (New York: The Macmillan Company, 1953), p. 43.

[7] Harry J. Baker, *op. cit.*, p. 63.

all children are to have equal educational opportunities. Since testing and diagnosis are often the task of the guidance person, working alone or in cooperation with medical specialists, the need for extension of guidance services is apparent.

6. Educational problems.

One of the areas in which the classroom teacher often seeks help is that of classroom learning. Children who exhibit slow or irregular developmental patterns in academic learning, non-readers, or children with spelling or arithmetic difficulties frequently cause concern to their teachers. Many questions, therefore, are asked by the teacher who feels that certain children are not learning at what they feel should be a satisfactory rate.

One of the ways in which guidance workers can help teachers and the general public think realistically about academic achievement is through thorough analyses of their classroom groups. This is especially true when a teacher (or parent) is concerned about a large percentage of children in a group "not measuring up." If this is the case, the need may be for a realization of the individual differences that exist within the group and for some planning based upon the child group rather than standards. A guidance worker may help a teacher immeasurably, for example, in the study of reading problems and needs within her classroom. Standardized tests will give part of the history. Through the charting of health data, recording of reading and speech patterns, study of home factors, child interests, and through classroom observations, the guidance person and teacher may collaborate to arrive at a tremendous appreciation of the complexity and diversity of any child group. Through such study, differences in language development, the extent or paucity of interests, the influence of physical factors, the relatedness of growth factors, the possible relation of parent attitudes to reading, and specifics such as ability to follow directions or to see likenesses and differences, should emerge in striking fashion. Such study is time-consuming, and probably is approached more willingly by the teacher when she has help. A study of this sort, even though demanding, is well worth the time, when one considers that approximately one thousand children could be benefited during the teaching career of even one individual, and when one considers, too, that the study may be used to good advantage for in-service discussions with other teachers. Any study that involves an examination of developmental factors in relation to curriculum planning should result inevitably in flexibility of planning.

Even after study and adjustments, some children will be found within a school who are in need of remedial help. These children should be of normal or better intelligence, in order that the program may be *remedial*—that is, they should have the capacity to profit from the instruction rather than being mentally retarded children who may already be achieving at expectancy. Because of normal individual variations in beginning reading patterns, referral should probably not be made during the primary grades. In other words, before remedial work is instituted, the remedial need should exist. A commonly applied rule for remedial referral is that children should be referred if they are achieving a year and a half (or more) below their mental age level.

Children for special help usually are selected by guidance workers, and planning becomes a joint enterprise of a curriculum resource, the guidance person, and the special remedial teacher. In small school systems without several resource personnel, screening and teaching responsibilities may be assumed by one person. The usual arrangement is one by which the children work with a special teacher for a period during the day, away from the regular group, individually or in small clusters if their needs are similar.

The guidance person, in addition to screening, has the responsibility of interpreting possible emotional, physical, and social factors that may have a bearing upon the child's performance. The remedial program is one of flexible placement, geared toward regular classroom performance eventually, and, regardless of which R is being remedied, requires close and constant study of the child and his progress.

Guidance workers are frequently asked by special and regular teachers for suggestions regarding the child who has outgrown primary books, but who needs easy reading materials. The following lists will aid in the selection of materials for such a child, whether he is in a special group or not: [8]

[8] Adapted from a list compiled by David Fils, consultant in the education of the mentally retarded, Division of Research and Guidance, Los Angeles County Schools.

Barrett, Edward J., *List of Books for Retarded Readers.* Springfield, Illinois: Illinois State Library, 1948.

Books for Older Boys and Girls with Limited Reading Ability. Prepared by the committee of Georgia teachers and librarians appointed at the Instructional Supervisor's Conference in Atlanta, Georgia, Nashville 3, Tennessee, Division of Libraries, State Department of Education, 1946.

Durrell, Donald D., and Sullivan, Helen Blair, *High Interest, Low Vocabulary Booklist.* Boston 15: Boston University School of Education, 1950.

Dutton, E. P., *Attractive Story Materials Which Have Worked Out Well with Slow Readers.* New York: E. P. Dutton and Co., Inc.

Slater, Russell, *Books for Youth Who Dislike Reading.* Bulletin of the Ohio Conference on Reading, No. 2. Columbus, Ohio: Ohio State University Press, June, 1941.

Wurtz, Sindt, and Keyser, *A Bibliography of Reading Lists for Retarded Readers.* State University of Iowa Extension Bulletin No. 640. Iowa City: University of Iowa, November, 1949.

7. Work with parents and staff.

Parents of exceptional children need help that goes beyond group and individual discussions of normal children. They need assistance in relating facts about needs and characteristics to their own particular child. For example, the parent of a very bright child may be concerned because his child is not the eager member of a social group that he should be, but finds his pleasures instead in associations with a few individuals who are interested in geology, or the parent of a retarded child may want his child to play with others of his own age instead of younger children. Counselors can do much with parents, individually and in groups, to help them understand their own children.

Parents very frequently have guilt feelings concerning handicapped children. They may wonder whether familial taints or some defects within themselves have created the handicap in their child. As Abel indicates, social and cultural values often operate to foster rejection of a child who does not have normal intelligence:

> The mentally retarded is a deviant who is perhaps treated with greater rejection and less respect by parents, teacher, and the community than is any other deviant, perhaps with the exception of the person with Hansen's disease.[9]

[9] Theodora M. Abel, "Resistances and Difficulties in Psychotherapy of Mental Retardates," *Journal of Clinical Psychology, Monograph Supplement No. 9,* April 1953, p. 9.

Similar comments may be found in the literature concerning other kinds of handicaps. The cerebral palsied are another group who have been widely misunderstood and often confused with the severely mentally retarded or insane.

Individual conferences and study groups with parents can help them understand the fundamental likenesses of all children and the particular capabilities of their own. They can learn to avoid either overprotection or unrealistic demands, and the importance of treating the children as normal children as far as possible.

Counselors may help parents of physically handicapped children answer questions such as these:

> How can we educate other parents in the neighborhood?
> How can we get other children to accept our child?
> How can we help our child through his frustrations when he sees what other children can do?
> What about the older child who is handicapped and sees a younger child doing much more than he can do?
> How can we handle the slanderous remarks of an older child who calls the handicapped child "stupid," "brainless," etc.?
> How can I help my child "grow up"?

Study groups should include school personnel as well, and others concerned. Many of the misunderstandings of parents are due to conflicting opinions that they have been given by educators and medical personnel. If exceptional children are within the sphere of contact of either educators or nurses or physicians, it seems obligatory that they participate in studying and understanding them to the best of their ability.

Parent study groups may be set up on the basis of planned lectures, or they may involve more direct parent participation. An example of a lecture series is one conducted by the New York Association for the Help of Retarded Children:

PARENT EDUCATION COURSES ON MENTAL RETARDATION [10]

The Help of Retarded Children, Inc.

This is a series of lectures followed by question and answer periods to acquaint parents with the various aspects and implications of mental retardation. It is an educational course to help

[10] Joseph T. Weingold and Rudolf P. Hormuth, "Group Guidance of Parents of Mentally Retarded Children," *Journal of Clinical Psychology, Monograph Supplement No. 9, Counseling the Mentally Retarded and Their Parents,* April, 1953, p. 25.

parents understand their children's problems, and, through understanding, handle them intelligently, as well as with love. The schedule of lectures is as follows:

1. Definitions, Kinds and Causes: Nature and needs of mentally retarded children; definition; causes; types and classifications of mental retardation.
2. Trends and Problems in the Medical Study of Mental Retardation.
3. Psychological Testing and Its Implications: Nature of intelligence and personality; aims and objectives of the psychological examination; procedure of the examination; the examination battery; its findings and implications and relationship to mental retardation.
4. Child in the Home, Recognition, Impact and Acceptance: Methods in early detection of retardation; mental growth and personality patterns of the child; the impact of the child's retardation on the whole family; acceptance of the child as a person and his place in society.
5. Speech for the Retarded: A definition of language and speech; the development of language and speech; preparation for language and speech.
6. Implications—Personal and Vocational: Training of the whole child with special attention to what the home and family can do to help the child grow towards his full potential in the various elements of his total personality.
7. The Older Retarded Child—Social Implications in the Home and the Community: Impact upon the home life; duties and obligations in the home towards the older retarded child and the need for community education to insure better understanding, acceptance and respect for the older mentally retarded child.
8. The Older Retarded Child—Vocational Training and Employment: What the older retarded child can do; what jobs are available to him and what training he needs.

A program of group meetings[11] for the parents of cerebral palsied children was extended to include sociodramas to promote parent participation. The sociodrama included the following situations:

1. Mrs. W.—6-year-old c.p. who cannot walk.
   Miss W.—normal 4-year-old sister.

[11] Cerebral Palsy Unit, Highland School, Inglewood, California, *A Threefold Parent Education Program*, A Pilot Study Conducted by the Staff of the Cerebral Palsy Unit, 1952-53, 109 pp., mimeographed.

2. Mrs. M.—17-year-old c.p.—seriously handicapped.
   Mrs. D.—normal 15-year-old sister who is getting ready to
       go to a party.
   Mrs. H.—their mother.

3. Mrs. M.—parent of a c.p. child who has been playing with
       the other children in the neighborhood.
   Mrs. D.—a neighbor who has children near the same age.

4. Mrs H.—c.p.
   Mrs. W.—mother
   Mr. W.—father
   It is bed time.

5. Mrs. M.—c.p.
   Mrs. D.—mother
   It is lunch time.

The problems above were the outgrowth of previous group discussions and listings of problems perplexing to the parents. The use of such problems encourages interested and spontaneous group thinking.

Discussions were used by the Inglewood parents to relate the general needs of children to the specific problems of children with cerebral palsy. Considerations such as those that follow of ways in which families can help exceptional children could be used in a wide variety of ways to help parents. Situations and characters could be modified to meet the needs of almost any group.

SAMPLE OF SHEET DISTRIBUTED TO PARENTS; THE COMMENTS LISTED
UNDER EACH HEADING REPRESENT A COMPOSITE OF SUGGESTIONS
MADE BY MEMBERS OF DISCUSSION GROUPS*

Situation: Household Chores
Characters: Mother
Daughter . . . 14 years old, c.p., confined
           to wheel chair
Son . . . 8 years old

HOW CAN WE MEET HIS:

Physical needs:

Helps with flour sifter, potato masher, pots and pans.
Dry dishers, dust, clean and prepare vegetables.
Sort linens and fold towels; re-arrange cupboards.
Water the lawn, sew, knit, do useful things.

* Three groups chose to discuss this one.

Open drawers, straighten up.
Dry silverware.

Social needs:

List chores together, select their own jobs.
Help with dishes.
Help mix cakes, bring things to school and church for entertainment.
Share unpleasant tasks.
Games with family and entertainment preparations.

Emotional needs:

Beat up cakes (release hostility).
Take her place in family group.
Recognition through responsibilities.
Doing housework.

Intellectual needs:

Read to brothers.
Try new chores.
Read recipes, use of measuring equipment.

HOW HAVE WE HELPED HER:

Feel worthwhile?	Give her responsibilities.
	Include her in family group.
Feel loved?	Being included.
Accept what she has?	Help her in not feeling sorry for herself.
Take her fair part?	Making it easy for her to be accepted as part of family group.

8. *Evaluation and research.*

Guidance workers have an obligation to work with other educators in the evaluation of programs for exceptional children. Such evaluation can do much to promote intelligent understanding, and to reduce emotion and opinion. All fields of special education need planned research programs. Studies such as that of Fils[12] on a public school program for the severely mentally retarded serve to interpret the purposes and functions of special programs, and to promote acceptance of them by school personnel and the general public.

[12] David H. Fils, *A Pilot Study of a Public School Educational and Training Program for Children Who Are Severely Mentally Retarded* (Los Angeles: Office of the Los Angeles County Superintendent of Schools, Division of Research and Guidance, January, 1955), 35 pp. (mimeographed).

summary

One of the important areas of contribution by the guidance worker is that of the education of exceptional children. If properly trained, he plays a key role in identification and diagnosis. The special skills required for adequate measurement of exceptional children demand high clinical competency of the guidance person.

Screening is only a part of his work. He helps to interpret the special needs of the child to other personnel and works with the child, if necessary, to promote self-understanding. He serves as a liaison person in the use of community resources, he assists with educational problems, he works with parents, and he conducts needed research.

Teachers, of course, contribute much to good education for exceptional children. They do this through their own positive attitudes, through varied programs geared toward children's needs, through individual help and counseling, and through helping parents see the values of their children. Much of the work of the teacher is parallel to that of the guidance worker. The skills of all persons who work with exceptional children are used to strengthen the total program.

IN-SERVICE STUDY
OF GUIDANCE TECHNIQUE

Much of the time and effort in the pre-service and in-service education of teachers is directed toward the understanding of children. Modern education is as much concerned as ever with the content of the curriculum, but studies in psychology have fostered continued examination and search for improvement of methods for working with children. The development of understanding about group relationships, individual needs, and how children learn has brought about a transition from stress upon content *per se* to a stress upon the effective use of content in relation to children's learning needs. In other words, modern teacher education stresses heavily the guidance aspects of teaching. The work of the teacher is no longer a simple matter of doling out assignments.

Although pre-service teacher education has done much to acquaint young teachers with the complexities and variations involved in working with children, all teachers know that actual service brings forth countless and continuous questions. In-service study in guidance is essentially child study; its central aim is provision for the needs of all children.

Since guidance activities are centered upon the social and psychological well-being of children, in-service study in guidance ideally should involve all school personnel to some extent. This is important if we consider the limited numbers of special guidance personnel at the elementary school level, and the need for making

214

their services as effective as possible. Group work aimed toward increased effectiveness with children can serve to improve all the human relationships within the school.

ROLES OF PERSONNEL

Because teachers are responsible for classroom guidance activities, the impetus for the study of guidance problems and needs should come from them. Unless the problems studied are vital to the teachers, implementation and use of the ideas is doubtful. In-service study groups need first to work on matters of importance to the group, and not on topics that someone thinks they need or on something that "would be good for them."

If the teachers work in groups, the groupings may need structure and variation according to the interests of the individuals concerned. Several differentiated small groups may be better than a wholesale approach. Small groups serve to promote cohesiveness and participation not always possible in larger gatherings.

Groupings may need to be planned as independent units. Even though the central topic under consideration is guidance, teachers may not need large amounts of it in direct fashion. Informal groupings that operate through combined group intelligence often are tremendously productive with a minimum of outside assistance. Teachers often have excellent training. Many of them have Master's degrees or more, and have taken special work that can be used directly in study group activities. Group leadership, therefore, should be thought of as flexible. If a district has a guidance person, this individual may work with the group, but not necessarily as a designated leader.

The guidance worker in the district can help others in several ways in their in-service study. One of the first ways is to plan with teachers and facilitate arrangements so that they may study children. It is necessary for someone to convene groups initially and help them to start their work. Matters of rooms and schedules for meetings may be arranged by the principals and the guidance person working together.

From time to time teachers will want special resource help in their study. The guidance person can supply this in several ways: through group participation, through the loan of materials, through

215

the development of bibliographies and study lists, and through arrangements for outside resource assistance. The guidance person may also supply incentive for group study through initiating studies that emphasize children's needs. For example, a study of the attitudes of self and others entertained by children of superior intelligence who are achievers or non-achievers can stimulate much interest and participation.

The chief objective of the guidance worker in the in-service program is the development of guidance leadership in others. With this objective in view, in addition to developing teacher leadership opportunities and abilities in guidance, he may work with administrative and supervisory personnel so that they may assist teachers with guidance problems.

TYPES OF PROGRAMS

It is not possible to outline detailed programs for in-service training in guidance activities, because of the tremendous array of potential topics that might be studied and the differing approaches that might be taken. The purpose here is to describe in brief some approaches to the exploration of guidance problems, apart from the usual techniques of lecture, discussion, and use of films. The hope is that they may furnish some ideas that may find application in the reader's situation.

Informal, free discussions, by small groups, of daily incidents and situations that have actually occurred in classrooms can contribute greatly to understanding. Several situations may be outlined in brief on a study guide for use in the discussion, as these:

> Mrs. B. had been having trouble with some of her sixth grade boys. On one particular day, prior to Christmas vacation, she had to remind Jim T. several times to work on his arithmetic assignment. He continued to create disturbances, and paid little attention to his work. Finally she walked over to him, and said, "Jim, I want you to get to work right now and stay with it until you finish!" Jim replied, "Oh, shut up!"

> Mr. A. tries to carry on varied activities in his fifth grade. He finds that when he goes from group to group, the groups with which he is not immediately concerned go to pieces.

> Mrs. W's. children have caused a great deal of difficulty on the playground since school started. She says that she can't

understand it—she never has a bit of trouble with them in the room.

Jerry T. (a colored boy) objected when the others on the field said that he was out. He argued with the first baseman that he hadn't touched him. Jack, the first baseman contended that he had, finally lost his temper, and said, "You *are* out, you dirty nigger!"

Sometimes a single question may be listed for discussion, as:

How young can children be and carry on self-government in the classroom?

or

How can we get parents to put their children to bed early?

Any of the topics or situations above, if it is of local concern, could promote much group discussion and sharing of ideas.

Teachers have made tape recordings of classroom discussions and student government proceedings and used the tapes as the basis for in-service meetings. The attention of the in-service group can be centered upon ways in which children were given status and responsibility, upon leadership skills, or upon the relationships of individuals.

The study of individual children over a period of time has been of tremendous benefit to teachers in understanding children. The pattern outlined in Chapter 4 can be used by teachers, even when resource help is limited. The learnings accruing from the study of one non-problem child transfer to work with other children in a classroom. The advantage in concentrating study on one child is that small groups of teachers can work together informally without deadlines or unreasonable production pressures.

Many groups of teachers have found it profitable to make studies of their classroom groups, using materials such as those described in Chapters 4 through 7. Study groups can work together to prepare materials, exchange ideas, and discuss and evaluate their findings. Teachers who undertake such projects find that they are immensely valuable in terms of understanding children, and that the information gained can be used to good advantage in other teacher study groups, and with parents in groups as well.

Role playing has been used to good advantage in teacher study

217

groups. New teachers have found it particularly worthwhile to participate in parent-teacher conferences, in preparation for the real thing. By assuming the roles of teacher, parent, and observer, they are able to identify with their own role and with the other person as well, and are able to evaluate their own performances and needs. Role playing can involve teachers who become groups of children in a classroom, or groups of parents who want to discuss varied topics of interest.

The guidance worker serves as a resource to teachers in the study of children.

Self-study has been a topic in several teacher study groups. Teachers who feel that self-understanding is essential to understanding others have joined groups that have employed group tests of aptitude, achievement, attitudes, and personal adjustment, along with presentations on mental health, to assess themselves as teachers. It is necessary in such a group to work closely with a well-trained resource person, since skilled interpretation is essential. In order to keep the groups permissive and non-threatening, it is necessary, too, that the teachers score their own tests, and keep their own profiles. Some individual discussion time is needed, as well as general group discussions of results.

Activity on the part of teachers has produced much fine material in guidance. Many school systems have local libraries of tape recordings, slides, guidance manuals and conference guides that are due in large measure to the efforts of teaching personnel. Teachers have spent long hours on evaluation and improvement of cumulative records and report forms. Such activities mean that staff members study and participate in guidance work, understand the reasons for the kinds of materials that they have, and are able to interpret intelligently the reasons for their practices. Their personal interest and personal involvement mean that the entire guidance program has much more support than would otherwise be possible.

DESIRED OUTCOMES

Teachers who read, study, and discuss guidance in relation to their own children develop great interest in the children as human beings. They tend to center attention less upon non-essentials, and derive more satisfaction from watching the growth of children, and from fostering the growth in desirable ways. As they learn about children, they tend more and more to enjoy their work and to realize the importance of it. Guidance study, then, pays dividends in terms of teacher mental health.

The knowledge that teachers acquire concerning children benefits the children, too. When teachers discuss a topic such as "How young can children be and carry on self-government in the classroom?" they can teach one another much about ways to foster desirable independence in children at all grade levels. They can gain in appreciation of capabilities of children younger than their own, and also learn to relate growth principles to the subjects under consideration. Teaching becomes more scientific in the classrooms of these teachers.

Through active participation in planning and carrying out guidance activities, teachers develop leadership abilities. Instead of being passive attendants at meetings, they become resources to their peers, and work with all district personnel on a group basis. Their active participation means that the guidance program will not become static.

219

Finally, the teamwork approach assures stability for the guidance program. No one person operates as a prima donna, pushing ideas and a program that would become non-functional without him. With many persons interested and active, the guidance work within a district is much less dependent upon any individual, and could operate successfully in many respects even if the guidance person should move to another position. Teachers who speak of it as "our program" rather than "the program" are likely to carry on the many guidance activities they have learned regardless of the presence or absence of special personnel. The role of the resource is to foster teamwork and to assist the team members to improve their skills.

GUIDANCE PROFESSIONAL GROUPS

In many areas guidance discussion groups have been formed for the purpose of studying guidance problems and learning new techniques. Such groups may be rather highly specialized, such as school psychologists' study groups; they may be composed of special guidance personnel with varied training backgrounds; or they may be area groups open to anyone interested. In the latter case, a group might include school psychologists, teachers, counselors, general supervisors, principals, child welfare and attendance workers, nurses, and so on. The advantage of an open group is, of course, the added interest as well as learning and active participation.

Within a large urban area, guidance groups may be found in local systems, in single areas of a county, on a county-wide basis, and under organizational sponsorship. In less populous areas, it is necessary for interested individuals from several communities to meet together.

Guidance associations provide challenge and stimulation for guidance workers, and supply them with new ideas for their work. Through contacts with outside resource people and through an interchange of learnings, guidance personnel learn new ways of interpreting tests, new findings regarding exceptional children, new audio-visual materials of value in guidance, and new techniques for studying children. If the groups are heterogeneous in interests and training, the participants learn about the views of others, and understanding of the guidance program is promoted.

OUT-OF-DISTRICT RESOURCES

In addition to district programs that are largely self-contained, and professional guidance groups, another group of individuals contributes to the in-service program. These individuals are usually well-known professional personnel from colleges, universities, institutions, or private practice who speak or conduct workshops on specified topics. Such persons can contribute much to guidance growth in a school system. Local personnel have a great responsibility toward making the visits effective, however, by preparing for the meeting or meetings in advance.

Preparations may involve problem surveys, or, if the visitor is one of several, informing him of previous topics and coverage. He may need to visit one or several classrooms during his visit. He may need to have planning conferences with local participants. Close communication between the local group and the visiting expert can do much to make the outsider an insider.

summary

All school personnel should be involved in guidance study, with the ultimate goal one of desirable human relationships within the school. Leadership should be flexible, and groupings should be based upon factors such as interest, training, and needs. The guidance person serves primarily as a resource in the program, assisting others.

Programs should be planned to be informal and to promote maximum participation. Topics should be of direct local concern. The active participation of many means better understanding of children by teachers, better classroom procedures, the development of teacher leadership, and an improving, self-sustaining guidance program.

Guidance learnings can be developed through local district activities, through associations interested in guidance, and through the use of special resources. All require close planning and cooperative effort to insure success.

221

WORKING
WITH PARENTS

The current chapter is not on what parents need to know, or on teaching adults about their young. It is rather a discussion of the importance of parent-school collaboration, and of how to make home-school contacts effective. All individuals tend to view others from their own perspective, and in the process the picture sometimes becomes blurred. School people at times may weigh improperly the relative influences of home and school, even though all of them have read many times that "the home exercises a profound influence upon the behavior and attitudes of the child at school."

IMPORTANCE OF HOME-SCHOOL CONTACTS

One way of stressing the importance of the home is to look at the matter of contact arithmetically. By the time the child has gone to kindergarten for a half year and the teacher feels that she knows him well, she will have had somewhat under 300 hours of association with him as part of a group. By this time, the parent will have associated with him for something between forty and fifty thousand hours. These figures do not allow for absences from either environment or for other associations, and are, of course, highly speculative. They do not relate to training and ability to observe, or to emotional involvement. They should, however, serve to underscore the importance of the contributions that parents can make.

222

School people, or others, do not really know a child until they know his parents. Acquaintance with parents can tell teachers much about a child. The characteristics of the parents, what they like and dislike, their affection for the youngster (or lack of it), the kind of example they furnish for him—all add to understanding of the child. His personality and behavior are direct products of his family relationships.

The benefit to the child of understanding his environment is illustrated through the following example:

> I really couldn't stand Beatrice until I knew her family (wrote her teacher). She was bold, aggressive, cloying, and, all in all, highly obnoxious. She constantly did things in class to get the attention of the children, and had them feeling pretty negative toward her. Of course, she acted like she didn't care, although I knew she must.
>
> My first contact with her family occurred when her mother came to the school to vote. She was terribly overweight, unkempt, and quite drunk. I learned that she lived with a number of men, serially, and that alcohol was one of her main interests in life.
>
> My next contact was on a tour of the area when I drove by her home. It was a hovel, set apart from any other dwellings among the sand dunes. It couldn't have contained more than two rooms. Although I didn't visit, I heard from other teachers that the furnishings were of the poorest type possible.
>
> The third contact came when the parents came to school to pick Beatrice up one day. The "father" walked toward her, and I could see that he was unshaven, untidy, and that Beatrice was in an evident hurry to rush them away.
>
> These few insights helped me to understand the child's behavior better. I tried in a number of ways to promote Beatrice as a group member, and succeeded to some extent. My real understanding of her environmental deprivation came when she made a statement to me which was both pitiful and profoundly revealing: "Miss ―――――, I wish *you* were my mother!"

Direct contact with parents helps school people understand them too. Acquaintance with parents and their problems helps teachers to develop understanding and tolerance toward both parent and child. The personal contact can promote liking and respect between the teacher and parent, which is of tremendous importance to the emotional well-being of the child. Children at the elementary school

223

level usually enjoy having their parents come to school, and derive great satisfaction from the friendships between their adults.

Parent-teacher contacts can promote understanding of children when they are young, at a time when the adults can work together most easily. The understanding can work to the benefit of the pupil all through the grades. Parents may work with school people, and come to them for information regarding their children and the school program instead of relying on hearsay or misinformation. Similarly, school personnel can get accurate information from parents.

Through individual and group contacts, teachers are able to communicate information and work cooperatively with parents in the job of understanding children. Parents are better able to understand their children and the schools they attend. It happens too, that parents get to know other parents as well as teachers, and many a close neighborhood friendship begins at a classroom orientation meeting.

The interpretation of the school program and the promotion of increased understanding of children benefits the school. From the school point of view, the study of children should result in environmental improvement, if improvement is needed. Any improvement would reflect itself in easier teaching. So, despite the amount of time involved, close relationships between the home and school are worthwhile.

KINDS OF CONTACTS

Contacts between home and school are basically one-way or two-way. The one-way contacts are information-giving, while the two-way are geared toward information exchange. It is possible, through adaptations, to permit some combination of the two, but a report card or report letter that provides space for parent reaction is still primarily a one-way report. Two-way communication necessitates conditions that permit free exchange of ideas. Both types are of value.

One-way contacts range from simple one-line notes to elaborate television productions. Because many parents do not have personal contact with schools, these sources may be their only ways of learning about the schools, aside from conversations with their children or neighbors. Many school systems have made good use of local newspapers, television, and radio to send information home. Some have developed attractive illustrated booklets of information on topics such as *How Children Learn to Read in* X *School System,* or *Meet Your Children's Teachers.* For parents who are unable to attend meetings, summaries of meeting procedures have been prepared and sent to the home. When important surveys are made that affect educational planning, summaries of questionnaire results may be sent to all homes.

Many teachers have supplemented school publications with booklets or leaflets of information for their own parents. Summaries of growth characteristics at a given grade level, suggestions of activities that will provide valuable background experiences for children, or booklets about kindergarten activities and learnings are examples. A few teachers regularly send notes and letters to their parents. The letters may be concerned with activities of the previous week—the learnings that came from a trip to a newspaper office, the paintings that the children made, John's new sister who is named Karen and weighs almost eight pounds, the conquering of mixed numbers, new library books of interest, and so on.

One-way communication has the advantage of contacting all school patrons. If the school relies on this method alone, however, it is possible that the real needs and feelings of the community may be quite unknown. It is essential that personal contacts be a planned part of the communication program.

PREPARATION FOR TWO-WAY GROUP COMMUNICATION

Since schools in rapidly increasing numbers are carrying on organized programs of meetings and conferences, the training of teachers in this area has been an important activity. Colleges and universities are including courses in home-school communication in their offerings to school personnel, and local supervisors and guidance personnel are working together to help teachers with group leadership and conference techniques and materials.

The preparation of teachers and other school people for conduct-

225

ing group meetings may involve study groups and discussions. In study group sessions, teachers may review and evaluate the content of such resources as:

> Benne, Kenneth, and Bozidar Muntyan, eds., *Human Relations in Curriculum Change*. Dryden Press, 1951, 363 pp.
> Chase, Stuart, *Roads to Agreement*. Harper & Brothers, 1951, 250 pp.
> National Training Laboratory in Group Development, *Leadership and Participation in Large Group Meetings*. National Education Association, 1951, 17 pp.

The ideas may be tried out by teachers or resource personnel in group meetings, and the results discussed in staff meetings.

Role playing has been used by teachers to prepare for discussion meetings. They have found that preliminary discussions of topics are of value in learning desirable group procedures with adults, and in developing self-assurance. The preliminary meetings prevent dilemmas of the sort expressed by one teacher after her first group session with parents, when she said that the meeting was fine, but she was so "petrified" that she could hardly hold her coffee cup.

The meetings can be arranged so that faculty groups become parent groups, or better still, volunteer parents may come in to work with a leader in a demonstration session. Teachers then may serve as observers and evaluate the meeting in a non-threatening atmosphere. A few simple criteria, like those below, listed on a study sheet with room for recording comments, help to record impressions and suggestions:

> How did the chairman set the group at ease?
> How did the chairman establish the purposes of the meeting?
> Were the materials appropriate and well-planned?
> Did everyone participate freely?
> Were the purposes achieved?

Questions that are commonly discussed in group meetings may form the basis for training sessions. The following are a few examples:

> Why do they have groups in classrooms?
> Why don't children learn to read (or spell, or do arithmetic) nowadays?
> How can we keep children from fighting?

Why don't children learn phonics?
Should elementary children have homework?

Meetings may also be held in which experienced teachers demonstrate techniques and materials that they have found worthwhile in presenting their plans for the year, or in presenting culmination programs that illustrate the year's learnings. In these sessions, teachers may show how they use text materials and independent activities as they discuss the daily program, and may illustrate in detail some of the learnings within a specific content area such as reading.

In evaluating such a presentation, teachers may discuss the following areas, among others:

1. *Invitations*—how to make them attractive. Some teachers have their pupils participate through cutting out or designing illustrations to place on the invitation sheets. Older children may formulate a group invitation. The children's discussion of the purposes of the group conference and their taking some part in it usually mean that they will urge their parents to attend.

2. *Identification.* Introductions and the use of name tags may be planned.

3. *Room arrangements.* The work of individual pupils should not be exhibited unless names are deleted. Rooms should be attractive, but natural. Teaching aids should be accessible for parent inspection and discussion. Here again, pupils can participate in the discussion of things that would be of interest to their parents, and how they should be displayed.

Some teachers may want their pupils to demonstrate their use of science materials (or others) with the parents.

4. *Refreshments.* These should be kept simple. Both children and parents may wish to participate here.

5. *Participation of administrative personnel.* Resource people may be of assistance, especially with new teachers. It is important that they plan with the teachers so that they serve as resources and do not themselves conduct the meeting.

As an outgrowth of planning sessions and their own experiences, teachers at different levels may wish to work together on a teachers' guide for group conferences. Such a guide may include a presentation of general considerations like those above and may, in addition, list specific suggestions for inclusion in the outline of daily activities. These may include materials such as the following, from which teachers may select ideas:

227

PRIMARY

1. Values from sharing time and/or opening exercises such as—
   a) Number concept—by counting boys, counting girls, counting milk money, counting lunches, books, papers.
   b) Vocabulary building—learning names of articles and names of parts of articles shown and shared.
   c) Social poise—talking before a group—taking turns—lisening—courtesy—
   d) Etc.
2. Values from nutrition period—
   a) Food values—discussion.
   b) Cleanliness—example.
   c) Personal responsibility.
   d) Rest.
   e) Etc.
3. Values from basic reading text—
   a) Controlled vocabulary.
   b) All types of techniques and skills scientifically presented and reinforced by concrete drill. (Show and explain use of teacher's manual.)
   c) Use of state text and other series as enriching and reinforcing material.
   d) Aim of reading—enjoyment and enrichment.
4. Value and use of independent activities—
   a) As a means of allowing for small group instruction.
   b) As a means of developing self-reliance.
   c) As a means of reinforcing reading techniques.
5. Values from calsomine and easel painting—
   a) Expression of ideas for those who are not yet skillful in expressing ideas in oral or written form.
   b) Development of muscular control.
   c) Clarification of form—size—relationship concepts.
   d) Esthetic value in color.
   e) Success feelings. (If it tells to the painter what the painter had in mind, it is successful, even though it needs interpretation to others.)
   f) Helpful to organize ideas so that oral and written expression may develop more easily.
6. Values from physical education period—
   a) Relaxation.
   b) Learning group participation—
      (1) Take turns.
      (2) Abide by group decisions.
      (3) Self-reliance, etc.
      (4) Muscular control—ball bouncing, catching (writing readiness).

7. Values from committee membership and monitorship—
   a) Beginning of democratic procedures.
   b) Basic citizenship training.
8. Values from field trips—
   a) The planning—
      (1) Setting up the questions.
      (2) Forming committees—establishing responsibility.
      (3) Setting standards of behavior.
   b) The trip—gaining of concrete information.
   c) The evaluation and recording—organization of material.
   d) The application and use of information.
9. Value of film lesson—
   (See field trip.)
10. Values in music period—
    a) Enjoyment.
    b) Activity—dancing.
    c) Expression.
11. Explain some writing readiness procedures such as—
    a) Likenesses and differences—games.
    b) Painting.
    c) Playing games.
    d) Bouncing balls.
    e) Learning left to right progression.
    f) Writing supplies—
       (1) Why large pencil and paper in primary grades.
       (2) Why we delay the use of pen and ink in middle grades.[1]

Meetings that are introductory and meetings that serve to summarize the year's activities are the two types most usually held in schools. Some schools go beyond the minimal program to plan study and discussion meetings as needed during the year.

The central problem in planning group meetings is how to make them appealing. Refreshments help, but are not the entire answer. Much more important is the matter of structure. Local problems of concern *to the parents* should form the basis for their discussions. School people can facilitate the discussions by positive attitudes and by providing a comfortable atmosphere in which parents can do their own thinking. Teachers in the elementary grades are expert at carrying on discussions within their own classrooms in which they promote group thinking and group decisions. The techniques

---

[1] Reproduced by permission of Norwalk-La Mirada City School District, Norwalk, Calif., from *Conference Guide, Reporting to Parents, Group and Individual Conferences* (Norwalk, Calif.: 1952), (mimeographed).

they employ are what they term "just good teaching." These same techniques apply also to adult groups. The use of discussion, promotion of participation, clarification of ideas, evaluation—all are employed with both children and adults. Many skills that teachers employ every day apply directly in their work as adult group leaders.

Flexibility is important in the structure of meetings. If programs are planned for a year in advance, the matter of whether local needs are met sometimes becomes a matter of guesswork. It is easier to plan a short series of meetings, perhaps three or four on a weekly basis, as the need arises. Such meetings may include parents from one class group, or from several, depending upon topic and interest. With several series of meetings it becomes easier to keep groups small, and the school may be able to help parents to attend by providing baby sitters, through the assistance of other parents or older students.

A handbook of suggestions for new teachers might well include a section entitled *This We Have Learned*, in which suggestions of a general nature could be listed. Below are a few examples of suggestions based on experience that are helpful to new teachers, and that may suggest ideas to those with experience.

> 1. *You may wish to tell parents in your invitation* that they may either leave children with cooperative neighbors or take advantage of school baby-sitting facilities, so that they can participate with freedom in the meeting.
>
> 2. *Arrange the chairs informally.* It seems better to sit with your group rather than at the desk.
>
> 3. *Think of ways in which you would make the parents feel at ease* if they were in your home. You are the hostess, although your room mother is helping.
>
> 4. *Don't overcrowd the room.* Try to choose varied materials of interest.
>
> 5. *Arrange materials with brief explanations* when needed, as "Games to Develop Coordination"—or—"To Learn the Meaning of Numbers."
>
> 6. *It helps to have books available* for use when discussing them. Illustrate whenever possible.
>
> 7. *You may wish to survey your parent group for hobbies,* talents, or special skills that can be used to enrich your year's work.
>
> 8. *If parents bring up the needs of particular children,* you may wish to suggest tactfully that they stay to arrange for an individual conference so that you can have enough time for dis-

cussion. This helps to keep the discussion centered upon the group.

9. *Try to avoid professional terminology.* Evaluate your statements in terms of meaningfulness. If you say children start reading before they come to school, give many concrete examples of what you mean. If you say many skills are needed in reading, illustrate profusely. It is better to cover a few points thoroughly. You can always have another meeting if you need one!

10. *In discussions of individual differences,* examples help. It is easy to delete names from papers and show differences in readiness, coordination, and skill. The opaque projector helps everyone to see the same thing, although materials can be held up to view fairly successfully. The projector may be used to show group differences in achievement areas, or even age, height, and weight, through charts.

11. *Write a summary report,* telling what you did, and what particular things were successful. This will help all of us, and will prevent duplication of approach. For example, if you use a chart story with meaningless symbols to illustrate the complexity of reading, the next teacher will avoid that approach with the same parent group next year. If the teacher before you stressed reading, you may wish to spend more time with social studies, and so on.

12. *The evaluation questionnaire* for parents (obtain from principal) gives much valuable information on how to improve group meetings. We feel that it should be used by all teachers whenever the meetings are over for the year.

PANELS

Panels are best used when a topic lends itself to the expression of several points of view. The discussion is informal, and does not necessarily result in a final consensus. Symposia, each comprising a series of short speeches, are not panels, although they are often mistakenly called by the name. The panel is conducted by a chairman who has the responsibility of promoting discussion, coordinating and summarizing points discussed, and bringing out discussion through questions.

Panels by children are often highly informative and interesting to an adult audience. Children may discuss such topics as grades, spending money, recreation, television, what they have learned in X subject area, what they want to do as adults, club activities, and so on. A panel of gifted children, for example, told about their

231

school experiences and needs through a discussion with their teacher of the following questions, among others:

What do you like to do best in school?
What is your favorite recreation?
What has been hardest for you in school?
How have you chosen your friends?
How have teachers helped you most?

Another group of children did much to enhance the prestige of the teaching profession through a discussion of teachers that involved questions like these:

Are teachers like other people? (Yes, only they need to know a lot more. They have to understand children better than persons who only see a few, etc.)
Can you think of special ways in which teachers have made it easy for you to learn? No names! (One teacher especially worked with us in groups a lot and made us think, but it was fun)—and so on.

Panels by teachers and parents have been used to integrate professional recommendations with practical considerations. Such discussions afford parents an opportunity to react directly to suggestions instead of waiting until the end of a formal presentation, when perhaps they feel hesitant about responding to the chairman's "Are there any questions?" A panel may explore such subjects as play materials for young children, and types of homemade materials that are inexpensive, interesting, and of creative value. Space in the home and yard, time of parents, other children and their interests, and neighborhood factors could be discussed as well. The point of view of the home is important to school personnel in keeping their recommendations realistic. The panel discussion often gives both parents and school people a better opportunity to question, clarify, and explore details.

Schools also may wish to utilize the panel approach for presentations by professional personnel. For example, a panel of specialists may relate their work to the elementary school experience of a mythical child and demonstrate clearly to parents the coordinated, carefully planned contributions of many persons to the welfare of their own children. The nurse and medical doctor may discuss the purposes, types, and schedules of examinations, records that they

232

maintain, and their use of community agencies; the guidance person may describe the guidance materials and resources that are used for all children; special curriculum resources may indicate how they enrich the learnings of the children, and so on. Such a panel may function before the entire parent group, and can do much to foster understanding and appreciation of the modern school program.

GROUP PARTICIPATION

The goal of group participation is the promotion and maintenance of active interest on the part of parents, as well as the proper interpretation of the school program. This type of activity goes a step beyond the panel in the involvement of the total group.

1. *Observation.*

Observation is one kind of group participation that has proved successful in clarifying school procedures to parents. Usually the type of observation that is planned is determined by the questions

Discussions of classroom observations add to parent understandings on school procedures. (*Courtesy Division of Elementary Education, Office of the Los Angeles County Superintendent of Schools.*)

233

expressed by parents in group meetings. They may ask how teachers can manage several groups in reading and make them good learning situations, or how dramatic play is valuable, or how children do rhythms in groups.

A good observation experience necessitates careful planning. Time must be provided for discussions with the parents both before and after the observation. The time before the observation may be scheduled before school opens or during a recess period, to allow the teacher to participate. If the activity to be observed comes at another time of the day, the teacher may plan with the proper resource person so that the individual may orient the parents to the demonstration, its purposes, and its content. The resource person may be a curriculum consultant, guidance worker, art or music supervisor, principal, or other special resource, depending upon the purposes of the observation. It is better to use the services of the resource person than to arrange for a substitute in the classroom immediately preceding the demonstration.

Definite schedules are important in observation arrangements. A written invitation, with a space for confirmation, will serve to notify parents, and will keep the adult group at a suitable size for the facilities. Because of the size of class groups and room space, many teachers prefer to divide the parent groups for visitations. The invitation may include suggestions to the parents on observation ethics as well. The form may be worded something like this:

Dear _____ _____,
You are cordially invited to visit the fourth grade on Thursday, December 4, to observe and discuss with the teacher a science lesson. Parents are asked to report to the conference room at 9:30 for a preliminary discussion of the lesson. The lesson itself will take about forty minutes, and the teacher-parent discussion afterwards will last about thirty minutes. We should be through at approximately eleven o'clock.

If you need someone to care for a younger child, we have older children who will be happy to take care of him.

We hope that you can be with us. Will you please let us know?

•   •   •

(Cross out one)
I shall, shall not, be present at 9:30 on Thursday, December 4.
I shall, shall not, need someone to care for a younger child.

Signed _____

Following the observation, the teacher should be released to meet with the parents. The principal or another teacher may substitute for her in the classroom so that she is free to confer with the parents in another place. The discussion should center upon group activities rather than upon individuals.

An observation sheet is useful in guiding observation and the ensuing discussion. It should be simple, confined to a few main points, and should allow room for recording of statements and questions. If the observation sheet were developed for use with the science lesson mentioned above, it might appear like this:

OBSERVATION—LESSON ON CONSERVATION OF NATURAL RESOURCES

This visit has been planned so that you may observe your children and their teacher in their classroom working relationship. Please notice any evidence of developing attitudes, interests, and insight. Use the five topics and questions below to guide your observation, and make free notes on your sheet so that you may share your reactions with us in the discussion later. (Please do not talk during the observation.)

1. What evidences do you see of self-control and self-direction?
2. How are individual differences provided for, and special abilities developed?
3. In what ways is the information gained of value?
4. What growth is evident in other skills, such as reading, problem solving, etc.?
5. How does this lesson contribute to the future lives of the children?

An observation sheet that is directed primarily toward the observation of children rather than curriculum areas *and* the children may be worded so that the attention of the observers will be directed toward the children as a group. For example:

This visit has been planned so that you will have an opportunity to observe the growth patterns of sixth-grade children. Notice the relationships within the child group. Use the items below to aid you in recording your reactions. Record them freely so that we may all share our ideas in the discussion afterwards.

1. What variations do you notice in growth and development?
2. What differences are evident between boys and girls in maturity?
3. How are physical needs being cared for within the room?
4. Note the differences in amount of energy and activity.

235

5. Do all of the children seem to feel that they belong to the group?

Observation programs may be based upon single meetings, or on any combination of topics, depending upon the wishes of the group. Thus, parents may wish to see several types of reading lessons to study the classroom reading program; they may wish to see a single lesson in several academic areas; or they may wish to observe creative art experiences. The plans should be flexible, subject to change, and based upon the expressed wishes of the observers.

2. *Activity by adult participants.*

A step removed from general meetings or panels is the meeting in which all those present are active. The usual types are the open discussion—for a small group—or buzz groups, for gatherings that are too large to permit total participation within a single unit. In such meetings parents may discuss such diverse topics as worthwhile home activities for children, what they like best about their child, television tastes, or how parents can work for adequate play space for their children. The meetings can be effectively combined with brief preliminary presentations in which facts, issues, and questions for discussion are presented. The success of the meetings is due in large measure to the extent to which the participants feel personally involved in the issue being discussed and much therefore depends upon the skill of the chairman in the buildup for the small groups. Sufficient time must be planned for presentation of the problem, for small group consideration, and for summary and discussion by representatives of the small groups involved. Unless the total group is aware of small-group reactions and can in turn react to them, much of the value of the buzz-group approach is lost.

Many parents have been brought into active participation in school activities through organized child groups and through special skills and talents that they possess. Mothers in many areas give time to Scouts, Campfire, and other groups. They provide "props" for programs, serve refreshments, and assist on study trips. Teachers have learned to capitalize on the talents of the parent who plays the violin or who works as an astronomer, a geologist, a policeman, or a farmer. When parents visit the school to talk about other parts of the country or world or to show costumes or to demonstrate dances, the curriculum is vitalized and the relationships among parents, teachers, and children are strengthened.

Often teachers follow demonstration lessons with similar activities for the parents. Parents who watch their children using work sheets in reading that check on ability to follow directions or word meaning may work on a lesson of the same type afterwards. Teachers have found that parents who do this develop a profound respect for the complexity of the work their children do. One parent (with a Master's degree), after misreading a direction and skipping one step necessary in a response for a second-grade lesson said, "I didn't know that the children had to think so much to do their work."

Whether parents are able to come for observations or not, they learn a great deal and enjoy participating in the kinds of activities that their children have. Discussions of music activities develop more meaning to parents when they listen to the records that are being recommended, when they handle the rhythm instruments as they hear of their proper use, or when they try the folk dance steps their children learned that week. Finger painting means more to them than stained clothing and more laundry when they experience the freedom of expression and the satisfaction in creation that it brings. Parents whose children have brought them presents from school may make simple presents for their children in art work sessions, and acquire much knowledge of children in an accompanying discussion. Teachers who need simple equipment for the classroom have invited fathers and mothers on alternate evenings to saw, hammer, sew, drink coffee, and talk about children. Parents who see their children cooking on a make-believe stove that they helped construct from cast-off wood, or rocking in a chair that they helped to cover, have a real sense of belonging to the group, and should not be hesitant about visiting school.

In schools that sponsor child-study groups, reading materials for parents often are at a premium. Parents again can make a needed contribution through maintaining a loan service of magazines, pamphlets, and books dealing with child development. Committees that function to exchange materials and to facilitate their distribution perform a real service to the parent-teacher group.

Many parents have found role-playing of situations reflecting normal child behavior interesting and informative. Situations may be discussed and planned by a committee, then written or presented to the group. An episode like the following is but one of many that is experienced by many parents, and leads to thought-provoking discussion:

> Jerry, the next-door neighbor, and your daughter Susan, both six years old, are busy playing in the backyard. They have boxes set up, and empty cartons and cans on the "shelves." Both have worked busily to set up the store, and both want to wear apron and be storekeeper. Tussle ensues. Susan swings, knocks Jerry aside, and tears the apron. Jerry comes crying to you. You say:

In the episode, parents can take child and adult roles, discuss alternatives, and evaluate various approaches to the dilemma.

Achievement tests of junior or senior high school level have been used in some schools to underscore the reality of individual differences. The tests have been used with adult groups, scored, and reported anonymously on a group basis. When parents hear of ranges and differences in performance within their own peer group, they often identify more closely with the problems of individual needs and the resultant individualized instruction that is required.

3. Demonstrations by children.

Children can and should take an active part in interpreting their learning to parents. Many learnings can become more evident through child participation than through teacher presentation. Children who dramatize activities at the harbor, or take a trip across the plains, clearly demonstrate an intricate network of learnings simultaneously. When children stand before a parent audience and talk of science learnings in general, principles involved in experiments with nutrition or plant growth or pressure, demonstrate those experiments and summarize their results, they give excellent evidence of good educational practices within their classroom. They furnish also many excellent insights into children's abilities and differences.

4. Recreational activities.

Parents, teachers, and children often are drawn more closely together through play. The play may be child and adult participation

238

in picnics, baseball, folk dancing, or crafts. It may be a single episode based upon a holiday in which the children sing to their parents, the parents sing to the children, and a combined committee serves refreshments.

Many parents and teachers have joined forces to put on a pot luck dinner or an annual "fun night," in which small groups present chorus lines and skits that good-naturedly satirize adults in the participating group. Such events frequently are held to raise money for recreational facilities for children, or other projects

5. Extension of school contacts.

Schools have worked in two ways to extend their contacts with parents. One is through orientation activities; the other is through meetings for parents of pre-school children.

Through meetings and visits held prior to the opening of school for kindergarten children, the children and parents are able to visit school, meet the teacher, and learn about the facilities. Some schools have the visits for a period of a week or more, and use them as a gradual induction to school for the youngsters. The children may visit once or several times, and be with a few children prior to meeting the whole group. Such contacts make the start of school easier for both parent and child, and enable the parent and teacher to know each other better than if they met only once when the total group arrived.

Meetings for parents of pre-school children have more often been arranged by nursery associations than by the public schools. If we accept the premise that guidance should begin early, it seems that meetings with parents of very young children are an important contribution of the school. Schools can render a vital service through sponsoring study groups, arranging for discussion leaders, loaning books and films, and providing meeting places and baby sitters. The meetings would benefit parents through providing them with opportunities to study their children, and would benefit the school through the promotion of understanding of children who soon will be in school and through close contact with their future parent groups. It is possible that some future guidance problems may be circumvented through this type of early assistance to parents.

239

6. *Films*.[2]

Films should be brought into meetings to meet real needs, not because they are new or because something is needed for a meeting. Most films are best presented in context—that is, if a group of parents is discussing the effect of parental ambitions on a child, a film like *Preface to a Life* might be useful. Or, if they are studying developmental patterns in young children, *Life with Baby* might be the best film to use.

For best results the films should be presented when the audience is ready for their use. This implies that some films will not be shown until a group has been oriented to their context through one or several lectures. Whenever any film is shown, the group should be given an adequate introduction to it, including content to observe and evaluate, and a skilled, well-trained leader should be available during the discussion period.

TRENDS IN HOME REPORTING

The evaluation of pupil progress became a major area of concern in American education with the development of the testing movement after World War I, and the increase of knowledge in psychology. Educators have become increasingly aware of the contradiction between their realization of individual differences, mental health needs, and the competitive type of evaluation that has been widely used in the schools, and is still employed in some today. Within the present century, the development of universal education through the secondary school level, the extension of the curriculum, provisions for differing abilities and skills, and the realization of the complexity of effective reporting of child development all have increased the need to re-examine and improve systems for reporting pupil progress.

The task of the modern educator in evaluating and reporting is not easy. The assignment of *ABC* or *1-2-3* grades on a curve limited to academic areas is infinitely simpler than that of evaluating individual growth in all curriculum areas and in physical, social, and emotional areas as well. Yet the educator realizes that unless evalu-

[2] An annotated listing of films is given in Appendix *A* for those who wish to have a listing of guidance films on various topics.

ation is done in meaningful and comprehensive terms, it does not keep pace with modern educational knowledge. The limitations of the traditional method are illustrated through a parallel drawn between the reporting of weather and the reporting of children's progress in which the writer facetiously suggests that traditional home reporting methods be applied to weather prediction to save time and money.[3] Since a *B* or *C* is acceptable in reporting complex variables in a complicated human being, *B* or *C* might be substituted as a single symbol to cover comprehensively such factors as wind velocity, precipitation, or cloud ceiling. The problems with either children or the weather are obvious!

BASES FOR CHANGES

Modern schools have shown an increasing dissatisfaction with the limitations of traditional marking systems, and have directed their efforts toward the development of continuous and comprehensive evaluation. They realize that evaluation and the total educational system are interrelated, and that evaluation procedures are basic to and based upon the educational philosophy of the school. Thus, it is impossible to say that we recognize and provide for individual differences, and yet mark all of the children on a single standard.

A number of trends in the total educational program have contributed to the increasing revision of reporting procedures:

1. *Education for all American youth is near realization.* Under the old evaluation system, a high percentage of children dropped out of school throughout the elementary and secondary grades. The need of all children for an education is recognized in the modern school, and necessary curriculum variations have been made.

2. *Education is becoming increasingly professionalized.* The teacher no longer drills all children on the same subject at the same time. Teaching methods, child study methods, and methods of evaluation have improved greatly, and with the new learnings, teachers have come to realize the complexity and variability of the learning process and the learner.

[3] R. P. Brimm, "The Weather is B Minus. Is an 'Average' Mark Enough?" *Clearing House*, XXVIII, May, 1954, pp. 534-35.

3. *Evaluation has become more complex than periodic judgment*. Education is a day-by-day process, and evaluation is a concomitant aspect of that process. Children and teachers work together in all learnings to evaluate the results.

4. *The need for two-way communication has been recognized*. The term "reporting" is becoming inadequate in the modern school. Home-school communication is no longer exclusively a *telling* process, but rather an exchange of information and plans in which the teacher, child, and parent participate. The relationships have become closer and more continuous than in the past.

5. *Accurate evaluation has become an increasing concern*. Research studies in great numbers since the beginning of the century have shown that "objective" evaluation is no simple task. Factors such as the variability of performance from one group to another; differences in judgment from teacher to teacher; differences of standards from school to school; the advantages of having social position, good manners, and being a girl in getting grades; occasions when effort was considered; and the problem of interpreting the real meaning of a single mark—all have caused educators to search for more meaningful ways to evaluate and report progress.

6. *Sound mental health is recognized as necessary for effective learning*. All persons, whether child or adult, need to derive satisfactions rather than failure from their work. They need to learn to evaluate themselves honestly and realistically. Competitive marking does not indicate what the slow learner *can* succeed in doing; neither does it give a true picture to the bright child who attains top rank with slovenly work and little effort in terms of what he could do. Thus, emotional and intellectual damage can occur to both the bright and dull child. Another problem is that of student-teacher relationships, when the teacher performs as judge rather than as guide.

7. *Learnings in child development have stressed the uniqueness of the individual*. Educators have recognized the need for evaluation that is based upon individual differences in potential and performance. Traditional evaluative methods failed either to foster uniqueness or to stimulate the desire to learn, particularly in bright children.

8. *Schools are becoming increasingly concerned with the de-*

velopment of sound social ideals. Education in academic areas is no longer the sole aim of education. The academic learnings are still highly important, but more important is the use of those learnings constructively and cooperatively. Success is not beating others, which an emphasis on competition rather than cooperation would imply.

The modern teacher is vitally concerned with the attitudes toward themselves and others that her children develop. Her search in all areas of education is directed toward methods and materials that will foster sound mental health.

DEVELOPMENTS IN REPORTING

The changes in American education noted above have been reflected in accompanying changes in reporting forms and methods. Chief among these have been the following:

1. Emphasis on reporting development of the child within several growth areas rather than the academic alone.
2. Change in emphasis to reporting of growth and progress of the individual rather than rating.
3. Fewer reporting periods, and staggered reporting within those periods.
4. Less use of comparison with classmates, and less use of specific marks, such as *ABCD, F, P,* 89%, or 1, 2, 3.
5. Pupil participation through self-evaluation with teacher as counselor.
6. Personal interviews with those concerned.
7. Use of multiple reporting methods, such as letters and/or individualized reports alternately with conferences.

PLANNING FOR CHANGES IN REPORTING PRACTICES

Changes in home reporting are difficult to effect. Change in any area of living necessitates adjustment, and people do not accept easily any alteration in the customary pattern. Changes that have meant increased comforts and extended contacts have been initially viewed with skepticism and foreboding by many. The automobile, the airplane, radio, motion pictures, television, and nuclear fission —all have been greeted by negative prophecies during their introductory periods.

The difficulty of change extends into the realm of education as well. All people have had some contact with schools, whether they be parents or professional educators, or both. Evaluation tends to occur in the light of one's own experiences. Therefore, part of the problem of modernizing the evaluation and reporting procedures in the schools is that of extending the experiences in this area of those individuals who are concerned—which includes everyone in the ' community as well as the professional staff and children. This is no easy task.

To illustrate the difficulty of effecting change in an area of public concern, we may use the example of education for women. Today we accept college education for women. Debate still goes on in terms of needed emphases, as it does for men, but most people feel that women should attend colleges and universities if they choose to do so, and are able to go. This idea did not come about without a struggle. The following editorials are two examples of many that appeared in newspapers during the early 1800's, when the notion of college training for women came into being:[4]

> *College for Ladies.*—The Kentucky Legislature has conferred upon Messrs. Van Doren's Institute for Young Ladies, in Lexington, the chartered rights and standing of a college, by the name of Van Doren's College for Young Ladies. By the power granted by the Board of Trustees and the Faculty of the College, we understand from the Daily Reporter, that a Diploma and the honorary degree of M.P.L. (Mistress of Polite Literature) will be conferred upon those young ladies who complete the prescribed course of studies; and that the same honor may be conferred upon other distinguished ladies in our country; and also that the honorary degree of M.M. (Mistress of Music) and M.I. (Mistress of Instruction) may be conferred by this College upon suitable candidates.

> *Female Degrees.*—Yesterday we gave some accounts of the degrees conferred in the Young Ladies College in Kentucky.— In addition to those, we would recommend the following, which we think will be of more use—namely—M.P.M. (Mistress of Pudding Making), M.D.N. (Mistress of the Darning Needle), M.S.B. (Mistress of the Scrubbing Brush), and especially M.C.S. (Mistress of Common Sense). But in order to fit the girls for those degrees, it will be necessary to organize a new department —and we recommend to the faculty of the institute to apply to

[4] Florence Davis, "Education of Southern White Women from 1730 Through the Antebellum Period" (Ph.D. Dissertation, University of Chicago, 1951), pp. 233-34.

244

the Legislature immediately for an enlargement of its powers, to enable it to confer these new and more useful degrees—and we furthermore recommend to them to procure some well-qualified Professors, from among the farmers' wives, and especially from some of the best regulated kitchens, to teach the young ladies the useful art of housewifery. When they have done this in the proper manner to fit them for taking charge of the family, and making their husband's fireside comfortable, then let the degrees we have recommended be conferred, in due course; and then, in due season, if they succeed according to their merits, they will attain to the honorable degree, to which, we dare say, they are all looking forward, namely that of R.W. (the Respectable Wife) and H.H. (of a Happy Husband) and M.W.R.F. (Mother of a Well-Regulated Family).

——*Republican and Journal*, Springfield, Massachusetts
March 14-15, 1835

Today the criticism and verbal denunciations that greeted the ideal that women could profit from education and contribute to society seem fantastic. Yet they serve to illustrate the difficulty of change.

A program of action for improvement of reporting procedures should involve many people. Whether the work goes on with the faculty, parents, or children at different stages, or with combined groups, this should be true. Unless the program of change represents the work and thought of many, it becomes an imposed program, and therefore is more likely to encounter resistance. With this central criterion in mind, then, a school staff might use the following steps as a general guide if improvement of their reporting procedures is a current problem:

1. *Within the staff, work toward agreement on the district philosophy and the place of district reporting procedures within it.* This is an important preliminary to any district-wide discussion of reporting. The professional staff should agree on the educational framework that will serve as the basis for any reporting change. Unless this step is taken, the school personnel may find that later some staff members may take exception to the plans of their peers in public contacts, and that the dissensions will serve to undermine the confidence of the public in the professional ability of the educators. Study and discussion of philosophy will help the teaching staff to interpret their beliefs and attitudes effectively in future discussions with lay groups.

2. *As early as possible, and long before decisions on change*

245

are made, include lay representatives in study groups. Parents who study professional literature with teachers and discuss its implications in planning for their children often become the strongest supporters the schools have. Participation in such groups often serves also to impress parents with the high professional calibre of the teacher group.

3. *Study the existing system in relation to the district educational philosophy.* If, for example, the teachers agree that a child is entitled to learn at the pace best for him without either the threat of failure or unrealistic approbation, then they will wish to evaluate the form or method used in terms of this statement. Or, if they feel that the children and parents should take part in educational planning, this factor would be one evaluated.

4. *Study developments in other school districts.* Many school districts have developed forms for individual progress evaluation, and handbooks for conference programs. Schools that are launching studies can profit greatly from the experience of others and avoid duplication of effort by asking for forms and materials. The form that follows this listing is one that can be used by a district that has reached this step. The questions, developed by a study group, served to guide teachers in their evaluation of sample forms.

5. *Prepare a* tentative *plan.*

6. *Introduce the plan.* Various methods of communicating should be used, including grade-level meetings, school gatherings, bulletins, informal discussions, and so on. Communication cannot be overworked. Difficulties usually arise from lack of communication rather than too much.

7. *Try out the plan.* Refinements probably will occur as school personnel and parents work with it.

8. KEEP EVERYONE INFORMED AND PARTICIPATING CONTINUOUSLY. This is particularly important. The American population is mobile, and a school district may find little resemblance between the parent group of five years ago and that of the present day. The same is true of the teacher group. If the school personnel and the parents work out a plan that is educationally sound and acceptable to the majority, review and study should be a part of that plan. Such review and study should be scheduled frequently and regularly.

9. *Improve child study procedures.* In a sense, the better the knowledge of children, the better the reporting procedures. The teacher who knows her children thoroughly derives more from her parent contacts than the one who knows them superficially, and the former is able to help parents and children more.

REPORT CARD EVALUATION

Please use the squares provided on this page to evaluate the sample report cards located in the Teachers Room. Find the *number* of the first card you evaluate on the left side of the squares. Write in U (upper grades), M (middle grades) or P (primary) beside this number to denote the grade level for which this card is intended. *Beside* this number write in either Y (yes) or N (no) across horizontally as you answer each of the lettered questions below in relation to this particular card. Use the top 0 line for a sample of how your valuation should be made. Please check over as many cards as you can and turn this sheet in to your principal.

a. Are the symbols clear and would they mean the same to teacher, parent, and child?
b. Do the marks indicate progress in relation to the child's own ability?
c. Does the report fit the material that is being taught at the level for which it is designed?
d. Is the organization clear and not too involved?
e. Is there a sufficient number of symbols to clarify, but not so many as to confuse?
f. Does the report cover all the important phases of child growth?
g. Does it provide for communication from home to school as well as from school to home?
h. Is the philosophy of the school expressed on the card?
i. Is the card appropriate for use in conjunction with parent conferences?

Comments:

	a	b	c	d	e	f	g	h	i
0-U	Y	Y	N	Y	Y	N	N	Y	N
1-M	Y	Y	Y	Y	Y	Y	N	N	Y
2-M	Y	N	N	Y	N	N	N	N	Y
3-M	Y	Y	Y	Y	Y	Y	N	N	Y
4-M	Y	N	Y	Y	N	Y	N	Y	Y
5-M	Y	Y	Y	Y	Y	Y	N	N	Y
6-M	Y	Y	Y	Y	Y	Y	N	Y	Y
7-									
8-M	Y	Y	Y	N	Y	Y	N	Y	Y
9-									
10-M	Y	N	Y	Y	Y	Y	Y	Y	Y
11-M	Y	N	N	Y	N	N	Y	Y	N
12-M	Y	Y	Y	N	Y	Y	N	Y	Y
13-									
14-M	Y	Y	Y	Y	Y	Y	Y	Y	Y
15-M	Y	N	N	Y	N	N	N	N	N
16-									
17-									

INDIVIDUAL CONFERENCES

In the preceding section, certain trends in home reporting were noted, and the reasons for the changes were given. After searching for methods of reporting that will meet modern criteria, many educators have turned to the individual conference as the answer. The conference provides a means for utilizing two- and three-way communication. It provides a way of evaluating child growth without threat to the individual, and permits truly individualized reporting. The verbal communication is centered upon one child, and eliminates, therefore, the element of comparison, which the written report presents even when geared to the child's own ability.

ADVANTAGES

The individual conference is the only means through which the teacher may report satisfactorily on all phases of child growth—intellectual, physical, social, and emotional. On the report form, one may find items devoted to these categories, but meaningful discussion of a child's growth in ability to work with others, or of his progress in learning to read, is limited at best when it is done on a small space within a report card. Certain areas of growth may need a great deal of interpretation at given times.

Through the conference the teacher and parent may center their attention upon one person—the child. The result usually is an increased sensitivity of both adults to the individual and his needs. Because the conference is devoted to the individual, the adults are able to consider reasonable and realistic planning in terms of his own ability. The planning is done for the child's best growth, with the emphasis governed by his needs. For example, in addition to discussing the children's academic progress, the teacher may spend additional time exploring the reasons for Charles's dependency, or Susan's dislike for games, or how the parent may help Tim develop further his skills and interest in geology.

Personal contact with the parent enables the teacher to learn about the child. The parent may contribute information that explains a great deal about a child's interests, his attitudes toward others and himself, and parental feelings toward him. Parents may

248

have suggestions to make to teachers that prevent or alleviate difficulties for the child. Nearly always they help the teacher greatly in understanding the child and his behavior.

The individual conference increases adult understanding of the child.

Through understanding the child's environment, the teacher understands him better. It makes a difference whether a child has his own room and plenty of toys and books, or whether he shares a room with three others and has no toys. It makes a difference, too, when a child's father works nights, or when the child frequently prepares his own meals, or when he stays up late to watch certain programs. One child may be proud of his home and be encouraged to bring his friends to play, while another may live in an opposite situation. Teachers learn much through the information that parents give regarding schedules, diet beliefs, physical living arrangements, and group relationships within the family. The learnings that the teacher gains concerning the child's cultural environment are tremendously important to her in planning for him.

249

Person-to-person communication facilitates the interpretation of the school program. Group conferences are held in many schools for this purpose, but often questions are not completely answered, or questions arise relative to the program of one child. When parents can ask questions and have them answered by the professional educator, understanding and cooperation between the home and school are increased.

Another advantage in parent-teacher conferences is that of benefit to the child himself. With the most important adults in his life working together for him, adjustment problems should decrease. The good relationships that come out of a successful parent-teacher conference promote a sense of well-being in the child. All is right in his world when friendly home-school relationships exist.

In a face-to-face situation, the teacher and parent are able to communicate accurately, and to clarify understandings. All educators know the multiplicity of interpretations given to such terms and expressions as "socially immature," "social studies," "average," "A," and "satisfactory growth for this child." Language that is understandable to the parent is sought in all forms of home reporting, but the problem of varied backgrounds and differing interpretations makes the search difficult. If the parent and teacher talk together, any questions or problems of meaning may be resolved as they arise.

Finally, the conference enables the teacher to know the child as a person and to appreciate him. She has studied his records thoroughly in preparation for the conference, has probably collected materials concerning him and his work for a period of time, and has learned much in the conference about him in his out-of-school life. In the words of one teacher:

> I didn't look forward much to parent conferences. To me they spelled work. I'd been accustomed to report cards, and couldn't see the value in talking with all of the parents. Now that we have finished them, I can say that I was right—it was work, but I didn't count the benefits. Teaching has been much easier ever since. I feel that I know my children, and it's made a tremendous difference in my relationships with them. I wouldn't trade the conferences for anything, even though we put in long hours.

CRITERIA FOR PLANNING

The parent conference should be planned as part of the total reporting program. If other means of reporting are used, the school staff should plan their conference procedures in such a way that the conferences will serve adequately as a means of informing parents and gaining information from them. For example, the emphasis in a parent conference may be quite different when a report form accompanies the conference. In such a case, the discussion of academic areas may center upon the content of the form and an interpretation of it, with proportionately more time spent on other growth areas in the total time. If the conference is used as a substitute for any written report, more time in interpretation of academic progress may be desirable.

The duplication of reporting procedures—that is, the use of a conference *and* a written form—is undesirable from the standpoint of teacher time and needless overlap of information. When parents are accustomed to written reports, some schools have alternated conferences with the written report, so that the parents may have either one conference and three written reports (or fewer), or two conferences and perhaps two written reports. The transition from written reports to conferences is made most easily at the primary level, with conferences in the middle and upper grades introduced later. When parents have worked with teachers in conferences, they are generally as enthusiastic about them as the educators.

Any development of a conference program should be thoroughly discussed, evaluated, and supported by the professional staff. The understanding and acceptance of administrators and teachers is necessary before successful procedures can be planned. Conferences are time-consuming and demanding, and, unless teachers are thoroughly convinced of their value, they may fail. In some schools, conferences are held by part of the staff at first; these persons then work with others to communicate the gains they have derived, and assist in the professional training for the program.

Parents, too, need help in understanding the conference program and its purposes. The pattern of talking with parents only when the child has had difficulty has existed in many schools in the past,

251

and parents often think of conferences negatively. For this reason, the group conference often has been used in part to prepare parents for the individual conference program, and to orient them to the positive, inclusive nature of the contact.

Interpretation to the children likewise is of importance. Teachers who discuss the purposes of the conferences with their pupils find that the children accept the conferences when they understand that all parents come and that the conference is centered upon their growth and progress. Many teachers have held individual conferences with their pupils prior to the conferences with parents in which the pupils have evaluated their progress, discussed their needs, planned any needed remediation, and planned the materials that might be used in showing their progress to parents. Unless children are included in the planning and evaluation, they may feel anxious about the contact.[5]

The inclusion of the child in the conference itself has been advocated by some writers. This would depend upon knowledge of the child and his family, and might prove undesirable in some cases. The procedure would seem to have more merit with older children than with the primary or middle groups, but with only selective inclusion, questions inevitably would arise. The inclusion of the child would seem most feasible in those conferences confined to verbal reporting of academic progress. Discussions that involve physical, social, or emotional phases of growth may be curtailed by the presence of the child, or may actually be damaging to him.

TRAINING PROCEDURES

Professional staff members have employed varied methods in preparing for parent conferences. Usually they have planned a series of in-service meetings designed to improve any skills that they acquired in their teacher training, or to give them some contact with conference methods if they have had no previous training.

The first step in training often is a consideration of criteria for successful conferences. Several resources, the best known and most

[5] Sybil Richardson, "How Do Children Feel About Reports to Parents?" *California Journal of Elementary Education*, XXIV, No. 2, November 1955, pp. 98-111.

widely used of which is probably D'Evelyn's monograph,[6] can be used by teachers for preliminary study and discussion. Summaries of suggestions like the one following are useful to teachers in evaluating their conference techniques:

PARENT CONFERENCES

1. A time and place for the conference should be planned so that the teacher and parent may be unhurried, relaxed, and uninterrupted. Informality and friendliness should keynote the conference.

2. A parent is very closely identified with his child, and therefore cannot be expected to be "objective" about him. A critical approach to a child's problems will probably produce a defensive attitude in the parent. On the other hand, a positive attitude toward the child on the part of the teacher will do much to foster rapport.

3. Since the parent has had much more contact with the child than the teacher has, the contributions of the parent should play a large part in the conference. An accepting, listening teacher can gain much in understanding the child. Statements of the parent should be accepted without obvious emotional reaction. The parent should be encouraged to talk.

4. Discussions of a child's needs should center on factors concerning which a parent can help. Otherwise a discussion can deteriorate into a complaint session, and feelings of frustration may develop.

5. Planning for the child should take place on a cooperative basis. We need to assume at least as much intelligence, maturity, and interest on the part of other adults as we possess.

6. Accept statements of the parent. Help clarify the child's needs by asking questions that lead to causes.

7. Avoid argument or advice. Argument destroys a cooperative relationship. Giving advice sets the teacher on a "voice of authority" level, and reduces the possibility of working together. Advice may go wrong, and the teacher may be open to criticism. Advice creates dependence in the parent.

8. Parents should participate in planning for the child. If suggestions are required, alternate ideas may be used, or the parent may be asked what he thinks about possibilities. He may then accept a plan as his own.

9. Establish a feeling of on-going interest in the child and a desire to continue cooperative planning with the parent. Project future conferences at definite times if further discussion is needed.

[6] See the list of suggested reading for this excellent resource and others of value in conference training.

Some training sessions have utilized role-playing in which teachers have briefly presented information about a child, have discussed together the needs to be met, the roles they will assume, how the conference should be conducted, and then have held the "conference," which is followed by evaluation. It is possible to discuss children, to plan as a total group, and then to proceed in a variety of ways. For example, small groups may work independently in conferences about different children, or in small groups in conferences about the same child, or in single demonstrations before a group. The small group conferences are perhaps more acceptable to teachers at first than the demonstration.

After the teachers have studied and discussed criteria for good conferences, and have some understanding of counseling techniques, they may work in mock conference relationships, with one person assuming the role of teacher, another that of parent, and a third (or several) the role of evaluator. A simple listing of evaluation criteria, like the one below, may be planned by the group and utilized to analyze the conference content:

1. Was a positive working relationship established?
2. Was the interaction natural and "easy"?
3. Was the purpose of the conference clarified?
4. Did the teacher and parent plan on a cooperative, equal basis?
5. Did the parent have adequate time to talk?
6. Did the conference deal with items of real importance?
7. Were definite plans made?
8. Did the plans fulfill the purpose?
9. Was further contact planned or implied?

A sample of the type of writeup that teachers might use appears below. The writeup, supplied by a teacher, is considered by the group from the standpoint of child needs, the purpose of the conference, and what approach would be feasible. Then, after the conference has been carried on, the evaluation is made on the nine points above.

Name—Judith C.
C.A.—7-4
Test results—
  Detroit Group Intelligence: C.A. 6-9; M.A. 7-4; I.Q. 109
  Reading Readiness tests—Scott Foresman: High, very high.
Family: Father, business executive in late forties. Mother,

unusually poised, cultured, extremely well dressed, does not work outside the home, lives in upper middle class subdivision. One sister, junior college age.

Mother reports that Judy plays almost entirely with a second-grade girl who lives next door. "Are inseparable." Judy's parents are very proud of her maturity and her unusual capability and dependability in the home. Standards for Judy at home are very high. Mother expects quiet, grown-up behavior. On one occasion when both parents attended P.T.A. they brought Judy, because Mother said "You know how it is when children get an idea." Judy often tells of attending sports events with her sister and the sister's boy friend.

Judy seems very mature for a first grader. She is very attractive and affectionate. She has very good coordination. She is always spotless, seems over-concerned by any loss of clothing or the many fancy pins, scarves, and purses she wears. She was taught the words in the pre-primer which we use before entering first grade, but knew no other words. She seems very happy as long as she can excel but seems very glum if she has difficulty. Judy is very competitive in her attitude toward other children and comments on her improvements on them. Plays with various children at school but frequently will stop playing as soon as she has had her turn. Enjoys keeping score for the boys' games. There are two boys whom she seems to prefer and who appear to enjoy her. On one occasion when she was left with her sister for several days she complained of stomach pains at school. She has done this on three occasions when she complained that other children were getting more opportunities to help than she did. Other children frequently choose her to work with them and she is always chosen for group games. Frequently she organizes them herself. At recess, she often seeks the attention of the teacher on yard duty, the student teacher, or her own teacher.

Another approach to the training of teachers in conference techniques is the use of narrations. Illustrative conferences may be read, with group members taking roles, and then discussion may be directed toward either positive or negative factors within the conference. The following conference illustrates this type, in which a brief description is given of the situation, and the narration follows. This conference is one that was actually held, and then recorded by a teacher.

Conference Subject: Jim, age 6, superior intelligence. Teacher concerned about aggressive behavior, which has involved hitting, kicking, pushing, and punching other children at frequent intervals during the day. The family consists of a widowed mother,

Jim, and the maternal grandparents. Because the mother is her-self a teacher, and had had previous professional contacts with Jim's present teacher, it is possible to have all three adults attend the conference. Jim's teacher suggested this, and his mother urged the grandparents to come.

Conference Participants: Mr. and Mrs. Lewis, grandparents, mother, teacher.

Teacher: (after introductions) I am so glad all of you could come, because I know that you can help me a great deal in working with Jim. He is a very inter-esting, capable fellow, and frankly, I don't feel that I understand him as well as I should. Could you help me out by giving me a picture of him at home?

Mrs. Lewis: What's he been doing?

Teacher: I feel that he's striking out for some reason. He has much difficulty in his social relationships, and many of his contacts with other children involve punches and blows. Because of these contacts, he has trouble in working successfully with the group. I thought that if you could describe him as you know him, it would help me to understand him better.

Mrs. Lewis: Well, frankly I'm surprised. He behaves very well for all of us at home. I can't imagine why he should do such things at school.

Mr. Lewis: If he does do something and gets bawled out, he comes to me for petting. (laughs)

Teacher: He comes to you when the others bawl him out?

Mr. Lewis: (apologetically) Yes—I suppose I shouldn't give him the attention I do at that time. When he comes to me and asks me to read him a story, I guess he's just using me to escape from the others.

Mother: I'll say you shouldn't. He just plays us against each other.

Mr. Lewis: Well, if I didn't do that, he'd have a pretty tough row to hoe. I just feel sorry for him sometimes.

Teacher: You feel that he has a pretty tough row to hoe. What do you mean?

Mrs. Lewis: I know what he means. He means that Jim is try-ing to get along with three adults, and that he takes a lot of bossing. We've talked about that before.

Mother: Well, it's true. There's always someone picking at him. I've thought about moving away and es-tablishing a home of our own so that he wouldn't have so much direction, but truthfully I can't

	afford it. I don't have enough money to get along on, and besides I'm not sure that it would be an advantage. He worships my dad, and I think he looks upon him much as he would a father. I don't think I could play father and mother both to him.
Mrs. Lewis:	When I think about it, I think the time when we have the most trouble with Jim is in the morning.
Teacher:	What happens in the morning?
Mrs. Lewis:	Well, you know that six-year-olds are famous for dawdling. It's a constant struggle to get him ready for school. He gets up at 5:30 or 6, and we battle with him from then on to get him to dress and get ready for school. Most of the time it's a matter of getting him dressed at the last minute, and rushing him out of the house to catch the bus.
Teacher:	What would happen if you waited until shortly before departure time to help him with the dressing?
Mother:	I think we ought to try that. It would save a lot of bickering.
Teacher:	I was interested in your statement that Jim gets up at 5:30 or 6.
Mrs. Lewis:	He wakes up at that time. We wish he wouldn't, but he does.
Teacher:	It means that he's had a pretty long day by the time afternoon comes, doesn't it?
Mrs. Lewis:	I think I'll try to get him to lie down with me to read a story when he comes home from school. He loves to be read to, and maybe he would go to sleep.
Teacher:	That's a wonderful suggestion. Now—I wonder if we've had other suggestions during our talk that might be of help to him.
Mr. Lewis:	Maybe I'd better stop giving him attention when he's been in trouble.
Teacher:	Or—since he's so fond of you, maybe the attention is needed. Are there other times when you could give it?
Mr. Lewis:	Oh, sure. He likes to play games with me, and listen to records.
Mother:	And—I think we need to think about the amount of bossing we do. We ought to keep hands off even if we don't agree.
Teacher:	I think we have some ideas here which will be of much help to Jim. I would like to talk with you again soon so that we may work together as much

257

as possible. Would it be possible for you to visit us
here from time to time? You would be very welcome whenever you could come.

Mr. Lewis: We'd like to. Jane can't because she teaches, but
we can get away.

Mrs. Lewis: Can we come? I'd like to very much.

Prepared scripts may also be used to illustrate good and poor
conference techniques. This approach might be termed the "before
and after" approach. A conference that demonstrates poor techniques may be read and analyzed by the group. Then a conference
that covers the same topic and employs largely the same terminology
may be read to illustrate improved conference procedures. The
group may follow the second presentation with further analysis and
suggestions. The two conferences that follow illustrate this technique:

Conference Subject: Jerry, grade 2, C.A. 7-1, I.Q. 93
Mother calls, wants conference regarding Jerry—feels he's not
learning to read.

Conference:

Teacher: (abrupt) So you feel Jerry isn't learning to read?

Mother: I certainly do! When I was his age, I read anything,
independently. He can't read the simplest material.
I have to help him with every other word. I've
spent hours struggling with him!

Teacher: I haven't felt that he's done so badly. He has shown
quite a good deal of progress since the first of the
year.

Mother: Maybe our ideas of progress are different. I have the
feeling that if he had some work with phonics, he
might be able to figure out words better. I've given
him help, but it's hard.

Teacher: Phonics aren't the panacea that some parents think.
Children need a reading vocabulary of some sort before phonetic aids can be used successfully.

Mother: You mean that I shouldn't be helping Jerry with
phonetics?

Teacher: It seems to me that it would be better to wait until
he's had more experience with reading. Then reading
might be more fun for both of you and less source of
conflict. If we start out with phonics and make reading a battleground, serious problems may result. I'd
like to have you visit school and see how we work

with the children. You could see Jerry in his group then, too.

Mother: That would be nice. I didn't know we could do that.

Teacher: (rather pompous) We're glad to have you at any time.

Analysis by the group:

The teacher started negatively.	She talked too much.
She argued with the mother.	She did establish an on-going
She used "pedaguese."	relationship.
	They were not co-equals.

Second Conference:

Teacher: I'm very glad you came to see me, Mrs. Smith. I feel that Jerry is a very interesting, likeable child, and that you can be very helpful to me in working with him. You wanted to talk with me about his reading?

Mother: Well, yes I did. When I was his age, I read anything, independently. He can't read the simplest material. I have to help him with every other word. I've spent hours struggling with him.

Teacher: Helping him has been a struggle to you?

Mother: Yes, it has! It seems that every time we sit down to read a fight develops.

Teacher: How does Jerry react?

Mother: He enjoyed reading at first, but now he groans when I mention it. Maybe it does more harm than good.

Teacher: Why do you say that?

Mother: Well, maybe I'm making him hate reading instead of helping him improve in it. I don't use the right methods probably. But what can I do?

Teacher: What methods have you used?

Mother: I've tried to get him to sound out words. He doesn't seem to know how. I have the feeling that if he had some work with phonics, he might be able to figure out words better. But I don't know if I'm doing it right. I'm not sure that what I am doing is the thing to do.

Teacher: Would it help you to visit school and see how we work with the children in reading? You could see Jerry in his group then, too.

Mother: That would be nice. I didn't know we could do that.

Teacher: Well, yes, as a matter of fact, since you live near here, could you come several times to visit the reading groups? I'll get the principal to come in so that we can talk for a few minutes afterwards and plan things we both might do to help Jerry. I think we can work together and do a lot for him.

259

Group comments:
    That was a lot better.
    Might the mother not resent so many questions?
    The teacher got the mother to think.
    They would be working together.
    The teacher is smart to make the approach to reading gradual. It's
        a complicated field.

Commercial materials, and materials prepared by districts as audio-visual aids, also play an important part in conference training. For example, districts have prepared colored slides to accompany narrations that take the teacher through the conference program from initial preparation to the final handshake. Tape recordings have been used effectively to illustrate good techniques. Films like *The Counseling Interview*,[7] while concerned with a secondary school counseling situation, have many learnings applicable to the teacher-parent relationship.

Discussions of questions that arise in parent conferences also are of value, regardless of the experience of the teacher. Teachers may compile questions like those listed below, and discuss them in group meetings. Not only will responses be suggested, but also teachers will tend to re-evaluate their beliefs and procedures.

    Why don't you give John homework? His cousin is a sixth-grader too, and he always has homework.
    Why don't you teach the alphabet?
    When do the children learn real writing?
    Where does Jim stand in relation to the others in the class?
    What do you mean by "socially immature"?
    What is my child's I.Q. score?
    Why doesn't Susan do better, if you say she can?
    Shouldn't Jack be a better reader than he is? (slow learner)
    Why isn't Jane learning to read?

Teachers may also discuss with profit questions that perplex them. Some questions that frequently arise are these:

    How do we tell parents about a child's ability?
    How can we tell parents that a child has an emotional problem?
    How can we get parents to avoid teaching the three *R*'s wrong at home?

[7] See Appendix *A* for list of films.

How can we keep parents from telling secrets they shouldn't tell, or gossiping about others?

Teachers need help also in writing conference summaries. Questions on when to write the summary, how much to write, the wording of content, and other items need consideration. In general, the summary should be brief, should be written immediately after the conference, should include the main content of the conference, and should reflect the attitudes and feelings of the parent. If recommendations are made by either party, the recommendations should be noted so that they may be known to future teachers of the child.

CONFERENCE SCHEDULES

In planning conferences, the primary concern of the administrator should be the teacher's time. Conferences should be planned in such a way that teachers are able to conduct them without undue fatigue. Otherwise, the conference period can be detrimental to both teachers and children.

Some districts close school during conference periods. In others minimum days are scheduled for a period of two weeks. Others hire substitute teachers to relieve teachers for conferences. In the opinion of the writers, the minimum-day schedule is the most desirable arrangement. Teachers are able to work with their children themselves, the daily program can go on without interruption, and the teachers are not required to crowd many conferences into a short period of time.

Regardless of the administrative arrangement used, the important need is that the bulk of the conference time fit into the teacher's work day. If teachers are expected to conduct conferences after working hours, an unfair burden is imposed upon them, and they may lose their enthusiasm for an activity that they actually feel is educationally desirable.

In order to give teachers time to prepare for conferences and to conduct them, administrators should avoid other demands on their time. In-service meetings or parent-education activities should be eliminated during conference periods. Any other district professional activities should be postponed until the end of the conference sessions.

Administrative personnel should plan with the teachers so that they may have privacy during their conferences. In schools on single sessions, this is not a problem. In schools on half-sessions, however, teachers need to plan in advance to use offices, benches outdoors (weather permitting), or even the seating in automobiles. Ideally, teachers should have a comfortable place indoors in which they could serve a cup of coffee if they desire.

The majority of conferences should be scheduled at school rather than in homes. If teachers are expected to go to homes, a great deal of time is consumed, and the teachers are subjected to travel expense. The conference in the home should be arranged only when the parent cannot come to school, when it is desirable to talk with both parents, when parents both work during the day, or when the teacher wishes to go to the home for a special reason. Many things may be learned from a home visit, but teachers need smaller groups and fewer other demands upon them before universal visiting is required.

Teachers need to discuss arrangements regarding the number of conferences scheduled during a given day, and time arrangements. They will need to think of the kind of conference they may anticipate. They may wish to schedule the parents of well-adjusted children first, if they are new at conferences, to get the "feel" of working with individual parents. They will need to schedule the conferences at intervals that are long enough to permit an unhurried talk and the writing of a brief summary before the next appointment.

CONFERENCE GUIDES

The organization of a successful conference program depends in large measure upon the forms and guides that are developed for teacher use. With adequate guides and with orientation to their proper use, teachers are able to organize their preparation and conduct of conferences satisfactorily. The necessary forms include invitation and orientation forms for parents, child study and conference summary sheets, appointment sheets, and reminders to parents. Simplicity, flexibility, and brevity are desirable in these forms. Sample forms from several districts are shown here.

INVITATION AND ORIENTATION[8]

Downey Elementary School District
Downey School

Dear Parents:

During the first two weeks of February, teachers will be holding individual conferences with the parents of each pupil in each class. Many of you have been awaiting this opportunity to come to school to talk about your child's progress during the first half of this school year. The teachers, too, have been anticipating a chance to get better acquainted with you and are looking forward to the conference as a means of exchanging helpful information.

In order that the teachers may have more time for conferences, we are having a minimum school day. This means that the primary grades (Grades one, two and three) will be dismissed at 1:30 P.M., instead of 1:45 P.M. The fourth, fifth, and sixth grade classes will be dismissed at 1:50 P.M. with the noon hour shortened to one half hour. Kindergarten and second grade morning and afternoon schedules will be the same as at present. These plans may necessitate some change in the home schedules due to the fact that the pupils will be home much earlier than usual, particularly in the upper grades.

You will receive an appointment blank from your child's teacher on which the date and time for your conference will be stated. We know that you will make every effort to attend.

Our past experience has made us feel individual parent conferences are the most helpful means of reporting your child's progress. You will also receive a written report at this conference.

Cordially yours,

Principal

HEB:bs

⊏⊟

OFFICE OF THE SUPERINTENDENT[9]

Bellflower Unified Schools

Dear Parent:

At mid-year the Bellflower Schools have parent conferences in place of report cards in grades 1 through 6. The purpose of this

[8] Permission to use the above form has been granted by the Downey Elementary School District, Downey, California.
[9] Permission to use the above form has been granted by the Bellflower Unified Schools, Bellflower, California.

263

plan is to provide additional opportunity for the parent and teacher to work together in the interest of the child.

We would like to have you come for a conference on_____
day

_____. Please go to _____
date   from   to
when you arrive at school.

If this time is not convenient, please suggest another time when you could come. If, for example, you have no one to care for your younger children at this time, we will work out a change. If you are working, we could probably see you on your day off or on the evening which will be scheduled for a few parents.

Parent-teacher conferences are built around what parents and teachers want to learn from each other. Following are some ideas to help you plan toward your conference.

Parents may like to ask teachers:
1. It is important to learn about a child's successes. What does he like best in school?
2. The child should be encouraged to do the best he can. Is his school work as good as it ought to be for him?
3. Successful and happy school experiences are possible only when teacher-child relationships are good. How does he seem to get along with you?
4. A playground is one of the best places to see how children are accepted by other children. How does my youngster get along on the playground?
5. Little shoulders often carry big burdens. Does my child seem to be worrying about anything at school?
6. Children often worry when they are very different from other children. Does my child have about the same ups and downs as the other children in the class?

Teachers may like to ask parents:
1. Health is an important factor in a child's school life. Do you have any health information which might give us a better understanding of your child's school activities?
2. A child's friends are an important part of his life. With what children does he play in the neighborhood?
3. Doing interesting things out of school helps the child in school. What does he like to do at home, by himself and with the family?
4. The school is concerned with the child's happiness. What does he seem to think about his class and school in general?
5. We always welcome suggestions from parents. What general ideas do you have for ways the school can help your child?

We hope your conference will prove valuable to you. We shall be interested in your reaction to it.

Very truly yours,

_____ Teacher

_____ Principal

W. Norman Wampler, Superintendent

. . . .

Tear off and return bottom section.

Check one:

_____I shall come for conference at the time suggested.

_____I could come for a conference on _____,

at_____ or _____ at _____.
(hour)   (date)   (hour)
(Indicate two possibilities, please.)

_____
(Parent's signature)

☞

EAST WHITTIER CITY SCHOOL DISTRICT[10]

Dear Parents:

For many years the East Whittier School District has used the Parent Conference as a method of reporting to parents. We consider these conferences important to the total educative program of elementary school children. The additional time and energy spent by the classroom teachers in planning and organizing for the conferences is well justified, since parents and teachers working together can develop better methods of assuring growth for each individual child.

Our first Conference Period for this year will be held on Monday and Tuesday, November 9th and 10th, previous to the Armistice Day holiday on November 11th. Children will not attend school on these days in order to allow time for teachers and parents to hold their conferences.

It would be most helpful if, before your conference, you

[10] Permission to use the above form has been granted by the East Whittier City School District, Whittier, California.

would think through questions that you may have concerning the child and his work at school. Perhaps it might be well if you jotted down a few notes to bring with you. The teachers will be happy to explain and clarify any details in which you might be particularly interested.

Most of the conferences can be covered in two days. When necessary, arrangements will be made by the teachers for additional appointments. The time reserved for your conference is given below. We will appreciate your keeping this appointment promptly.

Sincerely,

CHARLES T. SAMUELS
Superintendent

· ·

APPOINTMENT BLANK

Dear _____:

You have been scheduled for a conference concerning_____'s

school work on _____, _____, _____.
                     Day of Week   Date   Time

· ·

PARENT'S REPLY

Please check *one* of the following and return to teacher.

_____I will come to school at the stated time.

_____I cannot come at the time scheduled. Will you please arrange another appointment?
_____It will be impossible for me to come to the school for a conference because

_____

_____

_____
Parent's Signature

CHILD STUDY AND CONFERENCE SUMMARY SHEET

West Covina School District[11]
Parent Conference Summary

NAME OF CHILD _____ DATE _____

PERSONS PRESENT _____

PLACE _____

CONFERENCE   SUMMARY   AND   RECOMMENDATIONS:

CHILD NEEDS

CHILD INTERESTS

ILLUSTRATIVE MATERIALS USED

TEACHER PLANS

PARENT PLANS

PARENT ATTITUDES

Signature _____

BELLFLOWER UNIFIED SCHOOL DISTRICT[12]

Record of Parent-Teacher Conference

Pupil's Name _____   _____   _____
                                          Grade   Date

Areas discussed and most immediate needs determined:

Teacher's immediate plans or   Parent's immediate plans or
  suggestions   suggestions

Parent's attitudes (toward conference, child, school)

                              _____
                              Teacher's signature

[11] Permission to use the above form has been granted by the West Covina School District, West Covina, California.

[12] Permission to use the above form has been granted by the Bellflower Unified School District, Bellflower, California.

267

APPOINTMENT SHEET FOR PARENT CONFERENCES

Week of _____

Date

DAY	HOUR	SCHEDULED APPOINTMENTS	VERIFIED BY PARENT
MONDAY			
TUESDAY			
WEDNESDAY			
THURSDAY			
FRIDAY			

Dear Mrs. _____:

This note is to remind you that we have an appointment on

day	date	from	to

to discuss _____'s work and needs.

I am looking forward to this opportunity.

Cordially yours,

_____

Teacher

summary

Home-school contacts have become important in education with the realization of the value of parent contributions to educational planning. School personnel must know parents before they can fully or adequately know their children. Parents and teachers can work together for the understanding of children and understanding of the school program.

Schools have worked to develop varied ways to facilitate home-school communication. Illustrated booklets about children and school activities, notes to the home about school learnings, and information disseminated through newspapers, radio, and television have been used. Teachers have planned together for effective meetings in which parents and children are active participants. Panels, observations, classroom participation, participation in children's learnings, book exchanges, role playing, children's demonstrations, and other activities have been used to good advantage.

Because of the need for two-way communication and complete reporting, changes have been made in home reporting procedures. Written reports have become more inclusive and individualized, and have been supplemented or supplanted in many places by individual conferences.

269

Conferences have the advantages of better communication, complete reporting and interpretation, parental contribution to planning, and increased understanding of the child.

Planning for effective conferences demands thorough understanding by teachers, parents, and children. Studies of criteria for successful conferences, evaluation procedures, experiences in conference techniques, discussions of conference content, the writing of summaries, planning of schedules, and effective guides, all are part of the preparation for conferences by teachers.

CHARACTERISTICS OF AN EFFECTIVE GUIDANCE PROGRAM

The guidance program in the public schools exists for one purpose—to promote the optimal adjustment of all pupils and thereby facilitate the teaching process. The development of forms, use of tests, analysis of learning data for public relations programs, parent study groups, in-service activities of teachers, and other concomitants are auxiliary and subservient to this central purpose. If the program is successful, evidence will appear in several ways.

Children who live in a guidance-centered atmosphere are free to be children. They grow and develop at the rates best for them, and are allowed to learn freely, even from mistakes. They relate to their teacher as a guide who encourages them in the process of learning new things. If they have problems, they are given assistance by the teacher and by any necessary specialists. All possible skills are employed to help all of the children to grow satisfactorily. Children who live in an atmosphere that is guidance-centered live in an environment of sound mental health. Regardless of age, children in such an environment like school, enjoy their associations, and derive satisfactions from their learnings.

Teachers who are part of a guidance-centered environment have learned much about children and their growth patterns and needs. They understand the significance of behavior; they look at behavior in terms of causes and symptoms. They are constantly in the process of learning new things to help them guide children skillfully.

Teachers who accept child behavior listen to their children and watch what they are doing so that they may develop further understandings that will help them teach successfully. The curriculum is geared as far as possible to the potential of each individual child. The children are given time to learn. Teachers recognize that variations exist in children in all growth areas, and are willing to accept emotional retardation as well as slow learning ability or shortness or obesity.

The uniqueness of the individual is valued in the classroom of the guidance-minded teacher. Uniqueness and individuality make necessary her professional training and skill. She is aware of the continuity of growth as an individualized process, which gives her the ability to accept and be positive about differences. For the individual, she fosters a classroom climate conducive to sound mental health and therefore to creativity.

In a guidance-centered school, the teachers are trained in techniques of classroom child study and group study. They use all of the materials within the scope of their training to understand children. They have learned and are learning further skills to identify serious needs and to refer them for help.

Continued in-service study and improvement is a characteristic of the guidance-minded staff. They utilize the talents and abilities of all staff members in improving their effectiveness. For example, a teacher who has employed sociodrama with success may conduct in-service sessions in which she teaches others through discussions and taped demonstrations. Or—a group of teachers may work together informally to evaluate their recording of child behavior. Active participation causes the teachers to identify with the program and take pride in its progress.

Within the diverse activities of the group, a thread of planned coordination exists. The person or persons responsible for coordinating the guidance activities work for wide participation. Definite and comprehensive plans are made for improvement in guidance activities. The efforts of all are unified and centered upon the best total growth of children, so that the program becomes the concern of all.

272

Special personnel in guidance possess the proper qualifications to serve as resources to the staff in relation to both individual and group needs. They work on both a remedial and preventive basis, with the realization that their contributions should be geared to contacting and educating many people rather than a few. Preventive group work therefore is an important concern to them, and training others in the proper use of guidance methods and materials is a vital aspect of their work.

In the guidance-centered school, home-school contacts are made early. They remain constant and continuous, with a unifying of efforts for the benefit of the child. Teachers and parents work closely together, and understand their relationships to the school guidance resources. Parents and teachers communicate freely to inform those working with the child of his needs.

If the guidance program is successful, staff morale is high. The staff's participation in planning guidance activities should bring about an in-service program based upon their needs and requests. The clarification of duties and responsibilities of all personnel should promote understanding. With all persons participating in some way, the program belongs to all. The increased understanding and pacing of teaching to the needs of children should lead inevitably to professional satisfaction in a job well done. If the staff is active in guidance, all will realize that evaluation of results will be done on a long-range basis. The program may have a slow growth pattern, and at times may develop sporadically. The staff needs to examine results on the basis of long-term improvements.

The staff of the guidance-centered school maintains interest in a continued study of guidance. Teachers and others are involved in the development of guidance materials. They search constantly for improvements in their activities and for additional resources at school and in the community that will improve existing facilities.

The successful guidance program is recognized as a continuing and worthy service to all persons in the community. Teachers and school patrons realize that any function that contributes directly or indirectly to the adjustment of future citizens is to be valued highly. They are aware of the many ways in which guidance workers make their contributions, and they endorse the existence of organized guidance activities at the elementary school level. Because the community recognizes the value of the guidance program, support is given for adequate professional service within the school environment.

Follow-up studies are planned methodically in a successful guidance program. All school personnel work together to insure optimum and continuous adjustment for the children. Assessment of the adjustment at higher grade levels serves as a gauge and guide for planning future guidance activities in the elementary school.

summary

The effective guidance program can be identified in several ways. The children work in an atmosphere conducive to satisfactory learning and living. The teachers are professionally oriented to their proper function as guides to the learning experience. They utilize all of their professional skills and the skills of special resources in their study and understanding of children's needs. Their attitudes toward children and their professional contributions are constructive, and their interest in improving their skills is continuous.

Special personnel work closely with the staff and with the community to improve the total program. The program is one in which all work together to improve their skills and to help others.

274

EVALUATION OF
GUIDANCE SERVICES
IN ELEMENTARY SCHOOLS

Evaluation is an area of education that has expanded greatly in terms of definition during the past decade. Formerly it was thought of principally in relation to objective devices, or tests that could be applied to the areas to be measured. More recently it has become more than testing or measuring and has been extended to include many methods, many persons, and many aspects of the educational program. Wrightstone, a recognized authority in evaluation, indicates its changing scope in his definition:

> Evaluation is a relatively new technical term, introduced to designate a more comprehensive concept of measurement than is implied in conventional tests and examinations. Distinction may be made between measurement and evaluation by indicating that the emphasis in measurement is upon single aspects of subject matter achievement or specific skills and abilities, but that the emphasis in evaluation is upon broad personality changes and major objectives of an educational program. These include not only subject matter achievement but also attitudes, interests, ideals, ways of thinking, work habits, and personal and social adaptability.[1]

[1] J. Wayne Wrightstone, "Evaluation," *Encyclopedia of Educational Research* (New York: The Macmillan Company, 1950), p. 403.

Evaluation conceived as broad and inclusive of more than academic achievement is important in guidance, since guidance as an integral part of the educational program is concerned with the total child.

PURPOSES OF EVALUATION

The central purpose of any evaluation within the educational system is the improvement of the program. In other words, the school staff is concerned not only with needs within the program, but also with methods and means for improvements that should be made. The evaluative process then becomes a positive force enabling all personnel to work toward better methods, materials, and procedures in the business of educating children.

Improvements in guidance through evaluation involve all personnel, since all have some contributions to make to the guidance program. As they participate in the planning of improvements, their own procedures likewise should improve. Improvements in a program involve more than administrative changes or the addition of supplies. If needs are carefully and completely considered by many persons, changes also occur in attitudes and beliefs. Improvement of the program, then, involves also growth in stature educationally and psychologically for the planners.

Evaluation in guidance that involves not only school personnel but also parents may be used to clarify the purposes of the guidance program to the community. Parents who participate in studies of relative costs of preventive and remedial guidance programs, for example, become strong supporters of the school guidance program in board meetings. Parents who study and understand the psychological bases for changes in home reporting procedures rebel against horse-and-buggy methods of evaluating pupil progress.

Evaluation is a constructive, dynamic process that has as its purpose not only examination of procedures but also the planning of better programs, improved understandings, and increased support by the participants.

PROCEDURES

Evaluation should be based upon definite objectives or goals. Criteria should be developed cooperatively within the school or

276

system. The process should be long-range and continuous rather than a single occurrence.

The planning of evaluation procedures is an in-service experience for the participants, and should involve them from the beginning. "Experts" or consultants have a definite contribution to make, but they should be brought in to assist as the need arises instead of entering the system to inform educators of what they should or should not do. Unless local personnel define needs, understand their needs, and plan for improvements, changes will not be understood or advocated by those who will live with them.

Evaluation methods should be flexible, subject to change with needs. In some instances questionnaires may be used; in others committee discussions may be best. The method should be adapted to the problem and to the stage of progress. Since participation should be voluntary, changing participation should be part of the flexibility.

Many means of evaluation should be utilized to insure completeness. The methods and materials chosen depend upon their appropriateness in the situation being evaluated. Check lists are useful, but may prove to be only starting points in the evaluation process. Schools may find that they want to make use of observations, sociometry, individual case study data, interviews, attitude surveys, tape recordings, guidance materials from other districts, and so on.

The scope of the evaluation process should be planned carefully. Aspects of the program, such as report cards or cumulative records, may be evaluated during certain periods. At other times, the district may look at personnel needs or physical facilities. The person within the district who is in charge of the guidance program can work with other personnel to insure comprehensive evaluation on a planned basis.

Some procedures that have been used in evaluating guidance programs are listed here to suggest possibilities for evaluation in this field:

1. Committees of guidance, supervisory, and administrative personnel define purposes of the guidance program and discuss the effectiveness with which the purposes are being met. Pupils and parents are involved in some cases.

2. Interviewing of administrators by the guidance person

to determine needs in guidance and the effectiveness of the program.

3. Interviewing children to determine their conception of the guidance program.

4. Follow-up studies of children.

5. Evaluation through meetings with county and state consultants.

6. Analysis of follow-up reports on children who have had special study.

7. Analysis of changes in teachers' reasons for asking for special studies.

Two additional illustrations require more detail. In the first, a teacher acquired a newly formed class group of mentally retarded children. She found that the children needed much help in learning to work together. She described their behavior on the playground, in the lavatories, at rest time and in other situations, and then formulated plans for helping them. Her evaluation consisted of looking at the various situations described, and making periodic assessments of progress and further needs. A situation like bus behavior (hit, yelled, pounded on door) was approached through group planning in which the children decided that they wanted people to like them, and that if they walked from the bus to the classroom everyone would feel that they were "big." [2]

A second illustration might be that of teachers in study groups deciding that they wish to evaluate a given area of group relationships, such as discipline. They may formulate guide questions for their own use, such as these:

Is there evidence of self-discipline?

Is there evidence of self-direction by the pupils while at work?

Do the children take responsibility for keeping the room in order?

Do they assume responsibility for their behavior?

The following guidelines to effective evaluation, adapted from Michaelis, are of assistance in planning procedures:

1. Should be based upon a cooperatively developed point of view.

[2] Reported by Josephine Rightmire, Special Training Teacher, Culver City, California.

278

2. Should be carried on as an integral part of instruction.

3. Must be carried on as a continuous process.

4. Should be carried on as a cooperative process—teachers, children, parents, supervisors, administrators.

5. Must be done in terms of the purposes of the program—all of them.

6. Must be done in a variety of situations.

7. A variety of devices and procedures should be used in the evaluation program.

8. Self-evaluation by children should be provided in many situations, and make use of many devices.

9. Evaluative evidence must be organized and summarized in a manner that facilitates interpretation.

10. Evaluative evidence must be interpreted in terms of the child's level of development.

11. Evaluative evidence should be put to use.[3]

GENERAL EVALUATIVE FORMS

Much of the preceding discussion has been based upon the need for flexibility and specific purpose in the evaluative process. The general type of evaluation has merit, too, in making preliminary or periodic examination of the total program. The two forms that follow are intended as general guides relating to the guidance program in the elementary school.

[3] Adapted from William Michaelis, *Social Studies for Children in a Democracy* (New York: Prentice-Hall, Inc., 1950), p. 374.

A SCALE FOR EVALUATING GUIDANCE IN ELEMENTARY SCHOOLS[4]

Adapted from a scale prepared by Inga C. McDaniel
formerly Director of Guidance
San Bernardino County Schools

Three-point rating on ten items:

1	2	3
Inadequate.	Meeting essentials (minimum adequacy).	Excellent or optimal guidance resources.

I. Understanding needs of students

1	2	3
Little attention to children as individuals. Traditional assignments to grades. Traditional classroom environment.	Teachers study children and modify education program to meet needs of children (meeting individual differences). Good classroom climate.	Teachers participate in on-going program of child study and also utilize findings of specialists in case study techniques; emphasis on individuals; mental health needs considered essential; optimal classroom environment; understanding developmental tasks and behavior patterns in children.

II. Records and student data

1	2	3
Teachers keep registers, attendance records, health records, and achievement lists.	Comprehensive cumulative records are kept and used. (Including health, psychological, socio-economics, growth in skills, knowledge and attitudes, special recommendations.)	In addition to cumulative records, teachers make anecdotal records, sociograms, and keep such helpful material as folders of children's work, autobiographies, self-appraisal reports, and parents' notes.

[4] Permission to use the above material has been granted by Inga C. McDaniel, San Bernardino, California.

280

III. Evaluation and testing program

1	2	3
Some testing at intervals during elementary years (e.g. reading tests and occasional mental tests). Results used to measure achievement.	Skills test each term for diagnostic use; findings carefully analyzed; mental tests spaced regularly throughout elementary grades; concepts of mental ages used, individual testing used when needed.	Evaluation concerned with changes in pupils; uses of student self-appraisal; testing an integral part of total program; testing program flexible; evaluation based on curricular and behavior objectives; much individual study.

IV. Articulation with preceding and subsequent levels

1	2	3
Requirement of proof of birth for entering kindergarten students; sending on to junior high required lists or report cards.	Including in cumulative folder health record of pre-school illnesses and notations from birth certificates; sending to junior high cumulative records and test scores; meetings with mothers of incoming kindergarten children.	Including in cumulative materials data from well-baby clinics and pre-school examinations, pre-school home visitation, orientation for mothers of kindergarten with regular meetings; preparation for first grade program; orientation to junior high or senior high to include parents as well as students; ample data regarding each student sent to junior high or senior high; meetings with junior high staff or senior high personnel.

V. Working with children with special needs

1	2	3
Teacher finds children with special needs through test results and observation; plans classroom work according to span of differences.	Assistance by central office personnel in diagnosing needs; principal helps with remedial groups or individual "tutoring"; occasional help from speech correctionist.	Special classes for physically and mentally handicapped; availability of reading specialist or speech specialist; definite plan for helping individuals with special needs including gifted; special facilities for helping emotionally disturbed children; special study groups for parents of these children; special service for partially blind and hard-of-hearing children; close cooperation with home and with resource facilities in meeting needs of children.

VI. Working with parents

1	2	3
Teachers attend PTA and welcome parents when they come to visit school.	Plan for parent contact to include occasional home visits; conferences as needed; exhibits of children's work special programs.	Regular schedule for parent-teacher conferences; regular plan for home visitation; grade group meetings; parent education series; frequent exchange of notes with parents; parents on school councils and committees; parents helping with school activities (e.g. educational trips; kindergarten furniture).

282

VII. Coordination with other agencies for effective study of children's problems

1	2	3
Meager information kept in school files; extent of information only as wide as number of previous teachers child had had; usually test scores and minimum records only information available.	Information received from health department; joint attendance at teachers' institutes and in community groups to hear special speakers or reports; reports received from special clinics and information given upon request; referral of children to clinic by special personnel.	Representatives from school meeting with mental hygiene association, social planning councils, etc.; cooperation with other agencies such as family welfare, health, youth organizations; use of special facilities in community for enriching school programs and for referral of cases.

VIII. Mental health needs of teachers

1	2	3
Teaching is a job and the teacher receives no special attention apart from required faculty meetings and the filling of her supply orders and acceptance of required reports.	There is a teachers' room where teachers can lie down and where they can secure a modicum of privacy. There is a teachers' book shelf available. Occasional social affairs are planned. The PTA honors the teachers at the beginning and the end of the term.	Teachers have a free period during the day. There are frequent informal parties and several trips and meetings. Yard and bus duty are planned equitably. Teachers have a voice in school policies. Counseling services are available. There is a housing committee. There is a single salary schedule. Teachers receive advancement when warranted. They are carefully selected and there are tenure AND retirement plans. Health service is inexpensive and easily available.

283

IX. *A plan for teacher growth in guidance*

1	2	3
No training program beyond that of minimum preparation for credential.	Teachers attend lectures, take extension or summer courses; read articles for reports to faculty meetings.	Continual and growing program in study opportunities through workshops and child study programs; teacher participation in planning, conducting and evaluating these projects; sabbatical leave; exchange teaching plans.

X. *Availability of special personnel in meeting guidance needs of the school*

1	2	3
Elementary teacher provides any necessary guidance service; either she or principal administers tests; quality of service dependent upon understanding and resources of teacher and principal.	Referral of children's needs to nurse, to central office personnel, to special counselor; teacher participation in conference; joint plan.	Full-time counselor in every elementary school; special guidance personnel available when requested; facilities for referral of children to guidance or mental hygiene clinics; teacher participation in case conference; plan for coordination of city or county-wide facilities for child study.

SUMMARY PROFILE

Characteristic	Evaluation Scale (Points)		
	1	2	3
1			
2			
3			
4			
5			
6			
7			
8			
9			
10			
	10	20	30
	Lowest	Minimum Adequacy	Optimal or Excellent

EVALUATION OF GUIDANCE IN THE ELEMENTARY SCHOOL

Child Study Procedures

Testing

Are teachers administering and using group tests properly?

Does the evaluation program provide systematic information on ability, acadamic status, and personal adjustment?

Do teachers use tests to plan for individual needs?

Are teachers given expert help in test interpretation?

Individual study

Are complete studies made of children who have special needs?

Is special planning evident for all types of exceptional children? (gifted, academically retarded, mentally retarded, physically handicapped, emotionally maladjusted).

As exceptional children go from group to group, are their needs interpreted to the teachers concerned?

As exceptional children change schools, are follow-up interpretations made of their needs?

Do all teachers understand and support the program for exceptional children?

285

Groups

Do the teachers understand needs within their regular classroom groups?

Are classroom relationships democratic?

Are the children growing in responsibility and consideration of others?

Do the children participate in planning their experiences?

Do the children participate in the evaluation of their progress?

Is there evidence of increasing self-direction?

Records

Are records complete and up-to-date?

Is essential information recorded systematically? (home and family, health, personal adjustment, abilities, educational progress, interests, special needs).

Are records in the most accessible location for ready teacher use?

Is a folder-type record used for flexibility?

Is the record information sent to the school to which a child transfers?

Teachers as Guidance Participants

Are teachers developing increased understanding of pupil needs?

Do they use knowledge of individual differences in curriculum planning?

Are they making curriculum improvements based upon mental health needs?

Are they gaining ability to identify special needs?

Do they participate in staff conferences regarding individual children?

Do they accept behavior as motivated?

Do they respect children?

Do they seek help to understand children?

Do they participate in the formulation of guidance policies?

Do they understand the responsibilities and functions of special guidance personnel?

Do they understand referral procedures?

Do they study children's needs prior to referral?

Do they work closely with special resources?

Are they assuming increased responsibility in guidance?

Do they help plan and participate actively in an in-service guidance program?

Do they use guidance materials and techniques in a professional manner?

Do they study guidance literature?

Do they take professional courses in guidance?

Do they work closely with parents, individually and in groups?

Parents as Guidance Participants

Do parents work with the school before their children enter kindergarten?

Do they participate in planned child study programs?

Do they feel welcome at school?

Is parent participation in school activities increasing?

Is parent understanding of child growth and development increasing?

Do parents work closely with teachers to improve parent and teacher understanding of their children?

Do they make use of publications on child growth and guidance?

Do they participate in orientations to junior high school?

Do they understand and support the school guidance program?

Administrators as Guidance Participants

Has the chief administrator provided for adequate financial support for the guidance program?

Has the chief administrator designated one well-qualified person to coordinate the district guidance program?

Does the district have adequate special consultant services for exceptional children and in-service activities?

Have provisions been made throughout the district for adequate physical facilities for special testing, records, and individual conferences?

Are the guidance facilities attractive?

Do principals assist in the coordination of guidance activities within their buildings?

Do the administrators participate in planning guidance activities?

Do the administrators provide time for teachers to carry on guidance activities?

Do administrators help to interpret the program to the community?

Are the administrators increasing their understanding of good guidance procedures?

Do the administrators have a planned in-service program in guidance for themselves?

Special Guidance Personnel

Are the guidance personnel well trained for the work they are doing?

Are they taking training to improve their competencies?

Do they use a team approach to guidance?

Do they work toward the improvement of guidance skills in others?

Are they loyal to their colleagues?

Do they work as a part of the total educational program?

Do they have a well-defined, coordinated program?

Are they developing and acquiring professional study materials for staff use?

Do they make adequate use of available resources in and out of school?

Do they work closely and effectively with parents, teachers, and other district personnel?

BENEFITS OF EVALUATION

In the process of periodic evaluations, school personnel are able to indicate areas in which improvements are needed. Since they participate, the program becomes theirs, and the improvement is their concern. They improve the relationships of personnel within the school, and improve the school and community relationships as well. Continuous improvement and increased professional effectiveness are an inevitable outcome.

summary

Evaluation is a continuous, dynamic process of assessing and planning improvements in the guidance program. It includes all personnel, and involves many methods. Flexibility, continuity, completeness, and scope should be considered in planning a comprehensive program. Any evaluation, whether of a specific aspect of guidance, or of the entire program, should be based upon district needs. Evaluation procedures, to be of value, need to be put to use.

ORIENTATION TO
THE SECONDARY SCHOOL

No text on elementary school guidance would be complete without some attention to problems of transition to junior or senior high school. Unless careful plans are made by all concerned, much of the value in a comprehensive school guidance program may be lost at the transfer point. Three groups are involved: school personnel, parents, and the students themselves. Questions relating to program, activities, and philosophy need clarification so that each group may achieve full understanding.

Many parents and students, as well as elementary school personnel, have been confronted by incorrect and sometimes distorted information about practices at the next level. Parents and children may develop completely unjustified fears about "What Goes On At *That* School." Stories relayed by other students or uninformed neighbors may be given unwarranted credence unless correct information is available. When such information is given, fears are allayed and both children and adults are given proper bases for reacting to future rumors. Transfer should be planned so that students may enter the next level with complete understanding, readiness, and enthusiasm for the coming new school life. Sufficient information must be available to them and about them so that the transition is a positive educational experience.

Sixth grade students or eighth grade students may be involved in a transition problem in many respects as crucial as that of transfer

289

from the home environment to the school at the kindergarten level. They are entering or going through a period of important physiological and psychological growth change. They are entering new surroundings from a familiar environment. In many instances the new surroundings involve several buildings instead of one, and many more students. From being the oldest students and frequently the leaders in a school, they become the newest and youngest of the group. Although many junior and senior high schools have established blocks of time for home room groups, in many places the new student may find himself in a school in which he moves from one teacher to another each period, in contrast with the unity of the elementary school classroom.

Even when in many instances students, faculty, and parents may be involved in activities simultaneously, certain separate programs may be planned as well. Orientations for the three groups will be discussed briefly in the following sections and then an attempt will be made to correlate through a simple chart the activities discussed.

ORIENTATION OF SCHOOL PERSONNEL

Personnel at both levels need understanding of the purposes and values in school programs in the elementary and secondary school. Such understanding may be achieved through articulation meetings involving elementary grade personnel and teachers, counselors, and administrators from the secondary school. Discussion and evaluation of programs, information needed, and planning for individual students will contribute much to pupil welfare and increased mutual respect. Teachers and counselors may work together to plan orientation materials and activities for use with elementary students in the spring of the year. Teachers and others together may plan visitation activities that will help orient the students to them, and enable both the elementary and secondary personnel to increase their understanding of the others' educational program and practices.

The effective transfer of school records is a primary factor in planning for new students. Faculty members of both levels need to know the importance of complete, continuous records, and the kinds of information of most value to the secondary school. Special testing programs or special data records should be planned cooperatively so that all participate with understanding.

ORIENTATION OF PARENTS

Parents as a group are as much in need of information concerning the secondary school and its activities as elementary teachers and students. Because they are not in direct, daily contact with either school, they are perhaps more subject to misinformation and occasional misgivings than either of the other groups. Orientation programs therefore are being planned increasingly to involve parents as well as children and teachers. Programs have included visitations, conferences, demonstrations, and publications.

Visitations may include days for parents at the secondary school, at which time they visit some classes, become acquainted with some of their child's future teachers, meet with counselors and administrators, and discuss mutual questions and problems. Evening meetings may be arranged during the last elementary school year, in which parents meet with counselors and school personnel from both levels to develop understanding of the future school program. Many schools have used the "back to school" night, in which parents are given a preview of their child's future program by going through briefly the class activities in which he will be assigned.

Parent-teacher organizations have planned programs for parents designed to acquaint them with the new school program. Many parent organizations send invitations to new parents and make personal contacts to involve them actively in the new parent group.

Many questions of parents may be answered through bulletins and handbooks giving such information as the length and divisions of the school day, daily schedules, special expenses for physical education and other activities, resource personnel available, parent study group activities, student clubs, lunch programs, and so on. These are used to supplement personal contact, and to give information to parents otherwise not contacted.

ORIENTATION OF STUDENTS

The group most directly involved in orientation programs is the students. Through their contacts with varied activities at both levels, they undoubtedly experience more orientation activities than either school personnel or parents. Through visitations, through prepared materials, and through planned groupings, they learn what to expect of their new school.

Varied visitation programs have been successful in many schools. In some instances, student leaders who are "old grads" of the elementary school, accompanied by counselors and administrators from the secondary school, have met with elementary students in groups to discuss problems about which the students have expressed concern, and to describe phases of their own student lives. Such visits may be combined with a springtime Saturday at the secondary school, at which time the new students are introduced by student hosts and guides to their new homeroom groups, are given assembly presentations of activities, are taken on tours of their new school, are shown special facilities such as the nurse's office and the guidance office, and are served simple refreshments. Visitation may be extended further to include special visits for interested individuals to club activities, or may involve return visits for special groups. Some schools have arranged for students from the elementary school to visit classes in which they are especially interested.

Visitation programs are of value to all. Students from the secondary school who are involved develop ability to plan and to perform leadership functions. If careful plans are developed within the secondary student body for adequate assimilation of new students, much valuable learning about human relations occurs. New students who visit are able to obtain a feeling of personal relationship with their new school that cannot be obtained in other ways. Teachers are able to learn something about their new student groups prior to the opening of school in the fall.

Prepared materials have been used in many instances as effective supplements to visitation. Films and slides are used by many schools in student or faculty presentations about their activities. Charts and bulletins as well as handbooks have been developed for student information. Such simple devices as maps showing the location of important facilities within the school plant have been of help in assisting the new student to find his place.

Planned groupings involve close coordination between the elementary school and the secondary school so that students may be placed in groups that not only will mean adequate programs for them, but also will place them with friends. Elementary teachers and counselors may furnish much assistance to secondary personnel in helping them to understand individuals and their personal relationships.

The following simple chart is presented to indicate the extent to which all those within the schools may be involved in orientation activities:

EXTENT OF ORIENTATION PARTICIPATION

Activity	Participants				
	Secondary personnel	Elementary personnel	Parents	Secondary students	Elementary students
Meetings, teas	X	X	X		
Visits to secondary school		X	X	X	X
Visits to elementary school	X		X	X	
Orientation materials	X	X	X	X	X
Friendship groupings	X	X			X
Record transfers	X	X			
Audio-visual materials and presentations	X	X	X	X	X
Handbooks, bulletins	X	X	X	X	X
PTA contacts	X		X		
Classroom visits (secondary)	X	X	X		X
Visits to clubs			X		X
"Back to school"	X		X		
Welcoming plans	X			X	

The most elaborate orientation programs may fail through over-organization and lack of the personal touch. Simple contacts that enable students to identify with fellow students and with the school are often more effective than complex presentations by top school administrators. Informality and student-student contacts planned by student leaders with faculty assistance have been found more helpful than formal adult presentations.

Evaluation of the success of well-laid plans must come after a

293

period of time. Evaluation may take place through the use of prepared evaluation guides and through observation of the new students as they go through their first year. If students evidence positive reactions to both the elementary and secondary school, if they evidence a feeling of group belonging, if they are involved in a suitable program of activities, if they have made new friends, and if they have made the transition with minimal confusion and frustration, then the orientation efforts have had some measure of success.

summary

Orientation to the secondary school should be carefully planned on a cooperative basis to insure a continuing positive educational experience. Transition at any level is difficult, and students who transfer into the secondary school face growth and educational changes that make careful planning mandatory.

All persons concerned with the education of the student—teachers, parents, and the student himself—need to participate in orientation activities. Such participation promotes understanding and cooperation on the part of all. Transition activities should involve much student participation, and should be open in many instances to parents as well as students. Evaluation should be a planned part of the orientation procedures.

APPENDIXES

APPENDIX A

FILMS
FOR GUIDANCE

1. Individuals and Group Guidance

COUNSELING: ITS TOOLS AND TECHNIQUES. 22 min.
Mahnke Films, 1948. (Produced by Vocational Guidance Films)
How a well-trained counselor works. Shows what tools and technique to use in counseling and how to use them to best advantage. Included are interviewing, tests, questionnaires, the use of films.

DISCOVERING INDIVIDUAL DIFFERENCES, PART II. 25 min.
McGraw-Hill, 1954.
Shows how a fifth grade teacher studies systematically the differences in background, abilities and needs of the children in her room. She uses: observation, cumulative records, behavior journal, discussion with other teachers, interviews with parents, and staff conferences.

MAINTAINING CLASSROOM DISCIPLINE. 14 min. McGraw-Hill, 1947.
By contrasting methods of handling the same class, techniques are shown for securing class discipline and stimulating the interest of students. (Note: teachers often disagree with the conclusions implied by the film; this initiates effective discussion since all have the common background the film provides.

MOTIVATING THE CLASS. 19 min. McGraw-Hill, 1950 (Ed. Psych. Series).
A young student teacher of mathematics learns that adequate motivation is basic to all good teaching, and is obtained by translating the values of the subject matter into terms the pupils can understand.

OF PUPS AND PUZZLES. 11 min. Encyclopedia Britannica Films.
A study of individual differences and techniques in fitting applicants to

297

positions. Observing animals' reactions to certain stimuli helps one judge better what to expect from human beings.

PRACTICING DEMOCRACY IN THE CLASSROOM. 21 min. Encyclopedia Britannica Films, 1953. (Produced in cooperation with Michigan DAR & Kalamazoo Public Schools)

The development of a teaching method to foster democratic practices in a high school social studies class. Begins with the class setting up goals for the year's work with the guidance of the teacher. Smaller study groups work up specific topics for each unit; each group organizes its work plan and assigns individual responsibilities. The teacher's functions are clearly shown. The final stage of reporting results to the entire class is shown. Applicability of the method to all classes at all grade levels is briefly suggested.

WILLIE AND THE MOUSE. 11 min. Teaching Film Custodians, 1946. (Produced by Metro-Goldwyn-Mayer) (Passing Parade)

A comparative study which shows that experiments with laboratory mice have implications in educational procedure in the classroom. The mice are trained by sight, sound, and touch, and the commentary draws attention to the ways in which the experiments with mice illustrate the necessity for variety of approach in the teaching of children.

2. Understanding Behavior

ANGRY BOY. 33 min. International Film Bureau, 1951.

Through psychiatric care, the emotional disturbance of a boy who is caught stealing in school is traced to its basic causes. At the end of the film, he is on the way to recovery and the audience has seen how unconscious motivation affects the behavior of both children and adults.

BABY MEETS HIS PARENTS. 10 min. Encyclopedia Britannica Films.

Points out how differences in personalities can be accounted for by heredity, by the human relationships and environmental factors experienced during the first years of life. Explains how the infant personality is influenced directly by the extent to which the baby finds fulfillment of his basic needs, food, elimination, and care.

CHILDREN'S EMOTIONS. 22 min. McGraw-Hill, 1950 (Crawley Films) (Child Development Series).

Discusses the major emotions of childhood: fear, anger, jealousy, curiosity and joy. Points out what parents can do to lessen fears and promote the child's happiness and natural development.

EMOTIONAL HEALTH. 20 min. McGraw-Hill.

Portrays problem of the college student who visits a doctor because he is worried about chest pains. Finding no physical causes, the doctor recommends consultation with a psychiatrist, who discovers a deep-rooted but unsuspected fear. After discussion, the student improves.

FAMILY CIRCLES. 31 min. McGraw-Hill, 1949 (National Film Board, Canada).
Shows how the interplay of home and school influences affects the development of today's youngsters. The experiences of three children illustrate how parental indifference, lack of imagination, and emotional conflict at home can destroy the confidence and enthusiasm necessary for child's success at school.

FEARS OF CHILDREN. 30 min. International Film Bureau, 1951.
Parent-child situation in which the mother tends to coddle her five-year-old son while the father advocates sterner discipline and encourages the child to do for himself. The advice of a friend helps to work out resulting conflicts.

FEELINGS OF DEPRESSION. 30 min. McGraw-Hill, 1950 (Mental Mechanisms Series; Produced by National Film Board, Canada).
The case history of a conscientious, hardworking business man in his early thirties, who suddenly suffers periods of great despondency. Factors underlying this behavior are uncovered and it is suggested that the resources of psychiatry may help him to understand himself and lead the way to a full, rich life.

FEELING OF HOSTILITY. 27 min. McGraw-Hill, 1948 (Mental Mechanisms Series; Produced by National Film Board, Canada).
The case history of Clare, an outwardly successful but inwardly incomplete personality. Resentment toward others and the resulting failure in personal relationships are traced in detail from childhood.

FEELING OF REJECTION. 23 min. McGraw-Hill, 1947 (Mental Mechanisms Series; Produced by National Film Board, Canada).
The case history of a neurotic 23-year-old girl, suffering from physical symptoms for which no physical cause can be found. She is referred by her doctor to a psychiatrist who is able to uncover the emotional basis for these physical reactions.

THE FRUSTRATING FOURS AND FASCINATING FIVES. 22 min. McGraw-Hill, 1952 (Ages and Stages Series). (Produced by Crawley Films for National Film Board of Canada)
At home at the age of four we see a boy's behavior deviate from childish helplessness to vigorous self-assertion, and at kindergarten, from imaginative craftsmanship to inconsistent destructiveness. Although the change is gradual, at five Roddy appears more independent of adult support with an insatiable curiosity about everything around him.

HEREDITY AND PRE-NATAL DEVELOPMENT. 21 min. McGraw-Hill, 1950 (Produced by Crawley Films, Canada, Child Development Series).
Step-by-step picturization of growth, subdivision and eventual union of male and female sex cells. Includes explanation of chromosomes and genes in determining sex and in transmitting physical and mental char-

acteristics to offspring. Emphasizes modification of these traits by training and environment. Shows development in the newborn child of the
basic physiological actions of breathing, eating, and elimination. Stresses
close connection between physical and emotional sensitivity in very
young children.

HELPING THE CHILD TO ACCEPT THE DO'S. 10 min. Encyclopedia Brittanica Films.

Portrays the child learning to live in a word of Do's and explains how
his personality is influenced by the extent to which the Do's are accepted. Illustrates the types of Do's a child must learn to accept; the
Do's for personal living, the masculine and feminine Do's and the Do's
for human relations.

HELPING THE CHILD TO FACE THE DON'TS. 10 min. Encyclopedia Brittanica Films.

Reveals how the young child meets a world of Don'ts and reacts by
conforming in his own distinctive ways, thus forming his individual
personality. Classifies the Don'ts as those that restrain him from taking
things that belong to others and those that teach him to respect the
rights of others.

HUMAN BEGINNINGS. 22 min. McGraw-Hill.

In the first part we see what a group of children believe about the
origin of human life as expressed in their own drawings. The second part
of the film shows how a young boy and his parents react to the coming of a new baby sister into the family. One of the main uses of the film
is to provide a basis for discussion by children of 5 and 6 years of age,
or older.

HUMAN GROWTH. 19 min. McGraw-Hill.

Presents facts of human growth in a straightforward, unemotional manner; includes biological facts of sex as a part of human growth and
development; establishes teacher-pupil relationship conducive to easy
classroom discussion.

HUMAN REPRODUCTION. 20 min. McGraw-Hill.

Explains structure and functions of human reproductive systems and
process of birth. Models and animation are used to describe reproductive
organs, fertilization, growth of embryo and fetus, process of delivery.

**LEARNING TO UNDERSTAND CHILDREN, PART I—A DIAG-
NOSTIC APPROACH.** 21 min. McGraw-Hill, 1947 (Teacher
Education Series).

A case study of Ada Adams, an emotionally and socially maladjusted
girl of 15. Records the efforts of her English teacher to study her case
sympathetically, to understand her and to plan remedial procedures to
help her. Diagnostic techniques shown in detail include observation of
behavior, study of previous records, personal interviews, home visitation, and formulation of a hypothesis for remedial measures.

300

LEARNING TO UNDERSTAND CHILDREN, PART II—A RE-
MEDIAL PROGRAM. 23 min. McGraw-Hill, 1947 (Teacher Education Series).
Continuation of the case study of Ada Adams in which the teacher develops a plan for remedial action by making use of Ada's talent in art.

LIFE WITH BABY. 18 min. *March of Time*, 1946.
The knowledge gained of the mental and physical growth of children
ages 1-6 by Dr. Arnold Gesell at the Yale University Clinic. Features
many candid-camera sequences.

LIFE WITH JUNIOR. 18 min. *March of Time*, 1949 (with Child
Study Association).
The camera picks up a ten-year-old boy at the start of a typical day and
follows him through his sketchy ablutions, a wolfed breakfast and a
dawdling trip to school. Emphasizes the anxieties of today's world, and
explains ways in which to cope with behavior problems.

OVER-DEPENDENCY. 32 min. McGraw-Hill, 1949. (National
Film Board, Canada)
The case history of Jimmy, an attractive young man whose life is
crippled by behavior patterns carried over from a too-dependent childhood. The patient retracing of childhood experiences in talks with a
doctor leads to understanding of the emotional causes of his illness and
fear.

PREFACE TO A LIFE. 29 min. United World Films, 1950. (Produced by Sun Dial Films, Inc.)
Shows the influence parents have on a child's developing personality.
Illustrated by a series of episodes showing the effects of an overly
solicitous mother and an overly demanding father; and, in contrast, the
healthy childhood resulting when both parents accept their child as an
individual.

PRINCIPLES OF DEVELOPMENT. 17 min. McGraw-Hill, 1950
(Child Development Series). (Produced by Crawley Films, Ltd. of
Canada)
Outlines the fundamentals of child growth and development from the
point of early infancy. After defining the principles of development,
the film considers the variables that make each child different from
every other one.

SHYNESS. 23 min. McGraw-Hill, 1953. (Produced by National Film
Board, Canada)
Shyness in children, its causes, and how, through a greater understanding by parents and teachers, this problem may be dealt with. From
the lonely existence of a typically shy adult, the film turns to a study of
three children: Anna, shy but wistfully wanting association with others;
Jimmy, whose excessive timidity is really a symptom of profound emotional disturbance; and Robert, aloof but happily independent. A psy-

301

chiatrist from the Child Guidance Clinic reveals the confidence-destroying demands of parents that predisposed the children to shyness. Together, teacher, psychiatrist, and parents bring about a change in the children's attitudes.

SOCIABLE SIXES AND NOISY NINES. 20 min. McGraw-Hill.
Four children illustrate the behavior that may normally be expected in children from ages six to nine. It illustrates positive parent-child relationships, and stresses that each age level has its own values in the child's life, in addition to being a stepping stone to adulthood.

SOCIAL DEVELOPMENT. 16 min. McGraw-Hill.
Film offers an analysis of social behavior at different age levels and the reasons underlying the changes in behavior patterns as the child develops. The film goes on to the emotional conflicts that come with the gang age, when home and family are no longer the center of the child's world. It stresses the point that while the child must meet and solve each problem as he reaches that level of growth and development, guidance from understanding adults can make the adjustment infinitely easier and smoother.

UNDERSTANDING CHILDREN'S PLAY. 10 min. New York University, 1948.
First in a series planned to show how adults can understand and help children through observation of their use of toys and play materials. Shows that by increased awareness of children's various play activities, adults can function more effectively in guiding children.

YOUR CHILDREN AND YOU. 31 min. McGraw-Hill.
Presents problems that parents face in teaching children from one month to four or five years to fit into the family routine. Includes weaning, toilet training, preparation for the arrival of another baby, temper tantrums, sex, and general mischievousness.

YOUR CHILDREN'S SLEEP. 23 min. Encyclopedia Brittanica Films.
In their everyday lives children have their own particular problems to overcome. Insignificant to an adult, to a child they are important and even frightening. They can cause sleeplessness or nightmares. This film stresses the importance of sound, healthy sleep and advises parents on the ways in which they can ensure it for their children.

3. Exceptional Children

A CLASS FOR TOMMY. 20 min. Los Angeles City Schools, 1950. $3.00.
Story of establishment of experimental training class for mentally retarded.

A DAY IN THE LIFE OF A CEREBRAL-PALSIED CHILD (sound and color). 30 min. National Society for Crippled Children, 1950.
Describes 24-hour training and treatment for rehabilitation of the

cerebral palsied. Made at Children's Rehabilitation Institution, Cockeysville, Maryland.

GOOD SPEECH FOR GARY. 20 min. McGraw-Hill, 1953.
Presents the entire scope of a well-organized speech program as it is carried out in the California schools (and elsewhere) today. Contributes to the understanding of children's speech difficulties and what schools can do to help children to speak clearly and well.

LET ME SEE (color). 20 min. McGraw-Hill, 1953.
Cooperative planning by home and school for nursery-age blind child. The role of the parent at home is stressed. Awarded the 1953 Screen Producers Guild Annual Inter-Collegiate Film Award as the outstanding university-produced film of the year.

LISTENING EYES (color). 20 min. John Tracy Clinic, Los Angeles.
Shows the work of a modern clinic in teaching speech to young deaf children, and the assistance given by the clinic staff to parents.

MY CHILD IS BLIND. 22 min. United World Films, 1951.
Shows how a blind child, given patient treatment and proper training at a special nursery school for the blind child, can be taught to do many things normal children can do.

PAY ATTENTION. 30 min. New York University Film Library.
$6.00.
Shows some of the educational and personality problems faced by the child who is hard of hearing but is not "deaf," and suggests some of the ways in which parents, teachers, and specialists can help. Stressed are understanding of the problem, its early treatment, the use of "context" methods of speech reading, and the early use of hearing aids where appropriate.

SEARCH (sound). 26 min. National Society for Crippled Children and Adults, 1950. (Produced by National Association of American Business Clubs)
Aid to understanding problems faced by cerebral palsied. Film portrays attitudes of cerebral palsied and of others toward him.

SPEECH READING. 28 min. U.S. Army, 1952.
Explains how persons with a hearing loss can learn, by careful interpretation of lip movements with total situation, to "see" what people are saying. Shows how vowel and consonant sounds are formed by the mouth.

THAT THE DEAF MAY SPEAK (color). 42 min. Ideal Pictures Corp., 58 E. South Water, Chicago, Ill. Free Film (service charge $2.50).
A gripping and compassionate portrayal of the problems faced by the deaf . . . and the patience, love and understanding necessary to enable deaf children to lead a normal life in a world of sound. (Lexington School for the Deaf.)

APPENDIX B

PAMPHLET
MATERIALS

The following organizations publish pamphlet materials that are of value to both teachers and parents. The topics covered range from home reporting to film guides, study group procedures, childhood problems and needs, and parent education materials. The list necessarily omits many fine state as well as national resource organizations, but it attempts to present key organizations that provide inexpensive materials of value in the guidance of children. Bibliographies of available materials may be obtained upon request.

Association for Childhood Education International
Washington, D.C.

Association for Supervision and Curriculum Development
Washington, D.C.

Child Study Association of America
132 East 74th Street
New York 21, New York

Department of Health, Education, and Welfare
Washington 25, D.C.

National Committee for Mental Hygiene, Inc.
1790 Broadway
New York 19, New York

National Congress of Parents and Teachers
600 South Michigan Boulevard
Chicago 5, Illinois

Science Research Associates
57 West Grand Avenue
Chicago 10, Illinois

Public Affairs Pamphlets
22 East 38th Street
New York, New York

Teachers College
Bureau of Publications
Columbia University
New York, New York

University of Iowa
Iowa City, Iowa
Child Welfare Pamphlets

APPENDIX C

BIBLIOGRAPHY

Child development and learning

Baldwin, Alfred L., *Behavior and Development in Childhood*. New York: The Dryden Press, 1955.

Breckenridge, Marian E., and E. Lee Vincent, *Child Development*.

Cronbach, Lee, *Educational Psychology*. New York: Harcourt, Brace and Co., Inc., 1952.

English, Horace B., *Child Psychology*. New York: Henry Holt and Company, Inc., 1951.

Havighurst, Robert J., *Human Development and Education*. New York: Longmans, Green and Co., 1953.

Hurlock, Elizabeth B., *Child Development*. New York: McGraw-Hill Book Company, Inc., 1950.

Jersild, Arthur T., *Child Psychology*, 4th ed. New York: Prentice-Hall, Inc., 1954.

Martin, William E., and Celia Burns Stendler, *Child Development*. New York: Harcourt, Brace and Co., Inc., 1953.

Olson, Willard C., *Child Development*. Boston: D. C. Heath and Company, 1949.

Seagoe, May V., *A Teacher's Guide to the Learning Process*. Dubuque, Iowa: Wm. C. Brown Company, 1956.

Thompson, George G., *Child Psychology*. New York: Houghton Mifflin Company, 1952.

Measurement and evaluation

Anastasi, Anne, *Psychological Testing*. New York: The Macmillan Company, 1954.

Buros, Oscar Krison, ed., *The Fourth Mental Measurements Yearbook*. Highland Park, N.J.: The Gryphon Press, 1953.

Greene, Harry A., Albert N. Jorgensen, and J. Raymond Gerberich, *Measurement and Evaluation in the Elementary School*. New York: Longmans, Green and Co., Inc., 1951.

Torgerson, Theodore L., and Georgia Sachs Adams, *Measurement and Evaluation for the Elementary School Teacher*. New York: The Dryden Press, 1954.

Exceptional children

Baker, Harry J., *Introduction to Exceptional Children*. New York: The Macmillan Company, 1953.

Cruickshank, William, ed., *Psychology of Exceptional Children and Youth*. Englewood Cliffs, N.J.: Prentice-Hall, Inc., 1955.

Goodenough, Florence L., *Exceptional Children*. New York: Appleton-Century-Crofts, Inc., 1956.

Heck, Arch O., *The Education of Exceptional Children*. New York: McGraw-Hill Book Company, Inc., 1953.

National Society for the Study of Education, *The Education of Exceptional Children, Forty-Ninth Yearbook, Part II*. Chicago: The University of Chicago Press, 1950.

Home-school relations and communication

Benne, Kenneth, and Bozidar Muntyan, eds., *Human Relations in Curriculum Change*. New York: The Dryden Press, 1951.

D'Evelyn, Kathryn, *Individual Parent Teacher Conferences*. New York: Bureau of Publications, Teachers College, Columbia University, 1945.

Erickson, Clifford E., *The Counseling Interview*. New York: Prentice-Hall, Inc., 1950.

Hymes, James L., Jr., *Effective Home-School Relations*. New York: Prentice-Hall, Inc., 1953.

Langdon, Grace, and Irving W. Stout, *Teacher-Parent Interviews*. New York: Prentice-Hall, Inc., 1954.

Rogers, Carl R., *Client-Centered Therapy*. New York: Houghton Mifflin Company, 1951.

Strang, Ruth, *Reporting to Parents*. New York: Bureau of Publications, Teachers College, Columbia University, 1947.

Symonds, Percival M., *The Dynamics of Parent-Child Relationships*. New York: Bureau of Publications, Teachers College, Columbia University, 1949.

Tyler, Leona, *The Work of the Counselor*. New York: Appleton-Century-Crofts, Inc., 1953.

Guidance programs and practices; child study

307

Association for Supervision and Curriculum Development, *Guidance in the Curriculum*. Washington, D.C.: National Education Association, 1955.

Association for Supervision and Curriculum Development, *Fostering Mental Health in Our Schools*. Washington, D.C.: National Education Association, 1950.

Buhler, Charlotte, Faith Smitter, and Sybil Richardson, *Childhood Problems and the Teacher*. New York: Henry Holt and Company, 1952.

Commission on Teacher Education, *Helping Teachers Understand Children*. Washington, D.C.: American Council on Education, 1945.

Cunningham, Ruth, and Associates, *Understanding Group Behavior of Boys and Girls*. New York: Bureau of Publications, Teachers College, Columbia University, 1951.

Department of Elementary School Principals, *Guidance for Today's Children, Thirty-Third Yearbook*. Washington, D.C.: National Education Association, 1954.

Detjen, Ervin W., and Mary F. Detjen, *Elementary School Guidance*. New York: McGraw-Hill Book Company, Inc., 1952.

Foshay, Arthur, K. D. Wann, and Associates, *Children's Social Values*. New York: Bureau of Publications, Teachers College, Columbia University, 1954.

Harms, Ernest, ed., *Handbook of Child Guidance*. New York. Child Care Publications, 1947.

Hatch, Raymond, and Buford Stefflre, *Administration of Guidance Services: Organization, Supervision, Evaluation*. Englewood Cliffs, N. J.: Prentice-Hall, Inc., 1958.

Hatch, Raymond, *Guidance Services in the Elementary School*. Dubuque, Iowa: William C. Brown Company, 1951.

Jennings, Helen Hall, *Sociometry in Group Relations*. Washington, D.C.: American Council on Education, 1948.

Los Angeles County Superintendent of Schools, *Guidance Handbook for Elementary Schools*. Los Angeles: California Test Bureau, 1948.

McDaniel, Henry B., *Guidance in the Modern School*. New York: The Dryden Press, 1956. (Chapters 1, 2, 3, 6, 7.)

National Society for the Study of Education, *Mental Health in Modern Education, Fifty-Fourth Yearbook, Part II*. Chicago: University of Chicago Press, 1955.

Traxler, Arthur E., *Techniques of Guidance*. New York: Harper & Brothers, 1945. (Chapters 1, 7, 11, 12, 13, 14.)

Willey, Roy de Verl, *Guidance in Elementary Education*. New York: Harper & Brothers, 1952.

INDEX

A

Abel, Theodora M., 208
Achievement tests, interpreting results, 137
Activities, questionnaire on outside, 73-75
Adams, Georgia Sachs, 128
Administrators:
  guidance-centered schools, 4
  guidance functions of, 173
  participate in parent-teacher conferences, 227
  relationship between guidance workers and, 168-169, 187-188, 190-193
  responsibilities of, 168-169
  role of, in group study, 124
  scale for evaluating work in guidance, 287
Agencies, that can help exceptional children, 204-205
American Council on Education, 34 n
American Psychological Association 15, 176, 180 n, 181 n
Anastasi, Anne, 128 n
Anecdotal records, 34-42
  criteria for use, 35
  method of recording, 35
  time sample and running accounts, 42-44
Appointment sheets, for parent-teacher conferences, 266, 267, 268
Aristotle, 8
Armfield, Virginia, 120 n
Armstrong, Beatrice, 120

Arrowood, Charles, 8 n
Art work, used to understand child's behavior, 44-47
Association for Childhood Education, International, 11
Association for Supervision and Curriculum Development, 34 n
Associations, professional guidance, 220-221
Audio-visual materials, for conference training, 260
Autobiographical data, 94-95
  outline for pupil autobiography, 94

B

Baker, Harry J., 205
Beers, Clifford, 11
Behavior:
  developmental, 29
  factors affecting, 66
  group, 67
  pupil behavior observation record, 107-111
Bellflower Unified Schools, Bellflower, California, 263-264, 267
Bender-Gestalt tests, 61
Benne, Kenneth, 226
Bibliography, on guidance, 306-308
Binet, Alfred, 9-10
Biographical data:
  example of, 95-107
  outline for pupil autobiography, 94
  place in elementary guidance program, 94-107

Blind children, special classes for, 205-206
Bogardees, Emory S., 90
Bogen, David, 26 *n*
Books and pamphlets:
about children and school activities, 237
lists for remedial classes, 208
orientation material, 291-292
Bowles, J. W., Jr., 199 *n*
Brewer, John M., 11 *n*, 12 *n*
Brueckner, Leo J., 142 *n*
Bulletins, orientation material for parents, 291, 292
Buros, Oscar Krisen, 10, 128 *n*
Buzz groups, 236

C

California, Pupil Personnel Services Credential, 177-178
California Association of School Administrators, 22
California, University of, 75 *n*
Carmichael, Leonard, 9 *n*
Carter, Jerry W., Jr., 199 *n*
Case studies, 49
cumulative records used for, 143
individual child study conferences, 62-64
Cattell, James McKeen, 9
Cerebral palsied children:
parents aided by guidance workers, 209
testing, 198-199
Certification, for guidance work, 176
Chase, Stuart, 226
Check lists:
pupil behavior observation record, 107-111
used to evaluate guidance program, 277
used to study group relationships, 107-114
Chicago, University of, 12
Child study:
development of, 10-11
goal of, 28
group study, 66-125 (*see also* Group study)
guidance worker provides leadership in, 183-184, 185

Child study (*Cont.*):
health reports:
ear examination, 54-56
eye examinations, 52-54
need for health adjustment, 59-60
nurse's findings and recommendations, 50
orthopaedic examination report, 57-58
physician's examinations, 51
individual, 28-65
anecdotal records, 34-42
approach to, 30-31
case conference, 62-64
children's art work, 44-47
follow-up, 64-65
forms used, 32-48
guidance worker coordinates, 185
individuals and groups that can aid, 62
informal interviews, 47-48
outcomes of, 30
problems in, 28-29
procedures, 31
roles of personnel, 49-61
teacher's description of child, 47
tests used, 61-62
therapy, 64
time sample and running account, 42-44
in-service study of guidance techniques, 214-221
scale for evaluating, 285-286
Child Study Association of America, 11
Children:
differences among, 9
exceptional (*see* Exceptional children)
in a guidance-centered school, 271
guidance program aids teacher in understanding growth and behavior in, 271-272
handicapped, 9 (*see also* Exceptional children)
home-school contacts help teacher understand environment of, 223
as members of a group, 66-125
understanding, 66
guidance workers aid parents, 186-187
Children's Apperception Test, 62

Children's Bureau, 11
Christianson, Dr. Helen, 75 *n*
Classrooms:
    parents participate in work of, 236-238
    storage of current records in, 18
Clinics:
    to assist juvenile delinquents, 10
    historical development of, 10
Colleges and universities:
    courses in home-school communications, 225
    guidance courses, 12
    personnel assist in planning record systems, 146
    professional people from, aid elementary program, 221
Columbia University, 12
    Horace Mann-Lincoln Institute of School Experimentation, 90
Committees, district-wide guidance, 192
Commonwealth Fund, 10
Communications:
    between home and school, 222-270
    preparation for two-way group, 225-231
Community:
    guidance program benefits whole, 273-274
    guidance worker coordinates school-community guidance program, 185-187
Conferences:
    case, 62-64
    group, 63
    parent-teacher, 222-270
        activity by adult participants, 235-238
        appointment sheets, 266, 267, 268
        "back to school" nights, 291
        book exchanges, 237
        classroom participation, 236-238
        demonstration lessons, 237
        demonstrations by children, 238
        evaluation of pupil progress, 240-270
        examples of some successful, 253-261
        flexibility in structure of meetings, 230

Conferences (*Cont.*):
    parent-teacher (*Cont.*):
        group participation, 233-240
        guides for teachers, 262-269
        importance of home-school contacts, 222-224
        individual conferences, 248-270
            advantages, 248-250
            criteria for planning, 251-252
        invitations, 227, 263-264, 265, 266, 267
        kinds of contacts, 224-225
        list of specific suggestions that could be discussed, 228-229
        material for, 227
        observation, 233-236
        orientation activities, 239, 291
        panel discussions, 231-233
        participation by administrative personnel, 227
        participation in children's learnings, 237
        preparation for two-way group communication, 225
        promote understanding of child, 224
        reading materials, 237
        recreational activities with children, 238-239
        refreshments, 227
        role-playing used in preparing for, 226, 254
        room arrangements, 227, 230
        schedules, 261-262
        summaries, 253-254, 261
        to report pupil progress, 248-270
        training procedures, 252-261
            audio-visual materials, 259-260
            role-playing, 226, 254
    use of films, 240
    use of self-ratings by pupils in, 113
Confidential information, method of handling, 18-19
Connecticut Association of School Psychological Personnel, 180-181
Contacts, home-school, 222-224
    kinds of, 224-225
Correctional institutions, cost of guidance program, 25
    elementary guidance program, 17-27
        compared with secondary schools, 20-26

Correctional institutions (*Cont.*):
elementary guidance program
(*Cont.*):
estimated year's cost of minimum
and optimum programs (*table*),
23-24
personnel, 21-25
physical facilities, 17-19
of caring for one child for one day
in juvenile facilities, 26
of guidance program in correctional
institutions, 25
Counseling (*see* Guidance)
Counselors (*see also* Guidance workers):
testing responsibilities of, 20
Creative writing, as a means to learn
about children, 117
Crosby, Joseph Wallace, 21-22
Cruickshank, William, 198 *n*
Cumulative records, 141-165 (*see also*
Records, cumulative)
Cunningham, Ruth, 91 *n*
Curriculum:
cumulative records aid in planning,
143
meaningful enrichment, 196
Curriculum consultants:
relationship between guidance workers and, 191
responsibilities in the guidance program, 2
role of, in effective use of tests, 138-
139
Cutts, Norma E., 13 *n*, 173 *n*, 176 *n*,
180 *n*

D

Data:
interpretation and application of, 3
organization and correct interpreta-
tion of, 29
Davis, Florence, 244 *n*
Definitions of guidance, 1-6
Demonstration lessons, 237
Demonstrations, by children, 238
Denver Public Schools, cumulative
record forms, 147-160
Dewey, John, 8
Diagnostic tests, 62
Diary, used to supply biographical in-
formation, 95-96

Differences among children, study of,
9, 10
Discussions:
by panels of pupils, 85-86
preparing for, 226-227
Districts, school, guidance committees,
192
Downey Elementary School District,
Downey, California, 263
Dramatizations, used to study children,
114-124
Drewes, Ruth, 117 *n*
Durrell-Sullivan Reading Capacity and
Achievement Tests, 62

E

Ear examination reports, 54-56
East Whittier School District, Whittier, California, 265 *n*
Eby, Frederick, 8 *n*
Educators, who influenced guidance
movement, 89
Elementary guidance:
child study developments, 10-11
cost of, 17-27
development of, 5, 7-16
child study developments and, 10-
11
contributions of measurement
techniques, 9-10
increase in personnel, 13-15
educators who influenced guidance
movement, 8-9
evaluation of guidance services, 275-
288
scale, 280-285
growth of organized programs, 12-
14
vocational guidance and, 10-12
Europe, development of guidance, 7
Evaluation:
cumulative records, 277
definition, 275-276
of group study, 286
guidance services, 275-288
benefits of, 288
general evaluative forms, 279-288
periodic examination of program,
279
scale for, 280-285
methods, 277-279

Evaluation (*Cont.*):
  orientation programs, 293-294
  procedures, 276-279
  programs for exceptional children, 212
  program for mentally retarded, 277-278
  of pupil progress (*see* Evaluation of pupil progress)
  purposes of, 275
  report cards, 277
  of teachers:
    growth in guidance, 284, 286
    mental needs of teachers, 283
  use of questionnaires, check lists, 277
Evaluation of pupil progress, 240-270
  bases for changes, 241-242
  developments in reporting, 243
  individual conferences, 248-270
    advantages of, 248-250
    criteria for planning, 251-252
    guides, 262-269
    planning for, 251-262
    schedules, 261-262
    training procedures, 252-261
  planning for changes in reporting practices, 243-247
  trends in home reporting, 240-241
Exceptional children, 194-213
  community agencies that can help, 204-205
  contributions made by teachers to the education of, 200-202
    child helped to work with others, 202
    each child shown to have value, 200
    individual help given when necessary, 201-202
    parents and community helped to see values in child, 202
    varied program utilized to meet needs of pupils, 200-201
  definition, 194-195
  evaluation and research, 212
  guidance workers and, 184, 202-212
    children referred to community agencies, 204-205
    constant study needed, 204
    helping the child, 204

Exceptional children (*Cont.*):
  guidance workers and (*Cont.*):
    interpretation of needs, 203
    work with parents and staff, 208-212
  needs of, 195-197
  number of, 194
  parents and staff aided by guidance worker, 208-212
  problems in identification of, 197-200
  remedial classes for, 207-208
  scale for evaluating work with, 282
  special classes for, 205-206
  testing program for, 61, 197-200
  therapy and treatment, 64
Eye examination report, 52-54

F

Films:
  for conference training, 260
  list of films on guidance, 297-303
  used in orientation program, 292
  used with parent-teacher conferences, 240
Fils, David, 207 *n*, 212 *n*
Fletcher, S. S. F., 8 *n*
Follow-up programs, 21
  individual child study, 64-65
  methodically planned, 274
Forms:
  case study, 20
  guidance, 19
  medical history, 82-85
  transfer, 20
Fostering Mental Health in Our Schools, 34 *n*
Froebel, Friedrich, 8

G

Galton, Sir Francis, 9
Gates Reading Diagnostic Tests, 62
Gesell, Arnold, 14
Gifted children, 196 (*see also* Exceptional children)
Goodenough Draw-A-Man Test, 61
Gordon, Lillian G., 12 *n*
Grace Arthur performance scale, 61
Gray Oral Reading Paragraphs, 62
Group participation, parents and teachers, 233-240

Group study:
anecdotal records, 34 *n*, 36
buzz groups, 236
complex nature of, 67
guidance worker helps with, 185-186
informal methods of, 66-125
in-service study of guidance techniques, 214-221
desired outcomes, 219-220
professional groups, 220-221
types of programs, 216-219
leadership, 216
materials for, 69-125
biographical data, 94-107
criteria for use of, 69-70
panels and discussions by pupils, 85-86
questionnaires and interest surveys, 70-71
rating scales and checklists, 107-114
reaction forms and dramatizations, 114-124
social distance scales, 90-94
sociograms, 87-90
measures of social relations, 85-94
questionnaires, 70-71
for children, 71-75
for parents, 75-85
roles of personnel in, 124-125
scale for evaluating, 286
values in, 68-69
Growth factors, variations in, 166
Guidance:
bibliography, 306-308
certification for guidance work, 176
consultant (*see* Guidance worker)
contributions of measurement to, 9-10
cumulative records in, 143-144
definitions, 1-6
educators who influenced movement, 8-9
elementary (*see* Elementary guidance)
evaluation of guidance services in elementary schools, 275-288
films on, 297-303
historical development, 7-16
need for, 4

Guidance (*Cont.*):
pamphlet material on, 304-305
personnel, 3 (*see also* Personnel, guidance)
need for, 166-172
philosophy, 2
physical facilities for, 16-19, 20
program (*see also* Program, guidance)
characteristics of, 271-274
planned program required, 1, 4-5
special materials for, 3
Guidance worker:
aims for wide participation in guidance program, 272-273
coordinates individual child study, 185
cumulative record system planned by, 146
duties, 182-183
exceptional children aided by, 184-185, 202-212
functions of, 170-175, 177
helps with group work, 185-186
helps with in-service study of guidance techniques, 214-221
leadership in child study provided by, 183-184
need for, 166-172
need for specialized training, 199
parents need, 167-168
qualifications and duties, 173-189
educational, 175-182, 199
personal qualifications, 173-175
teaching experience, 175-176
relationship between teachers and, 187-188
remedial and preventive aspects of work, 273
research conducted by, 187
responsibility delegated to many persons at the elementary level, 170-172
responsibility towards staff members, 190-193
role of:
in effective use and development of records, 163
in effective use of tests, 20, 138-139
in group study, 124-125

Guidance worker *(Cont.)*:
  rules for, 192
  specialized aid given to teachers, 184
  training program, 177-187

H

Hahn, Milton E., 161
Hall, G. Stanley, 8
Handbooks, used in orientation program, 292
Handicapped children *(see also* Exceptional children):
  providing for, 9
Hard-of-hearing children, special classes for, 205-206
Harms, Ernest, 10 *n*
Harsh, J. Richard, 110 *n*
Harvard University, 12
Hawaii, University of, 178-179
Health reports:
  ear examination, 54-56
  eye examinations, 52-54
  need for health adjustment, 59-60
  nurse's findings and recommendations, 50
  orthopaedic examination, 57-58
  physician's examinations, 51
Healy, Dr. William, 10
Helping Teachers Understand Children, 34 *n,* 36 *n*
Herbart, Johann Friedrich, 8
Hereditary Genius (Galton), 9
High school:
  orientation program, 289-293
  personnel assist in planning record system, 146
Hodge, Marian W., 144 *n*
Home-school contacts, 222-224 *(see also* Conferences, parent-teacher)
  are made early and are continuous, 273
  discussion meetings, 226-227
  importance of, 222-224
  important for teacher to understand child's environment, 223
  interviews, 49
  promote understanding of children, 224

Home-school contacts *(Cont.)*:
  trends in home reporting, 240-241
Horace Mann-Lincoln Institute of School Experimentation, 90
Hormurth, Rudolf P., 209 *n*
Human Relations in Curriculum Change (Benne and Muntyan), 226

I

Individual child study, 28-65 *(see also* Child study)
Individual differences, study of, 9, 10
Inglewood, California, Cerebral Palsy Unit, 209-210
In-service education:
  desired outcomes, 219-220
  in guidance techniques, 214-221
  out-of-district resources, 221
  professional groups, 220-221
  roles of personnel, 215-216
  scheduling meetings, 215-216
  types of programs, 216-219
Intelligence tests *(see also* Tests and testing):
  development of, 9-10
Interest surveys, 70-71, 89
Interviews:
  area provided for, 19-20
  home, 49
  informal, used in individual child study, 47-48
Invitations:
  to observe classes, 234
  parent-teacher conferences, 263-264, 265, 266, 267
Iowa Tests of Basic Skills in Reading, 62

J

Jennings, Helen Hall, 89, 118
Journal of Consulting Psychology, 14-15
Junior high school, orientation program, 289-293
Juvenile delinquents, clinics to assist, 10

K

Kanner, Leo, 10 n, 44 n
Kindergarten:
 obtaining basic family data from parents, 161
 orientation program for parents, 239
 questionnaire for parents, 75-85
Kluckhohn, Clyde, 29 n

L

Leadership, guidance, 216, 219
Lee, Dorothy, 29 n
Leiter International Performance Scale, 61
Library:
 facilities, 19
 materials for staff and parent use, 20, 25
Los Angeles County Schools, 207 n, 212 n
 Elementary Research and Guidance, 107, 110 n
 guidance personnel, 13-14

M

McClung, Harrison, 71 n
McDaniel, Inga C., 280
MacLean, Malcolm S., 161
Marking systems, 240-270 (*see also* Evaluation of pupil progress)
 bases for changes, 241-242
 developments in reporting, 243
 planning for changes in reporting practices, 243-247
 trends in home reporting, 240-241
Martinson, Ruth A., 13 n, 171 n
Materials:
 for guidance program, 19
 for parent-teacher conferences, 227
 prepared by study groups, 219
Measurement and Evaluation for the Elementary School Teacher (Torgerson and Adams), 128
Measurement techniques (*see also* Tests and testing):
 contributed to the development of guidance, 9-10

Medical history, questionnaire form, 82-85
Meetings (*see* Conferences)
Mental health:
 development of child guidance and, 10-11
 organizations interested in, 11
Mentally retarded children:
 evaluating guidance program for, 277-278
 growth of interest in, 10
Mental Measurement Yearbook (Buros), 10, 128-129
Michaelis, William, 278-279
Mind That Found Itself, A (Beers), 11
Morale, guidance program promotes staff, 273
Moreno, J. L., 118 n
Muntyan, Bozidar, 226
Murphy, Gardner, 66-67
Murray, Henry A., 29 n

N

National Association of Guidance Supervisors and Counselor Trainers, 13-14
National Association for Mental Health, 11
National Committee for Mental Hygiene, 11
National Conference on Vocational Guidance, 11
National Congress of Parents and Teachers, 11
National Society for the Study of Education, 194 n
Nebraska Test of Learning Aptitude, 61
Needs:
 of exceptional children, 195-197
 problems in identifying, 197-200
 scale for evaluating needs of students, 280
Newspapers, used to inform parents about school, 225
New York Association for the Help of Retarded Children, 209
New York Regents' Inquiry, into cumulative records, 142

Nolan, Esther Grace, 144 n
Norwalk—La Mirada City School District, Norwalk, California, 229 n
Nurses, school:
  form for findings and recommendations, 50
  relationship between guidance worker and, 191
  responsibilities in the guidance program, 2
  role in individual child study, 49
Nursery school, questionnaire for parents, 75-85

O

Observations of school program, by parents, 233-236
  planning for, 234
  pupil behavior observation record, 107-111
  schedule and invitations, 234
  sheet to guide observation, 235
  time sample and running account, 42-44
  used in evaluating guidance program, 277
Olson, Willard C., 134
Organizations, guidance, 11-12
Orientation:
  bulletins and handbooks, 291
  extent of orientation participation, 293
  of parents, 291
  of pre-school children, 239
  personal touch important, 293-294
  programs:
    evaluation of, 293-294
    for parents, 291
    planned by parent-teacher organizations, 291
    for school personnel, 290-291
    for students, 291-294
    types of, 291
    visitations, 292-293
  of school personnel, 290-291
  to the secondary school, 289-293
  of students, 291-293
    visitations and prepared materials, 292

Orthopaedic examination reports, 57-58

P

Panel discussions, 85-86, 231-233
  by children, 231-232
  by parents and teachers, 231-233
  use of professional personnel, 232-233
Parent-teacher organizations:
  educational programs, 6
Parents:
  conferences with teachers, 222-270
    (see also Conferences)
    activity by adult participants, 235-238
    demonstration lessons, 237
    group participation, 233-240
    importance of home-school contacts, 222-224
    kinds of contacts, 224-225
    observation, 233-236
    orientation program for parents of pre-school children, 239
    preparing for, 218
    to report pupil progress, 248-270
    schedules, 261-262
    trends in home reporting, 239-243
    use of cumulative records, 143
  education program in guidance for, 4
  exceptional children, 208-212
  guidance publications available for use of, 25
  guidance worker helps parents to understand children, 167-168, 186-187
  interpreting test results to, 137
  orientation program for, 239, 291
  orientation program planned by, 291
  publications and booklets sent by school to, 225
  questionnaire for parents of nursery school children, 75-85
  scale for evaluating work with, 282, 286
  visitation programs for, 291
  working mothers, 167
Parsons, Frank, 11-12
Pedagogical Seminary (periodical), 8
Peer groups, 68

Pennsylvania, University of, Psychological Clinic, 9, 10
Personality, factors affecting, 66
Personality tests, 62
Personnel, guidance:
  accreditation, 176-177
  cost of guidance, 21-25
  counselor-child ratios, 26
  duties of, 182-183
  educational qualifications, 175-182
  elementary guidance (*table*) 13
  evaluating needs, 277
  exceptional children aided by, 202-212
  functions, 170-175, 182-187
  growth in elementary guidance, 13-14
  guidance involves special, 3
  helps with group work in the school, 185-186
  leadership in child study provided by, 183-184
  need for, 166-172
    from the standpoint of the administrator, 168-169
    from the standpoint of parents, 167-168
    from the standpoint of the teacher, 169-170
  orientation to the secondary school, 289-293
  per cent of schools with (*table*), 14
  personal qualifications, 173-175
  qualifications and duties, 173-189
  relationship between administrators, teachers and, 187-188
  relationship between school staff and, 190-193
  research, 187
  resource, 25-26
  responsibility has been delegated to many persons at the elementary level, 171-172
  rules for, 192
  scale for evaluating, 284, 287-288
  in secondary schools, 166
  teaching experience desired, 175-176
  training programs, 177-182
  work with community groups, 186-187
  work with parents, 186-187

Personnel, guidance (*Cont.*):
  work with school personnel, 184, 185-186
Pestalozzi, Johann Heinrich, 8
Philosophy, guidance, 2
Physical facilities, 16-19, 20
  area for testing and interviews, 19-20
  library, 19
  storage space for current records, 17-18
Physicians:
  form for report of examination, 51
  relationship between guidance workers and, 191
  role in individual child study, 49
Pintner, Rudolph, 9 *n*
Plant, James S., 28 *n*
Preventive guidance, at early levels, 27
Principals (*see also* Administrators):
  arrange group meetings in guidance, 215
  responsibilities towards guidance program, 2
  role of:
    in effective use and development of records, 163-164
    in group study, 124-125
    in testing program, 138-139
Program, guidance:
  characteristics of, 271-274
    children work in an atmosphere conducive to satisfactory learning and living, 271
    continuing and worthy service to the community, 273-274
    follow-up studies, 274
    guidance person works on a remedial and preventive basis, 273
    guidance worker tries for wide participation, 272
    high staff morale, 273
    home-school contacts made early, 273
    staff interested in in-service study and improvement, 272
    teachers understand children's growth and behavior, 271-272
  comprehensive, 4
  cost of, 17-27
  cumulative records are the framework of, 162

Program, guidance (*Cont.*):
  evaluation of, 275-288
  functions of, 4
  goal, 5
  growth of elementary guidance programs, 12-14
  in-service groups, 216-219
  interpreting school, to parents, 224
  periodic examination of, 279
  personnel records, 3
  planned program required, 4-5
  purpose, 3, 271
  scale for evaluating guidance in the elementary school, 280-285
  values of a planned, 4
Psychoanalysis, influenced development of elementary guidance, 10
Psychological Testing (Anastasi), 128
Psychological well-being of children, guidance stresses, 214-215
Psychologists, school:
  case conferences conducted by, 62-64
  demand and need for, 15
  growth in number of, 14-15
  training program for, 180-181
Publications, school:
  sent to parents, 225
  for staff and parent use, 25
Pupils:
  behavior observation record, 107-111
  orientation programs for, 289, 291-294
  self-ratings by, 111

Q

Qualifications, of guidance workers, 173-189
Questionnaires:
  for children, 71-75
  for group study, 70-71
  medical history, 82-85
  on outside activities, 73-75
  for parents, 75-85, 225
  sent to homes, 225
  television viewing, 71-72
  used to evaluate guidance program, 277
  wording and choice of questions, 71
Quintilian, 8

R

Radio, used to spread information about school, 225
Rating scales:
  self-ratings by pupils, 111-114
  used to study group progress, 107-114
Reaction stories:
  examples, 119-124
  used to study children, 114, 117-119
Reading:
  diagnostic tests, 62
  scheduling, 129-131
  materials for parent-teacher conferences, 237
Records, school, 141-165
  anecdotal, 34-42
  cost of, 22
  cumulative, 141-165
    characteristics of, 141
    contents of, 144-145
    Denver Public Schools forms, 147-160
    directions for recording data, 148, 161-163
    effective use of, 148, 161-163
    evaluating, 277
    folders for, 147-148
    importance of, 141-144
    improving, 142
    location of, 162
    plan for recording data, 162
    planning of record system, 146-149
    reflects philosophy of school, 144
    roles of personnel in effective use and development of, 163-164
    should demand a minimum of clerical time, 161-163
    uses of, 142-144
  guidance worker helps teacher in keeping, 183-184
  individual child study, 29
  observational, 40
  parent conference, 20
  personnel, 3
  scale for evaluating, 280, 286
  storage of current, 17-18
  time sample and running account, 42-44

Records, school (*Cont.*):
transfer of, to secondary schools, 290-291
Recreational activities, participation in, 238-239
Reed, Anna Y., 11 *n*
Referrals, 31
guidance worker can refer children to community agencies, 204-205
Refreshments, parent-teacher conferences, 227, 229
Remedial classes:
for exceptional children, 207-208
list of books suitable for, 207
Report cards or letters, 224
evaluating, 277
Reporting pupil progress (*see also* Evaluation of pupil progress):
bases for changes, 241-242
developments in reporting, 243
individual conferences, 248-270
advantages of, 248-250
criteria for planning, 251-252
guides, 262-269
schedules, 261-262
training procedures, 252-261
planning for changes in reporting practices, 243-247
trends in, 240-241
Reports, health:
ear examination, 54-56
eye examinations, 52-54
need for health adjustment, 59-60
nurse's findings and recommendations, 50
orthopaedic examinations, 57-58
physician's examinations, 51
Research programs:
for exceptional children, 212
use of cumulative records, 144
Resource personnel:
guidance worker as, 183
individual child study by, 32
role in individual child study, 49
Resources, out-of-district guidance, 221
Retarded children (*see also* Exceptional children):
parents aided by guidance worker, 208-212
Revised Stanford-Binet Scale, 61
Richardson, Sybil, 252 *n*

Richmond, California Public Schools, 204-205
Rightmire, Josephine, 278 *n*
Roads to Agreement (Chase), 226
Robinson, Helen, 198-199
Role-playing, 117-119
used in preparing discussion meetings, 226
Rorschach Test, 62
Rosecrance, Francis Chase, 13-14
Rosenzweig Picture Frustration Study, 62
Rousseau, Jean Jacques, 8
Running account records, for child study, 42-44

S

San Bernardino County Schools, California, 280
Scoring tests, 133
Secondary schools:
cost of guidance programs, 20-26
guidance personnel in, 166
orientation to, 289-293
Self-idea completion tests, 115-116
Self-rating scales, 111-114
Sentence completion tests, 114-116
Sevy, Jane, 120 *n*
Shaftel, Fanny and George, 118 *n*
Social distance scales, 90-94
Social relations:
measuring, 85-94
sociograms, 87-90
Social well-being of children, guidance stresses, 214-215
Sociodramas:
dangers in, 119-120
examples, 120-124
used to study children, 114, 117-119
Sociograms, 87-90
reasons for constructions, 87
sociometric tabulation form, 88
used to study status roles of children, 90
Socrates, 8
Special classes, for exceptional children, 205-206
Status, group, 86-87
sociograms used to study status roles of children, 89

Stories:
  reaction, 114, 117-119
  examples of, 119-124
  unfinished, 62
  used to aid children in the evaluation of their beliefs and standards, 117-119
Strange, Phyllis, 120 *n*
Students (*see* Pupils)
Summaries, parent-teacher conferences, 254-255, 261

T

Tape recordings:
  for conference training, 260
  used by in-service guidance study groups, 217
Teachers:
  clerical duties, 142
  developing guidance leadership, 216, 219
  evaluating mental health, needs of, 283
  evaluating teacher's growth in guidance, 284, 286
  of exceptional children, 195
    aided by guidance workers, 208-212
    ways in which they can be helped in the classroom, 200-202
  form used in writing description of child, 47
  forms used by, in understanding children, 32-48
  group study of children and, 68-69, 124-125
  in guidance-centered school, understand children's growth and behavior, 271-272
  guidance workers provide specialized aid for, 169-170, 184
  home-school communications, 225-231
  in-service education, 18, 36, 161 (*see also* In-service education)
  of guidance techniques, 214-221, 272
  key in the guidance program, 1-2
  morale improved through guidance program, 273
  need the assistance of guidance personnel, 169-170, 184

Teachers (*Cont.*):
  orientation meetings planned by, 290
  outline of pupil study, 32-33
  relationship between guidance workers and, 184, 187-188, 191-193
  responsible for classroom guidance activities, 215-216
  responsibility for recording data in cumulative records, 161
  role of:
    in child study, 49
    in effective use and development of records, 163
    in testing program, 139
Teacher's Journal of Anecdotal Records, 32 *n*
Teaching, guidance aspects of, 214
Teamwork approach, guidance study groups, 220
Television:
  questionnaire on viewing habits, 71-72
  used to spread information about school, 225
Tests and testing:
  achievement, 62, 137
    scheduling, 130-132
  area for, 19-20
  Bender-Gestalt, 61
  Children's Apperception Test, 62
  costs of, 25
  criteria for use, 127-129
  diagnostic, 62
  Durrell-Sullivan Reading Capacity and Achievement Tests, 62
  exceptional children, 61, 197-200
  Gates Reading Diagnostic Tests, 62
  Goodenough Draw-A-Man Test, 61
  Grace Arthur, 61
  Gray Oral Reading Paragraphs, 62
  group, 62
  individual child study, 49, 61-62
  intelligence tests:
    development of, 9-10
    individual, 61
    interpreting results, 137-138
    interpreting results to parents, 137
  Iowa Tests of Basic Skills in Reading, 62
  Leiter International Performance Scale, 61

Tests and testing (*Cont.*):
  Nebraska Test of Learning Aptitude, 61
  personality, 62
  preparation for the use of, 132-133
  procedures in use of, 132-133
  program in elementary schools, 125-140
    careful organization of, 125
    functions of, 125-126
    group testing, 131
    planned, 129-132
    reading readiness, 62
    scheduling, 129-130
  Revised Stanford-Binet Scale, 61
  responsibilities of counselors, 20
  roles of personnel in effective use of tests, 138-139
  Rorschach Test, 62
  Rosenzweig Picture Frustration Study, 62
  scale for evaluating testing program, 281
  scheduling appropriate, 129-132
  scoring by hand or machine, 133
  selection should be done by qualified persons, 127-129
  sentence completion, 114-116
  social distance scales, 90-94
  sources of information on, 128-129
  use of test results, 133-137
    to identify group variations and individual needs, 133
    to identify underachievers, 135
    to survey and identify individual needs, 135-136
  World Test, 62
Therapy and treatment of children with emotional problems, 64
Time sample records, for child study, 42-44

Torgerson, Theodore L., 128
Training program:
  for guidance workers, 177-182
  parent-teacher conferences, 252-261
  school psychologists, 180-181
Transfers, orientation programs solve problems of, 289
Traxler, Arthur E., 141

U

Unfinished story, used in study of children, 114, 117-119
Universities (*see* Colleges and Universities)

V

Vittorino da Feltre, 8
Vocation Bureau of Boston, 11
Vocational guidance, historical development of, 11-12

W

Weingold, Joseph T., 209 *n*
Welton, J., 8 *n*
West Covina School District, West Covina, California, 267 *n*
Why Pupils Fail in Reading (Robinson), 198-199
Witmer, Lightner, 9
Women:
  changes in attitude towards education of, 244-245
  working mothers, 167
World Test, 62
Wrightstone, J. Wayne, 275
Writing, creative, used in study of children, 114, 117